JESUS FOLLOWERS IN THE ROMAN EMPIRE

JESUS FOLLOWERS
IN THE ROMAN EMPIRE

Paul B. Duff

WILLIAM B. EERDMANS PUBLISHING COMPANY
GRAND RAPIDS, MICHIGAN

Wm. B. Eerdmans Publishing Co.
2140 Oak Industrial Drive NE, Grand Rapids, Michigan 49505
www.eerdmans.com

2019-01

ISBN 978-0-8028-6878-7

Library of Congress Cataloging-in-Publication Data

Names: Duff, Paul B., 1952– author.
Title: Jesus followers in the Roman Empire / Paul B. Duff.
Description: Grand Rapids, Michigan : Eerdmans, 2017. |
    Includes bibliographical references and index.
Identifiers: LCCN 2017026272 | ISBN 9780802868787 (paperback)
Subjects: LCSH: Church history—Primitive and early church, ca. 30-600. | Christian life—
    History—Early church, ca. 30-600. | Christianity and other religions—Judaism. |
    BISAC: RELIGION / Christianity / History. | RELIGION / Biblical Studies / New Testament
Classification: LCC BR162.3 D84 2017 | DDC 270.1—dc23
    LC record available at https://lccn.loc.gov/2017026272

For Ann Brooks Duff

Table of Contents

Acknowledgments

Many people have assisted me in the preparation of this book. Thanks first go to Allen Myers of Eerdmans, who initially suggested the idea to me, and to Trevor Thompson of Eerdmans for his help following Allen's retirement. Thanks also go to Andrew Langford and Alexander Bukovietski for their valuable assistance. I am grateful to Elise Friedland for helpful information about the gods, to Jennifer Glancy for allowing me to cite one of her unpublished papers, to John Granger Cook for sharing one of his unpublished papers as well as a published article, and to Heidi Wendt for generously sending me parts of her forthcoming book. Thanks are also due to Katherine Keller and Stefania Cotei for reading and critiquing earlier versions of various chapters and to Elizabeth Chacko for her advice on all things geographical. I am, of course, indebted to all my colleagues in the Department of Religion at the George Washington University, and particularly to Robert Eisen, the department chair. Thanks also go to the Office of the Vice-President of Research at George Washington University for a summer grant to help complete the book. I would also like to acknowledge my family, especially my children, their partners, and their children, for their support. For last-minute help, thanks especially to Ann Osborn, my brilliant and amazing wife. This book is dedicated to my mother, Ann Brooks Duff, in honor of her ninety-second birthday.

Abbreviations

Ancient Sources

1 Apol.	Justin Martyr, *First Apology*
2 Apol.	Justin Martyr, *Second Apology*
Ag. Ap.	Josephus, *Against Apion*
Ag. Her.	Irenaeus, *Against Heresies*
Agr.	Philo, *On Agriculture*
Alex.	Plutarch, *(Life of) Alexander*
Anab.	Arrian, *Anabasis*
Ann.	Tacitus, *Annals*
Ant.	Josephus, *Jewish Antiquities*
Ant. rom.	Dionysius of Halicarnassus, *Roman Antiquities*
Appar. Wom.	Tertullian, *The Apparel of Women*
Cels.	Origen, *Against Celsus*
Contempl. Life	Philo, *On the Contemplative Life*
Dial.	Justin Martyr, *Dialogue with Trypho*
Dial. Court.	Lucian, *Dialogues of the Courtesans*
Did.	Didache
Diogn.	Letter to Diognetus
Disc.	Epictetus, *Discourses*
Embassy	Philo, *Embassy to Gaius*
Eth. Nic.	Aristotle, *Nichomachean Ethics*
Goddess	Lucian, *Goddess of Syria*
Gos. Thom.	Gospel of Thomas

J. W.	Josephus, *Jewish War*
Jub.	Jubilees
Herm. Mand.	Shepherd of Hermas, Mandates
Herm. Sim.	Shepherd of Hermas, Similitudes
Herm. Vis.	Shepherd of Hermas, Visions
Hist.	Herodotus, *Histories*
Hist. eccl.	Eusebius, *Ecclesiastical History*
Lies	Lucian, *The Lover of Lies*
Lives	Diogenes Laertius, *Lives of Eminent Philosophers*
Med. Coll.	Oribasius, *Medical Collections*
Metam.	Apuleius, *Metamorphoses*
Moses	Philo, *The Life of Moses*
Or.	Aelius Aristides, *Orations*
Pol.	Aristotle, *Politics*
Prep. Gos.	Eusebius, *Preparation for the Gospel*
Rom. Hist.	Dio Cassius, *Roman History*
Sat.	Macrobius, *Saturnalia*
Smyrn.	Ignatius, *To the Smyrnaens*
Symp.	Dio Chrysostom, *Symposia*
Tib.	Suetonius, *Tiberius*
T.Levi	Testament of Levi

Modern Sources and Collections

ABRL	Anchor Bible Reference Library
BGU	*Aegyptische Urkunden aus den Königlichen Staatlichen Museen zu Berlin, Griechische Urkunden.* 15 vols. Berlin: Weidmann, 1895–1937.
CIJ	*Corpus Inscriptionum Judaicarum*
CIL	*Corpus Inscriptionum Latinarum*
GIBM	*The Collection of Ancient Greek Inscriptions in the British Museum.* Ed. Hicks, Newton, and Hirschfeld. Oxford: Clarendon Press, 1874–1916.
HUT	Hermeneutische Untersuchungen zur Theologie
IEph	H. H. Engelmann and R. Merkelbach, *Die Inschriften von Ephesos.* IGSK 11–17. Bonn: Rudolf Habelt, 1979–1984.
IG II²	Johannes Kirchner, ed. *Inscriptiones Atticae Euclidis anno anteriores.* 4 vols. Berlin: Walter de Gruyter, 1913–1940.

IG XI.4	Pierre Roussel. *Inscriptiones Deli liberae. Decreta, foedera, catalogi, dedicationes, varia.* Berlin: Georg Reimer, 1914.
ILS	Hermann Dessau. *Inscriptiones latinae selectae.* 3 vols. Berlin: Weidmann, 1892–1916. Repr. Dublin: Weidmann, 1974; repr. Chicago: Ares, 1979.
JAJ	*Journal of Ancient Judaism*
JRS	*Journal of Roman Studies*
KTAH	Key Themes in Ancient History
LCL	Loeb Classical Library
LSAM	Franciszek Sokolowski. *Lois sacrées de l'Asie Mineure. Ecole française d'Athènes.* Travaux et mémoires 9. Paris: E. de Boccard, 1955.
NRSV	New Revised Standard Version
PHI	Packard Humanities Institute numbers for Greek inscriptions
SBLSBS	Society of Biblical Literature Sources for Biblical Study
SBLTT	Society of Biblical Literature Texts and Translations
*SIG*³	Wilhelm Dittenberger. *Sylloge inscriptionum graecarum.* 3rd ed. 4 vols. Leizpig: S. Hirzel, 1915–24.
SSRH	Sociological Studies on Roman History
YCS	Yale Classical Studies

Introduction

When Jesus of Nazareth began proclaiming the kingdom of God in the towns and villages of Galilee in the early years of the first century, he had no intention of starting a new religion, especially one that included former pagans. Rather, he believed that his mission was only to "the lost sheep of the house of Israel" (Matt 15:24). Even after his death, Jesus's original disciples continued to understand their beliefs and actions solely within the context of Judaism.[1] Those who had followed Jesus during his brief public ministry would have almost certainly still described themselves as Jews (albeit Jews who proclaimed Jesus as Israel's Messiah).

Nevertheless, a new religion did eventually develop, one that not only included former pagans but was soon dominated by them. How did this come about? Following Jesus's death, some (Jewish) Jesus followers took their message of a crucified messiah to the hellenized cities of the eastern Roman Empire. Oddly enough, they shared it with both Jews *and* non-Jews. Remarkably, the latter showed an interest. Shortly thereafter, Jewish missionaries such as Paul of Tarsus (known to later Christians as St. Paul) began to create assemblies of non-Jewish Jesus followers. Within a little more than a decade, the movement had established itself in some of the great cities of the Roman Empire.[2]

---

1. A significant portion of the Didache and a reconstructed document known only as Q (both to be discussed in the chapters that follow) each fit comfortably into a Jewish context. It is likely that the later Gospel stories about Jesus preaching to or healing non-Jews were used to explain the later presence of gentiles within the movement.

2. The earliest communities most likely appeared in Antioch (near the coast in northern Syria), Ephesus (on the western coast of what is now Turkey), and possibly Rome. It is also likely that an early community began in Alexandria (given its proximity to Judea). Unfortunately, we have no evidence to support the founding of a community there.

1

Despite the movement's Jewish roots, non-Jews who joined were discouraged from converting to Judaism. Indeed, figures like Paul *insisted* that they remain non-Jews. As a result, although the Jesus movement ultimately retained much of its early Jewish character—non-Jewish Jesus followers worshipped the God of the Jews and revered the Jewish Scriptures—it acquired a decidedly Hellenistic stamp. The hybrid character of the movement led one later author (whose name is unknown) to label its members *sojourners*.

Sometime in the second century, that unidentified author wrote a letter to an otherwise unknown person by the name of Diognetus, in which he defended the movement. He depicted its members as "no different from other people in terms of their country, language, or habits." The author continues, "Nowhere do they inhabit cities of their own, use a strange dialect, or live life out of the ordinary. . . . They live in their respective countries, but only as sojourners" (Diogn. 5.1–2, 5 [Ehrman, slightly revised]). In other words, the author insisted, these people did not behave like the various ethnic groups that otherwise populated the cities of the empire, each coming from a particular homeland, each holding to its own customs, and at times even using its own native language. Instead, they lived like those around them. Nevertheless they were sojourners—although they participated in the culture of the pagan empire, their true allegiance lay elsewhere, with the God of the Jews and his son, Jesus.

Although the epistle to Diognetus was written about second-century Christians, the metaphor of the sojourner is particularly applicable to the urban followers of Jesus in the mid-first century, when the movement was first taking hold. The members of the early movement lived "betwixt and between," in some ways retaining their urban, Hellenistic culture, but in other ways resisting the values of pagan society. In the chapters that follow, we will explore this give and take.

The book is organized into three sections. The first section, "Setting the Stage," consists of three chapters. The first chapter, "Hellenistic Culture, Jewish Religion, and Roman Power," opens with an exploration of the Hellenistic (i.e., Greek) cultural legacy of Alexander the Great. In so doing, it also examines the effects that Alexander's legacy had on Judaism, the religion from which the Jesus movement would eventually emerge. The chapter concludes with an assessment of the political situation in Judea, the homeland of Jesus and his disciples. As we will see, both the cultural legacy of hellenization and the politics of Judea played a formative role in the movement's origin.

The second chapter, "The Early Years of the Jesus Movement," provides a description of the Jesus movement's beginnings in the rural area of Galilee.

Since the New Testament Gospels, products of the late first century, represent our primary sources for the movement's earliest years, a methodological discussion regarding the separation of the Gospels' earliest layers opens the chapter. The chapter then presents an overview of the teachings and activities of Jesus of Nazareth. A chronicle of the events that happened after Jesus's execution follows this overview. These events include the initial gathering of disciples in Jerusalem, the preliminary expansion of the movement within Jewish territory, its subsequent expansion beyond Jewish territory, and the controversy over inclusion of non-Jews.

The final chapter of the first section, "From Idols to a Living and True God," opens with a survey of Greco-Roman paganism. It is followed by the often-repeated claim that paganism was in decline at the time that the Jesus movement took root. Although that claim is not endorsed, a description of some of the changes that paganism underwent in the Roman period is nevertheless provided. This is followed by a summary of Paul's preaching—reconstructed from his letters—to urban-dwelling pagans in the mid-first century. Although Paul was certainly not the only Jewish missionary recruiting pagans at the time, he is the only one about whom we have substantial knowledge.

The second section of the book, "Inside the Movement", consists of chapters four through six. It focuses on the kinds of people who populated the early assemblies. It also considers the status that these people would have held both outside and inside the movement. The three chapters derive their titles from the parallel phrases found in one of the movement's earliest baptismal formulas: "There is no longer Jew or Greek, there is no longer slave or free, there is no longer male and female" (Gal 3:28).

Chapter 4, "No Longer Jew or Greek", examines the Jesus movement in terms of its ethnicity. As we will see, the early movement was, as a whole, diverse; both Jewish and non-Jewish assemblies existed. The assemblies in Judea were made up of Jews, and those elsewhere—insofar as we are aware—consisted primarily of non-Jews. Individually, however, the assemblies seem to have been relatively homogenous. This chapter focuses on the non-Jewish assemblies in the cities of the empire. Although to our ears the phrase "no longer Jew or Greek" makes the Jesus movement sound multicultural, first-century pagan ears would have heard it differently. To them, it would have proclaimed a Jewish or quasi-Jewish movement that allowed non-Jews into its ranks. In light of this, the chapter poses the question: why did such a message attract non-Jews? The chapter then turns to pagan attitudes toward Judaism and focuses on the proclamation of a message about the Jewish God and his son in the context of Greco-Roman paganism. As we will see, certain aspects of the message of the earliest missionaries would have been attractive to a pagan audience. Furthermore, the missionaries themselves—wandering holy men, working wonders and preaching mysterious religious ideas from the East—would have been neither unusual nor unwelcome within the cities of the empire.

Set against the background of the patriarchal family's significance within Greco-Roman culture, chapter 5, "No Longer Male and Female," explores opinions expressed by those in the Jesus movement regarding family, sexuality, and gender roles. The chapter opens with an investigation of Jesus's attitude toward his own family as well as the families of his followers, both their families of origin and the families created by those of his disciples who were married. Although Jesus renounced the former, he nevertheless prohibited his followers from dissolving their families created by marriage due to his unyielding rejection of divorce. The chapter next turns to Jesus's attitude toward sexuality. Although evidence is slim, it seems likely that Jesus encouraged celibacy among his unmarried followers. Next, we explore Jesus's understanding of the role of women. The fact that a number of women disciples traveled with him as he moved throughout the rural villages of Galilee suggests that his attitude toward gender roles was at least to some degree egalitarian.

The chapter then considers attitudes regarding family, celibacy, and gender roles in the movement following Jesus's death. As we will see, Jesus's commands regarding how to relate to the family unit and, in particular, his own family of origin were downplayed by the later movement. This was in part because certain members of Jesus's own family, his brother James in particular, assumed important leadership roles in the movement shortly after Jesus's death. But despite the soft-pedaling of Jesus's sayings regarding family of origin, his rejection of divorce was maintained, as was his regard for celibacy for unmarried Jesus followers. The role of women within the movement varied considerably. In some assemblies, they played significant roles as teachers, prophets, or patrons. In others, the more traditional Greco-Roman role of women (as silent wives and mothers) was emphasized.

The sixth chapter, "No Longer Slave or Free," focuses on both the economic resources and social status of Jesus followers. After discussing the wealth (or lack thereof) and status of Jesus's original followers, it turns to the later Jesus movement in the cities of the empire. It also discusses the apostle Paul, his role as an artisan (a tentmaker according to Acts), and what that would imply about his economic resources and social status. The second half of the chapter highlights those who were enslaved. In this section, not only are slaves discussed but also freedpersons, those who had originally been enslaved but had subsequently gained their freedom. The chapter concludes with a look at some of the important Jesus followers who were freedpersons.

The book's third section, "Accommodation and Resistance," begins with chapter 7, "One in Christ Jesus," which has to do primarily with accommodation; in particular, it considers the assemblies of the Jesus movement against the background of various kinds of Greco-Roman clubs or associations. Although there were a number of different types of associations in ancient society, all of them had at least a nominal cultic function. As such, they were comparable to the assemblies of Jesus followers, particularly in their manner of worship. The chapter focuses specifically on the Lord's Supper as it was practiced in Corinth in the middle of the first century and on its parallels with other such meals in pagan associations.

Chapter 8, "Unstained by the World," examines interactions between Jesus followers and their pagan neighbors. It poses the questions of how and to what extent a Jesus follower could preserve his or her religious integrity while, at the same time, continuing to participate in pagan society. Especially problematic for Jesus followers were issues involving idolatry and marriage with outsiders. With regard to the former, this chapter takes up the controversial issue of food sacrificed to pagan gods. Both Paul, in 1 Corinthians, and John, the author of the book of Revelation, weighed in on this issue. A number of authors, including Paul and John, also addressed the issue of marriage to nonbelievers. Curiously, there were differences of opinion among Jesus followers on both of these issues in the mid-first century and those disagreements continued for many years, in some case into the second and third centuries.

This book is aimed at a diverse audience. There is no presumption that the reader has a background in Christianity. Those from other religious traditions (or those who hold no religious beliefs) will hopefully find the book informative; interested Christian readers will also benefit from it. However, because the book is intended for a diverse audience, it is necessary to say a few words about references and about terminology.

In the following chapters, I have kept footnotes citing scholarly literature to a minimum. I have only cited secondary sources where I felt it necessary. Nevertheless, I have included a significant number of explanatory footnotes. The reader is free to examine them for further information but the book can also be read without them. The purpose of employing these footnotes is to keep the main text concise but, at the same time, allow interested readers to pursue certain points further.

The next issue mentioned concerns terminology. Any terms that could be read as politically charged, sexist, or Christocentric have been avoided, as have anachronistic or misleading terms. Although I have consistently tried to avoid judgmental language, a number of problematic terms have been retained, usually for the sake of clarity or for lack of a better option. These terms are discussed in the paragraphs that follow, as are the reasons for retaining them.

Probably the most challenging of all are the labels applied to the religions under discussion, specifically *Christianity*, *paganism*, and *Judaism*. The reader may have already noted that I have avoided the terms *Christian(s)* and *Christianity* in the above paragraphs. There is no evidence that early Jesus followers used these terms to describe themselves. The label *Christian* appears in the New Testament only in two works, the book of Acts and 1 Peter. Both of these texts were written either at the very end of the first century or in the early years of the second. The term *Christianity* first appears in the letters of Ignatius of Antioch, written sometime in the early second century. Consequently, I employ the labels *Jesus followers* or the *Jesus movement* when addressing first-century issues. The terms *Christian* or *Christianity* will be reserved for discussion of the second century and the centuries that followed.

The term *paganism* is problematic for several reasons. First and foremost, it usually carries a negative connotation. The *Merriam-Webster Collegiate Dictionary*, for example, defines a pagan as "one who has little or no religion and who delights in sensual pleasures and material goods: an irreligious or hedonistic person."[3] But even if it carried no negative connotations, *paganism* is an overly broad term. Over time, it has been applied to all kinds of groups in any number of places, including the ancient Greeks and Romans, Africans, the inhabitants of South Asia, and American Indians, to name just a few. Furthermore, some present-day religious groups, in particular, Wiccans, have appropriated *pagan* as a positive self-descriptor.[4] In short, because of its breadth, *paganism* conveys little.[5] Unfortunately, despite all the problems

3. *Merriam-Webster's Collegiate Dictionary*, 11th ed. (Springfield, MA: Merriam-Webster, 2007), s.v. "pagan."

4. Originally, the term *pagan* referred to an inhabitant of a *pagus*, the smallest unit of the Roman territorial system. It probably, as a result, carried the connotation of a "country bumpkin," that is to say, an unsophisticated person. But regardless of its etymology, the term originally seems to have had nothing to do with religion.

5. Note the comment of Moshe Halbertal and Avishai Margalit: "From the point of view of practitioners, anthropologists, or historians of different pagan religions, the very general category of paganism—a category that includes an enormous variety of religious phenomena—seems empty. . . . The only perspective from which the category makes any sense is the non-pagan perspective" (*Idolatry* [Cambridge: Harvard University Press, 1992], 237), cited in Page Dubois, *A Million and One Gods: The Persistence of Polytheism* (Cambridge: Harvard University Press, 2014), 21.

with the term *paganism*, there are few viable alternatives. Other options, like *heathenism*, are no less broad and even more pejorative than *paganism*. *Polytheism*, although less pejorative, is not very descriptive since it focuses only on the *belief* in multiple gods. But belief is more characteristic of Judaism and Christianity; the ancient religions of the Greeks and Romans focused more on action than belief. Given the lack of viable options, therefore, the terms *pagan* and *paganism* will be retained.

The term *Judaism* is also problematic, although less so than *paganism*. One of the difficulties with the term *Judaism*—a problem that is also encountered with the terms *paganism* and *Christianity*—is that *Judaism* suggests a monolithic phenomenon. But, in the ancient world, as today, Judaism was not at all uniform. The Judaism of the High Priest in Jerusalem differed from the Judaism of the Egyptian philosopher Philo which in turn differed from the Judaism of the community that produced the Dead Sea Scrolls, and so on.

The second difficulty with the term *Judaism* is a basic problem of translation. The normal Greek term for a Jew is *Ioudaios*. But it can mean one of two things. On the one hand, it can indicate a "Judean," that is, a person from the territory of Judea. But, on the other hand, it can also mean a "Jew," that is, one who practiced the religion of the Judean people. Sometimes we can decide the better translation from the context, but at other times the English translation is ambiguous. What is important to keep in mind is that, in ancient times, the label *Ioudaios* (plural: *Ioudaioi*) pointed to both a nationality and the cultural (including the religious) practices of that nationality. So, while today we might compare or contrast Judaism and Christianity as *religions*, people in the ancient world would tend to see the former term (Judaism) as a description of a people that shared a common homeland, culture, and religion. We will discuss this issue in a bit more depth in chapter 4.

Besides labels for the religious and cultural groups, other terms also present problems. One is a territorial label, the name of the land in which Jesus was raised. In the past, scholars typically labeled this part of the world *Palestine*, a term used by the Greeks and Romans to describe the area between Egypt and Syria. But today that term is politically charged. The term "Israel" is also problematic. Two particular reasons stand out. First, Jesus's homeland was not called Israel at the time and, second, the borders of modern Israel and the territory in which Jesus was raised do not conform to one another.[6]

---

6. Israel was the ancient territory of the ancestors of the Jews. Following the death of Solomon, Israel's king, the territory of Israel split into two kingdoms, one in the north and the other in the south. "Israel" was the name of the former and "Judah" the latter. The nation

Consequently, when referring to the homeland of the Jews in Greco-Roman times, we will use the term *Judea*, the label that the Romans used in reference to the territory of their client king, Herod.[7]

Yet another label that presents challenges is *Old Testament*, because of its obvious Christocentric nature. For Jews, the books found in the Christian Old Testament constitute their Bible, not simply the first part of it.[8] Sometimes scholars use the label *Hebrew Scriptures* to designate this body of literature. But, since ancient Jews living outside Judea (as well as Jesus followers) read their sacred books in a Greek translation, called the Septuagint, the label *Hebrew Scriptures* is misleading. Consequently, I will use the label *Jewish Scriptures* or simply *the Scriptures*, although I recognize that the former is not ideal since these texts also serve as Scriptures for Christians, past and present. But since in this book these writings are mentioned in reference to a period of time in which it is anachronistic to speak of Christianity per se, *Jewish Scriptures* will have to suffice.

One last term that can be misleading is the label used by Jesus followers to describe their gatherings. The Greek term used was *ekklēsia*. The English word used to render *ekklēsia* in virtually all New Testament translations is "church." But there are a number of problems with "church." First, *ekklēsia* was not originally a religious term. Rather, it simply meant a "gathering" or an "assembly."[9] Second, the term usually calls to mind a *building* where worship

---

of Israel ceased to exist following 722 BCE when it was conquered by the Assyrians, although those in the Southern Kingdom continued to use the term to refer to themselves as a people, as did their descendents. But when the term was used this way, it did not refer to a territory (e.g., Jews in the diaspora would also have been counted as part of "Israel").

7. "Judea" is a variation of "Judah," the Southern Kingdom under the monarchy (ca. 1000–586). Following the Babylonian exile, when the area was ruled by the Persians, they called it *Yehud*. After Alexander's conquest, this area in turn became known as *Ioudaia* (as it was said in Greek). The Latin equivalent is *Iudaea* (anglicized as Judea). Unfortunately, Judea also can be used to refer to a smaller area, the area ruled by Roman governors after Herod's death, an area that did *not* include Galilee (where Jesus was born) or the area to the east of the Sea of Galilee that had originally been controlled by Herod.

8. It should be noted that the Old Testament and the Jewish bible (*Tanak*) are not exactly the same (The Jewish bible is often referred to as the *Tanak*, an acronym created by combining the first Hebrew letter of each of the sections: *Torah* (the Law), *Nevi'im* (the Prophets), and *Ketuvim* (the Writings) = TaNaK). Although the Protestant bible contains the same books as the *Tanak*, the order of the books differs. Furthermore, the Old Testament in Roman Catholic and Christian Orthodox bibles contains several books not found in the Protestant Old Testament or the *Tanak*.

9. Interestingly enough, the term *synagogue* (*synagōgē* in Greek) also originally meant a "gathering" or an "assembly." Consequently, at the time of Jesus, the terms *synagōgē* and

takes place. But, in the first century, Jesus followers did not have independent places of worship.[10] Instead, they gathered in homes, workshops, warehouses, and the like. Third, "church" can point to a hierarchically structured organization. But no such hierarchical structure existed within the Jesus movement of the first century. Consequently, the term "assembly," a term that suggests a gathering rather than a building or an organization, will be employed to stand for the term *ekklēsia* rather than "church."

Finally, translation of New Testament texts are from the NRSV. Translations of classical sources are from the Loeb Classical Library, unless otherwise noted. Translations from the Old Testament Pseudepigrapha are from James H. Charlesworth, *The Old Testament Pseudepigrapha*, 2 vols. (Garden City, NY: Doubleday, 1983).

---

ekklēsia were synonyms. It was only later that *ekklēsia* and *synagōgē* became technical terms, the former for a Christian gathering and the latter for a Jewish gathering.

10. The earliest freestanding "church" (building) that we know of comes from the mid-third century.

SETTING THE STAGE

CHAPTER 1

Hellenistic Culture, Jewish Religion, and Roman Power

In order to understand the Jesus movement, we must first understand something about the political and cultural environment of the society in which it took root. Of course, Jesus and his immediate followers were born and raised as Jews in Judea, the ancient homeland of Israel. But Judea, although Jewish, was hellenized (at least to some extent), like the rest of the eastern Mediterranean.[1] That is to say, it participated in the Greek culture that Alexander the Great had spread throughout the territories that he had conquered several centuries earlier.

But the Jewish religion and Hellenistic culture comprise only part of the background. Rome's political dominance also needs to be added to this mix. Each one of these three factors, Hellenism, Judaism, and Roman power contributed significantly to the world in which the Jesus movement came into existence. Each also influenced the Jesus movement as it later spread throughout the empire. We will open our examination of these three important phenomena with Alexander's propagation of Greek culture.

---

1. The influence of hellenization on Jesus and his original followers is disputed. Although the cities of Judea (including Sepphoris, a mere four miles from Jesus's home town of Nazareth) were hellenized, the countryside was less so. It is almost certain that Jesus spoke Aramaic as his first language. This by itself indicates that he would have been less hellenized than an inhabitant of one of the Judean cities, Jerusalem, for example. However, assuming that Jesus was a carpenter, as the Gospel of Mark tells us (6:3), it is reasonable to assume that he found work in nearby Sepphoris, in which case it is at least possible that he knew some Greek, if only at a rudimentary level.

Hellenistic Culture: The Legacy of Alexander

The man we know as Alexander the Great was born in Macedon (what is now the north central part of Greece) in 356 BCE, roughly three and a half centuries before the birth of Jesus. Alexander's father, Philip II, was the reigning monarch in Macedon and his mother, Olympias, was the daughter of the ruler of the neighboring kingdom of Epirus. Although at the time Persia was the dominant empire in the eastern Mediterranean, Alexander was nonetheless raised to appreciate the culture of the Greek city-states to the south. His father deemed it appropriate that he receive a Greek education and so, as a young teen, Alexander was tutored by the philosopher Aristotle, one of the great Greek thinkers of the ancient world.

Alexander's father Philip was an accomplished military leader. He had conquered all of the lands between the Dalmatian coast (modern-day Albania) and the Hellespont (the strait of water—now called the Dardanelles—between the Aegean Sea and the Sea of Marmara). But, Philip was not content with these conquests. His plan was to cross the Hellespont into Asia and challenge the Persian Empire, a kingdom that had dominated the area for two centuries. To that end, Philip sent an expeditionary force down the western coast of Asia Minor (modern-day Turkey) to build support for his invasion among the Greek speakers there.[2] Philip, however, was never to realize his goal; he was assassinated in 336. Nevertheless, a few years later, Alexander decided to implement his late father's strategy.

Alexander arrived in Asia in 334 BCE with almost fifty thousand troops. In the year that followed, he engaged and defeated the main body of the Persian army at a place called Issus, in southeastern Asia Minor, although the Persian king, Darius, managed to avoid capture. Alexander, rather than immediately pursuing Darius, marched south along the eastern shore of the Mediterranean, conquering cities in Syria, Phoenicia, Samaria, and Judea.[3] Alexander then continued along the coast into Egypt. Once in Egypt, he turned his attention to religious matters. As one ancient historian wrote, "A sudden desire now seized Alexander to visit and consult [the Egyptian god] Ammon in Libya, both because the oracle of Ammon was truthful and because [the Greek heroes] Perseus and Heracles had consulted it. . . . In any case, he set out with this in mind and imagined that he would obtain more precise knowledge of his own

2. This area had been colonized by Greeks centuries earlier.

3. Most cities, including Jerusalem, surrendered without a fight. However, the Phoenician coastal city of Tyre resisted. Alexander besieged the city and eventually destroyed it.

affairs" (Arrian, *Anab*. 3.3.1–2).[4] When he reached the temple of Ammon, the shrine's chief priest purportedly hailed him as "the son of the god." It was later alleged that shortly thereafter, the famous oracles at Didyma and Erythrae (both on the western coast of present-day Turkey) likewise proclaimed Alexander the son of Zeus.

Leaving Egypt, Alexander led his army into Mesopotamia where he again met Darius and the latter's reconstituted army at Gaugamela, a site east of modern-day Mosul, Iraq. Darius was decisively defeated but managed to escape once again. Alexander, although eager to capture the Persian king, nevertheless first took control of the important Persian cities of Babylon (in the southern part of current-day Iraq) and Susa (in what is now western Iran). He then resumed his pursuit of Darius, following him into Bactria (Afghanistan), where the Persian ruler was finally killed, not by Alexander but by one of his own former governors. Following Darius's death, Alexander continued east through what is now Pakistan and entered India. His army, however, after campaigning nonstop for almost a decade, would go no farther. At the Hyphasis River (now named the Beas), his soldiers rebelled. Reluctantly, Alexander turned his army around and headed west, back to Babylon.[5]

Shortly after his return to Babylon, in 323 BCE, Alexander fell ill. Within a few days, at the age of only 32, he was dead. Rumors quickly began to circulate that Alexander had been poisoned. It was alleged that Cassander, the son of Antipater—who had faithfully ruled Macedon in Alexander's absence—had slipped him wine mixed with a deadly toxin. Many believed the rumors. Antipater certainly had motive; shortly before, Alexander had summoned him to Babylon (Antipater had been feuding with Olympias, Alexander's mother). Fearing for his life, Antipater ignored Alexander's summons and sent his son Cassander instead, allegedly armed with the poison. But whether there is any truth to the rumor that Alexander was poisoned by Cassander is unclear. Although it is certainly possible, there are other possible explanations for his sudden death.[6]

4. Translation by Pamela Mensch in James Romm, ed., *The Landmark Arrian: The Campaigns of Alexander* (New York: Anchor, 2010).

5. There are a number of biographies of Alexander: W. W. Tarn, *Alexander the Great*, 2 vols. (Cambridge: Cambridge University Press, 1950); Peter Green, *Alexander the Great* (New York: Praeger, 1970); J. R. Hamilton, *Alexander the Great* (London: Hutchinson, 1973); Robin Lane Fox, *Alexander the Great* (London: Penguin, 1986). A concise summary of Alexander's conquests can be found in F. W. Walbank, *The Hellenistic World* (Cambridge: Harvard University Press, 1981), 29–45.

6. Did Antipater really try to kill Alexander? Unfortunately, ancient sources disagree. While

But regardless of how he died, Alexander had clearly not planned for his death; he had not named a successor. Who would take his place? Alexander's young Bactrian wife Roxane was pregnant at the time and her soon-to-be-born son was a likely candidate. Another possible successor was Alexander's half brother, Arrhidaeus (later renamed Philip). But neither Roxane's son nor Alexander's half brother were very strong candidates. The former, as a child, would have been incapable of ruling and the latter was mentally challenged. Consequently, the decades following Alexander's death were filled with instability and intrigue as many of those in the deceased leader's former inner circle vied for control.

Among those who seemed most likely to succeed were Perdiccas, a former page of Alexander's father, and two of Alexander's bodyguards, Ptolemy and Lysimachus. The latter two received control of Egypt and Thrace, respectively. Each of them would play important roles in the years to come. For the time being, however, Perdiccas was in the strongest position. He was named regent of the empire and retained control of the army. Although Alexander's son and his half brother Arrhidaeus were ultimately recognized as kings, they were in Babylon, under the control of Perdiccas; he ruled in their names.[7] But within a few years, Perdiccas was assassinated by his generals, one of whom was named Seleucus. This same Seleucus would ultimately come to control many of Alexander's eastern territories.

Besides Ptolemy, Lysimachus, and Seleucus, another important figure to emerge was Antigonus "Monophthalmus" ("one-eyed"). Antigonus, a generation older than Alexander, had not accompanied the conqueror in his eastern campaigns but had instead been assigned the task of protecting Alexander's supply lines. This he did from a base in Phrygia (in what is now west central Turkey). From that base, Antigonus was able to seize many of the conquered Near Eastern territories following Alexander's death. Indeed, within the span

---

some sources assert that he was poisoned, others blame Alexander's death on a combination of fever and fatigue. Scholars at a conference held at the University of Maryland School of Medicine recently re-examined the sources and concluded that Alexander was probably *not* poisoned. They concluded that his death was more likely the result of typhoid fever, perhaps complicated by other medical factors (possibly including one or more of the following: stress, exhaustion, heavy drinking, malaria, and multiple wounds). Unfortunately, we will never know for sure. For more, see Romm, *The Landmark Arrian*, 404–10.

7. Ultimately, Arrhidaeus (Philip), Alexander, and Roxane were all murdered. Arrhidaeus was killed in 318 on the orders of Olympias, Alexander's mother. Olympias arranged for Roxane and Alexander to leave Asia, for she had planned that her grandson should eventually rule. Nevertheless, Roxane, the child, and Olympias were all killed by Cassander.

of less than a decade, most of the territory between the Hellespont and Babylon was under his control.

Antigonus's rapid consolidation of power alarmed his rivals; they were forced to band together to challenge him. In 301 BCE, the combined forces of Cassander (the alleged poisoner of Alexander), Lysimachus, and Seleucus (one of the assassins of Perdiccas) faced the army of Antigonus at Ipsus, a site in central Asia Minor. Antigonus's forces were defeated and Antigonus himself was killed. His territory was subsequently divided among the victors: most notably, Lysimachus added western Asia Minor and much of what is now Bulgaria and eastern Greece to his territory in Thrace; Seleucus gained eastern Asia Minor, Syria, and Mesopotamia. Ptolemy, although he did not participate in the battle against Antigonus, nevertheless seized Judea and southern Syria and added them to his territory of Egypt; Judea and southern Syria were supposed to go to Seleucus for the latter's role in the defeat of Antigonus. But they were already in the possession of Ptolemy, and Seleucus was not in a position to get them back. The territories would remain contested for a century.

Although some political stability emerged following Ipsus, it was short-lived. Within two decades, Lysimachus was dead, killed in battle by the forces of Seleucus. Thereafter, his territory was fought over by the Attalids, who ruled the city of Pergamum (now Bergama, in the northwest part of Turkey); Seleucus and his successors; and several waves of Gauls (Celtic tribes that had invaded from the west in the first half of the third century BCE).[8] Cassander fell ill and died a few years after Ipsus; his territory was seized by Demetrius, the son of Antigonus Monophthalmus, but it was only held for a short time; Demetrius was soon defeated and imprisoned by Seleucus.

Of all of the would-be successors of Alexander, only Ptolemy and Seleucus would realize any kind of long-term success. Both established kingdoms that would last into the first century BCE. But their dynasties seemed incapable of coexisting in peace. Each seemed intent on destroying the other. In fact, in the early years of the second century BCE, the Seleucids nearly achieved their goal. But, at the gates of Ptolemy's city of Alexandria, the Seleucid ruler Antiochus

---

8. The Gauls were originally from what is now France (called Gaul by the Romans). Some tribes traveled to the east in the early third century BCE, invading Italy, Macedon, and Greece. They crossed the Hellespont into Asia in 278–79 BCE. They preyed on the local population until they were defeated first by the Attalids of Pergamum and later by the Romans. They were ultimately pushed into the central part of Asia Minor where they settled. Because of that, the area came to be known as Galatia. The Gauls were ultimately hellenized. Paul founded assemblies in the area and wrote a letter to the Galatian communities. That letter can be found in the New Testament.

IV was met by the Roman legate, Gaius Popilius Laenas, who ordered Antiochus to stand down and to evacuate Egypt immediately. If Antiochus refused, he would be answerable to Rome. The Seleucid ruler reluctantly complied. The fact that Rome could make such a demand of Antiochus IV illustrates the waning political influence of the eastern kingdoms. Rome had been gathering power in the West while the Seleucids and Ptolemies skirmished in the East. By the middle of the second century BCE, the power and influence of the eastern kingdoms had diminished notably in the face of Rome's rise to power.

Nevertheless, while neither Alexander nor his followers were ever to realize fully their *political* ambitions, their *cultural* influence on the eastern Mediterranean was significant. Greek-style cities emerged throughout the territories conquered by Alexander; Greek became the *lingua franca* of trade and government; indigenous Asian gods were identified with members of the Greek pantheon and so something like Greek religion arose in the East. In short, the Greek way of life became widespread.[9] Indeed, even after the arrival of the Romans, the Greek language continued to hold sway in the East.

Because of the vast cultural change that took place in the territories conquered by Alexander, the later writer Plutarch compared the conqueror to a philosopher. A philosopher's responsibility, Plutarch believed, was to civilize humans and Alexander had civilized the barbarian East. As Plutarch saw things, because of his conquests,

> Homer was commonly read, and the children of the Persians, of the Susianians,[10] and of the Gedrosians[11] learned to chant the tragedies of Sophocles and Euripides. And although Socrates, when tried on the charge of introducing foreign deities, lost his cause to the informers who infested Athens,

9. It seems that Alexander's dream had been to take the best of both Eastern and Western cultures and create a brand new civilization. To partially fulfill that end, he brought Greek culture with him on his march eastward. As he traveled, he founded a number of Greek-style cities and settled them with Greek mercenaries. But Persian culture was not just set aside. In fact, in a massive group wedding, he and eighty of his officers took native wives. Alexander also incorporated soldiers and cavalry from the east into his army. These soldiers came from Bactria (northern Afghanistan), Sogdiana (eastern Uzbekistan and western Tajikistan), and Arachosia (southeast Afghanistan and northwest Pakistan). Alexander's appreciation of eastern culture, however, was not shared by his Greek and Macedonian troops; his integration of native soldiers into the army provoked discontent. Ultimately, Alexander's attempt to create a culture fusing the best of the West and East failed.

10. The Susianians were the people in what is now southwest Iran.

11. The Gedrosians were the people of contemporary southeast Iran and Pakistan, along the coast of the Indian Ocean.

yet through Alexander Bactria[12] and the Caucasus learned to revere the gods of the Greeks. Plato wrote a book on the one ideal constitution, but because of its forbidding character he could not persuade anyone to adopt it; but Alexander established more than seventy cities among savage tribes, and sowed all Asia with Grecian Magestries, and thus overcame its uncivilized and brutish manner of living. . . . If, then, philosophers take the greatest pride in civilizing and rendering adaptable the intractable and untutored elements in human character, and if Alexander has been shown to have changed the savage natures of countless tribes, it is with good reason that he should be regarded as a very great philosopher (*On the Fortune or the Virtue of Alexander,* 5 [Babbit, slightly revised]).

While Plutarch obviously underestimated the positive aspects of eastern culture (or the idea that civilization even existed there prior to Alexander's arrival), his testimony nevertheless indicates the enormous cultural influence that Alexander's conquests had throughout the Mediterranean world and areas to the East. Sometimes the hellenization that followed in Alexander's wake was embraced enthusiastically. At other times, it was resisted. Regardless of the response, it significantly changed the character of the various eastern Mediterranean cultures, Judaism included.

Hellenization and Judaism: Two Encounters

From the time of Alexander until the Muslim conquest—a period of approximately a millennium—Judea was hellenized to one degree or another. As mentioned above, shortly after Alexander's death, Judea was occupied and controlled by the Hellenistic Ptolemaic dynasty. The Ptolemies held it until 198 BCE, when the Hellenistic Seleucid ruler Antiochus III "the Great" finally wrested it away from the Ptolemies. Although hellenization affected Judea and the religion of its people in a number of ways, for our purposes, two examples stand out. The first, the translation of the Jewish Scriptures from Hebrew into Greek, began while Judea was under the political control of the Ptolemies. The fact that the Scriptures were translated at all indicates that many Jews—specifically those living outside of Judea—could no longer read Hebrew. The translation enabled them to maintain a connection both to their cultural roots and to their homeland. Without it, diaspora Judaism would have unlikely remained as vital as it did.

---

12. Bactria is where Afghanistan, Uzbekistan, and Tajikistan currently meet.

The second example of Hellenism's impact on Judaism, the imperial suppression of Jewish practices in Judea, came about after control of Judea was surrendered to the Seleucids. For various complex reasons that are still not entirely clear, the desire of some in Judea to live in the Hellenistic style ultimately led to the Seleucid proscription of all native religious practices. Although the Seleucids were ultimately unsuccessful in this endeavor, the attempt left its mark. Among other things, it demonstrated Judaism's resilience in response to the threat that its cultural and religious practices would be swept away.

The Translation of Hebrew Scriptures into Greek: The Creation of the Septuagint

According to an account narrated in an ancient Jewish writing, the Letter of Aristeas, the Scriptures were translated into Greek because Ptolemy II desired a copy of them for his massive library (Let. Aris. 9–11). Since they were of no use in their original language to those with access to the library, they had to be translated. The account narrated by Aristeas, although a good story, has little to recommend it historically. It is much more likely that the motivation to translate the scriptural texts from Hebrew into Greek came from Jews living outside of Judea.

There were a significant number of Jews in the Hellenistic diaspora. Although actual numbers are hard to come by, we have evidence from both ancient literature and inscriptions that Jewish communities existed in Hellenistic Egypt, Syria, Asia Minor, the Balkan region along the north coast of the Black Sea, on the Greek mainland, and on a number of the Greek islands.[13] There were many reasons that so many Jews lived in so many places.

Some Jews were strongly encouraged to resettle in Hellenistic areas. For example, the Jewish historian Josephus tells us that, in order to stabilize western Asia Minor, the Seleucid ruler Antiochus III (who ruled 222–187 BCE) resettled two thousand Jewish families from Mesopotamia there. The migrating Jews were promised that they could follow their own customs; they were also given financial incentives (*Jewish Antiquities* 12.147–53). Once established in Asia Minor, these Jewish communities grew significantly. By the first century

---

13. These would have included the islands of Cyprus, Delos, Samos, Cos, and Rhodes. For more on Jews in the diaspora in Hellenistic and Roman times, see Emil Schürer, *The History of the Jewish People in the Age of Jesus Christ (175 B.C.–A.D. 135)*, rev. and ed. Geza Vermes, Fergus Millar, and Martin Goodman (Edinburgh: T&T Clark, 1986), 3.1: 3–86.

CE, the Jewish writer Philo reported that "Jews were numerous in every city [of Asia Minor]" (*Embassy to Gaius* 33 [245]). The large Jewish population of western Asia Minor in Roman times can be attested by the enormous synagogue that occupied a central location in the city of Sardis. This synagogue, discovered in 1962 and subsequently excavated, dates from the third century CE.[14] Since it was large enough to accommodate one thousand worshipers, we can assume that a very large Jewish population lived in that city, a population that could likely trace its origin to the time of Antiochus III.

While some Jews were encouraged to relocate, others were forcibly moved. The Letter of Aristeas, mentioned above, informs us that Ptolemy resettled one hundred thousand Jews from Judea to Egypt. Of those one hundred thousand, Aristeas further tells us, Ptolemy stationed thirty thousand of them in fortresses throughout Egypt (12–13). Although some Jews were forcibly settled in Egypt, others moved there voluntarily. An ancient historian named Hecateaus reveals that many fled to Egypt because of the political unrest in their homeland.[15]

But massive resettlements account for only a portion of the Hellenistic Jewish diaspora. Josephus claims that many Jews lived in Syria, particularly Antioch, because of "the success of [the] city" (*Jewish War* 7.43). By this he seems to have meant that, as the capital of the Seleucid Empire, Antioch offered opportunities to Jews that they would not have found in their native territory. Furthermore, he indicated that Jews were able to dwell securely there. Finally, Josephus claimed that Jews in Antioch received "citizen rights on an equality with the Greeks [i.e., native inhabitants]" (*Jewish War* 7.44). This latter claim, however, is probably exaggerated.

But whether such a large Jewish diaspora population resulted from voluntary resettlement, forced migration, flight from political instability, or better opportunities, the result was that Jews dwelled in most of the major cities of the eastern Mediterranean during Hellenistic and Roman times. After a few generations, most diaspora Jews probably spoke only Greek. Such a large number of Greek-speaking Jews consequently demanded a translation of their sacred writings. For unless the Scriptures could be read in Greek, diaspora Jews would lose their cultural heritage.

We know very little about the production of the Greek translation of the

14. The building was not originally built as a synagogue but was taken over and converted into one in the late 3rd century CE. It was later remodeled in the 4th century. Remains of other diaspora synagogues have been discovered at Priene (in western Asia Minor), the Greek island of Delos, Ostia (Italy), and Dura-Europos (in eastern Syria).

15. The comments of Hecataeus are recorded in Josephus, *Ag. Ap.* 1.194.

Scriptures that came to be known as the Septuagint.[16] The translation was likely made over a significant period of time, with the Law (i.e., the first five books of the Bible) being translated first, followed by the Prophets, and finally the remainder, the Writings.[17] While we know little about how or where the translation originated (the Letter of Aristeas says Alexandria, which is likely), we do know that by the late second century BCE, the majority of the canonical writings were circulating in Greek.[18]

The production of the Septuagint clearly demonstrates the cooperative interaction between Judaism and Hellenism. Obviously, the creation of the Septuagint benefitted the Jews living in the diaspora. But the translation also had another, likely unintended, effect: it made the biblical texts available to non-Jews.[19] A further unintended consequence of the translation was the ease with which Jewish missionaries who followed Jesus could later make the Jewish Scriptures available to their non-Jewish assemblies. Indeed, the enthusiastic adoption of the Septuagint by non-Jewish Jesus followers likely contributed to its later rejection by diaspora Jews. The latter group eventually turned to a different translation, created in the second century CE by a convert to Judaism, Aquila of Sinope.[20]

---

16. The title comes from the Latin phrase: *versio Septuaginta interpretum*, meaning the "translation of the seventy interpreters." According to the Letter of Aristeas, six scribes from each of the twelve tribes were commissioned to make the translation. However, since 6 x 12 = 72, it is unclear why the later title refers to seventy. The label *Septuagint* did not come into use until the fourth century CE.

17. As mentioned above, the Hebrew Bible (*Tanak*) is traditionally divided into three sections, the Law (*Torah*), the Prophets (*Nevi'im*), and the Writings (*Ketuvim*).

18. We know this because in the prologue of the apocryphal work, Sirach (sometimes known as Ecclesiasticus), the writer explained that he was translating the book—it had been written by his grandfather—from Hebrew into Greek. He apologized in advance that the Greek translation may not have accurately conveyed all the nuances of the original. He further explained that "not only this book, but even the Law itself, the Prophecies, and the rest of the books differ not a little when read in the original [language]." Given the traditional division of the Hebrew Scriptures (into Law, Prophets, and Writings), we can be fairly certain that the translator is speaking here of the differences between the original Hebrew texts of the Bible and the Greek translation of them. Since Sirach/Ecclesiasticus was translated not long after 117 BCE, the Greek translation of the Hebrew Scriptures must have been complete or close to it by that time.

19. In some places, non-Jews were attracted to Judaism and, it seems, welcomed in the synagogue. Some ultimately converted but most probably did not. The latter group, although they did not convert, nevertheless observed some Jewish practices, including the Sabbath rest. We will look more closely at the pagans who were attracted to Judaism in a later chapter.

20. On Christianity's use of the Septuagint as a contributing factor to its loss of legitimacy among diaspora Jews, see Schürer, *History of the Jewish People*, 3.1: 480.

The Limits of Hellenization: Jewish Resistance to Forced Assimilation

The next example of Judaism's encounter with Hellenism provides us with a quite different scenario. While the translation of the Septuagint illustrates Judaism's willingness to accommodate Hellenistic culture, Antiochus IV's attempt to force hellenization on the population of Judea demonstrates the limits to which hellenization would be tolerated by Jews. This attempt to force hellenization on the inhabitants of Judea (to the extent of abolishing Jewish practices entirely) took place during the reign of the Seleucid emperor Antiochus IV (175–164 BCE).

The exact series of events that led to the forced hellenization (and suppression of Jewish practices) in Judea is not entirely clear. 1 Maccabees, a Jewish work written several decades after the events it describes, blames the situation partly on the Jews (particularly the leadership in Jerusalem) and partly on the Seleucid ruler Antiochus.[21] Toward the beginning of the document, the author wrote:

> In [the] days [of Antiochus IV] certain renegades came out from Israel and misled many, saying, "Let us go and make a covenant with the Gentiles around us, for since we separated from them many disasters have come upon us." This proposal pleased them, and some of the people eagerly went to the king, who authorized them to observe the ordinances of the Gentiles. So they built a gymnasium in Jerusalem, according to Gentile custom, and removed the marks of circumcision, and abandoned the holy covenant. They joined with the Gentiles and sold themselves to do evil. (1:11–15)

According to this passage, the call for hellenization came from Jewish "renegades."

Shortly thereafter, however, the author seemed to provide a different cause. In this passage, the blame fell squarely on the shoulders of the Seleucid ruler:

> [Antiochus IV] wrote to his whole kingdom that all should be one people, and that all should give up their particular customs. All the Gentiles accepted the command of the king. Many even from Israel gladly adopted his religion; they sacrificed to idols and profaned the Sabbath. And the king sent letters by messengers to Jerusalem and the towns of Judah; he directed them to follow customs strange to the land. (1:41–45)

---

21. The date of 1 Maccabees is disputed. It could have been written anytime between 135 and 62 BCE. Most scholars, however, date it to around 100 BCE.

As this passage explained things, Antiochus was behind the forced hellenization; he attempted to unify his territory culturally. This particular text suggests that Antiochus did not target the Jews of Judea. Instead, it seems that he planned to force hellenization on his whole realm.[22]

Although the history is difficult to determine with any precision, nevertheless, the ultimate outcome for the Jews was the same: they were to both hellenize and, at the same time, abandon their native customs. According to a royal decree, also recorded in 1 Maccabees, the Jews were directed "to forbid burnt-offerings and sacrifices and drink-offerings in the sanctuary," and further, "to profane Sabbaths and festivals, to defile the sanctuary and the priests, to build altars and sacred precincts and shrines for idols, to sacrifice swine and other unclean animals, and to leave their sons uncircumcised." In sum, they "were to make themselves abominable by everything unclean and profane, so that they would forget the law and change all the ordinances." Finally, Antiochus commanded, "And whoever does not obey the command of the king shall die" (1:45–50). As 1 Maccabees tells the story, the temple in Jerusalem was subsequently defiled: "they erected a desolating sacrilege on the altar of burnt-offering" (1:54).[23] Regardless of what the motivation was for the action and who was ultimately to blame, the account presented in 1 Maccabees seems to oversimplify the series of events that took place. Regardless, the ultimate outcome—the violent suppression of traditional Jewish practices—is no doubt accurate.

There were different reactions from those in Judea. While some acquiesced, others resisted. In 167 BCE, a priest named Mattathias and his sons undertook guerilla action at Modein, a town approximately 10 miles northwest of Jerusalem.[24] This action quickly turned into a full-scale rebellion, commonly referred to as the Maccabean revolt (named for one of its

---

22. For detailed accounts of the forced hellenization of Judea, see Victor Tcherikover, *Hellenistic Civilization and the Jews* (Philadelphia: Jewish Publications Society, 1966), 39–203; Elias Bickermann, *The God of the Maccabees* (Leiden: Brill, 1979); John H. Hayes and Sara R. Mandell, *The Jewish People in Classical Antiquity: From Alexander to Bar Kochba* (Louisville: Westminster John Knox, 1998), 43–74.

23. It is unclear who actually erected the desolating sacrilege, presumably a pagan altar, on the altar of sacrifice. The term "they" is ambiguous. It could refer to the Seleucids but it could also point to the Judean leadership.

24. In 1 Maccabees, the origins of the revolt are depicted in almost exclusively religious terms. However, there were probably other forces at work, both political and economic. 2 Maccabees, for example, describes the revolt as motivated not by a desire to protect religious freedom but in order to throw off the yoke of foreign domination.

leaders).[25] The revolt dragged on for many years but ultimately resulted in an independent Jewish state ruled by the sons of Mattathias and their descendants. This dynasty is usually referred to as the Hasmonean dynasty, after its family name.[26] Although armed revolt was obviously the most dramatic response to forced hellenization, it was not the only one. A very different reaction appears in the biblical book of Daniel, a book written at about the same time. But the book of Daniel is not a call to arms; it is instead a call for endurance.

Although the book of Daniel purports to narrate events that occurred during the Babylonian exile (c. 587–539 BCE), the book was actually written during the time of Antiochus IV's suppression of Judaism.[27] The beginning of the book tells the story of Daniel, a young Jew, who arrived in the city of Babylon following the destruction of Jerusalem. In the early chapters, Daniel is portrayed as a member of the Babylonian royal court who possessed the God-given ability to interpret the dreams of the king, dreams that prophesied the king's future. In the latter half of the book, the part where our particular interest lies, the narrative changes considerably. In these chapters, Daniel describes his own dreams and visions of the future. Ironically, the interpreter of the king's dreams in the early chapters of the book was not able to understand his own dreams in the later chapters. Instead, a heavenly figure was needed to interpret his dreams and visions for him. Regardless, Daniel's first vision in this section is particularly instructive for understanding the book's response to Antiochus's policies (Dan 7:1–14).

In this vision, four great beasts emerge from the sea: the first looks like a winged lion, the second, a ravenous bear, the third, a multiheaded, winged leopard, and the fourth appears with "iron teeth" and horns on its head. The fourth beast is further described as "terrifying and dreadful and exceedingly strong" (7:7). As the angelic interpreter later explains, these beasts represent various kingdoms (Dan 7:17). The last beast is clearly the most important one; it signifies the Hellenistic kingdoms of Alexander and his successors. The horns on the head of the fourth beast, Daniel is told, symbolize kings. The last horn, described as a little one with "eyes

25. The title of the revolt comes from the nickname of one of Mattathias's sons, Judas, who was known as Maccabeus ("the hammer").

26. According to Josephus, Mattathias was the great-grandson of Asamonaios of Jerusalem (*Ant.* 12. 265).

27. Most scholars are convinced that the descriptions of the desecration of the Jerusalem temple (Dan 9:27; 11:30–35), although written as predictions, were instead examples of *vaticinium ex eventu* ("prophecy after the event").

like human eyes . . . and a mouth speaking arrogantly" (Dan 7:8) points to Antiochus IV. We know this because the interpreter later informs us that the little horn "shall speak words against the Most High, shall wear out the holy ones of the Most High, and shall attempt to change the sacred seasons and the law" (Dan 7:25).

Next, we see "an Ancient One," clearly the deity, who sits in his throne room surrounded by tens of thousands of attendants. The scene depicts judgment under way: "the court sat in judgment, and the books were opened" (Dan 7:10). The fourth beast is then put to death "and its body destroyed and given over to be burned with fire" (Dan 7:11). Finally, the vision tells of the arrival of a humanlike figure described as "one like a Son of Man."[28] This figure descends on the clouds of heaven. He is presented before the Ancient One who in turn gives him "dominion and glory and kingship, that all peoples, nations, and languages should serve him" (Dan 7:13–14).

By interpreting this vision, we are able to grasp its *apocalyptic* worldview.[29] The apocalyptic perspective perceives history's seemingly inexplicable tragedies as part of the divine plan. Although dismal circumstances might suggest to some God's absence (or even divine abandonment), someone thinking apocalyptically would instead understand these circumstances as divinely ordained. Such bleak conditions were, from the apocalyptic point of view, characteristic of the current age, an era dominated by evil powers.

The procession of predatory beasts in the early part of Daniel's vision provides a good illustration of the apocalyptic perspective; evil powers do and will continue (at least for a time) to control the world. But the domination of these evil powers is not to be considered permanent. Rather, the apocalyptic perspective looks forward to God's intervention in the very near future: soon, all things will be set right. There will be a reckoning; the evil powers that control the present era will be destroyed, as was the fourth beast in Dan 7:11. The vision in the book of Daniel next points to the establishment of justice; eternal "dominion, glory, and kingship" are handed over to the heavenly Son of Man (7:14). From that moment forward, God's rule would be established on earth by his divine agent, the Son of Man. Those who had remained faithful to the covenant (i.e., those who did not

28. The NRSV translates this as "one like a human being," which is a fair translation. However, it is important to note that the original language (Aramaic) says "one like a son of man." This is important because the notion of a "son of man" figure is picked up by later literature, both apocryphal Jewish writings such as 1 Enoch and some of the writings of the New Testament, including the four Gospels and the book of Revelation.

29. The term *apocalyptic* comes from the Greek word *apokalypsis*, meaning "hidden."

give up their Judaism under Antiochus, despite the consequences) would share in that rule.

For righteous Jews enduring persecution under Antiochus IV, Daniel's apocalyptic vision offered a more viable explanation for their distress than the classic justification of suffering found in older scriptural texts. Over and over again in those earlier works, Israel's suffering had been attributed to its own transgressions. For example, the Northern Kingdom's destruction at the hands of Assyria and the Southern Kingdom's exile to Babylon were both explained as consequences of the peoples' willingness to compromise their culture, and specifically to commit idolatry.[30] However, at the time of Antiochus's violent suppression of Judaism, such an explanation made little sense. At that time, Jewish suffering resulted from the peoples' steadfast *refusal* to compromise their Judaism and to worship other gods.[31]

The two examples of Judaism's interaction with Hellenistic culture that have been discussed in this section—the translation of the Scriptures into Greek and the rise of apocalypticism—demonstrate, in the first case, the accommodation of Judaism to the widespread hellenization of the eastern Mediterranean and, in the second case, the limits of that accommodation. For our purposes, these two examples are particularly relevant. Each, in its own way, paved the way for the creation and propagation of the Jesus movement. On the one hand, as the Jesus movement made its way into the non-Jewish world, its missionaries were able to introduce the Jewish Scriptures—in their Greek incarnation—to their pagan audiences. On the other hand, Daniel's apocalypticism provided the context for both Jesus's message and the message spread about him by his disciples following his death. Indeed, the vision that we have seen in Daniel was particularly appropriate for members of the early Jesus movement. After Jesus's death, they identified him with the "Son of Man."

30. While there are many biblical examples, perhaps the most instructive is Ezekiel's allegory of the two promiscuous sisters, Oholah and Oholibah, in Ezek 23. Oholah represents the Northern Kingdom, centered at Samaria; Oholibah symbolizes the Southern Kingdom, with Jerusalem as its capital. Both of the sisters are depicted as whores, because they lusted after the Assyrians and Babylonians (as well as their idols) respectively. As a result, the prophet anticipates their punishment. He states: "Your lewdness and your whorings have brought this upon you, because you played the whore with the nations, and polluted yourself with their idols" (Ezek 23:29–30).

31. Although the origins of apocalypticism are earlier than the persecution of Antiochus IV, its relevance during that time gave it a prominence that it probably did not have earlier.

The Collapse of the Hellenistic Kingdoms and the Coming of Rome

As we have seen, in his apocalyptic visions, Daniel anticipated the collapse of the Hellenistic kingdoms. But he did *not* foresee another earthly empire arising to take their place. That, however, is what happened. Approximately a century after the book of Daniel was written, the Seleucid Empire was no more. A new earthly power from the West now ruled in its stead. A later Jewish apocalyptic author, writing approximately two and a half centuries after Daniel was composed, attempted to come to terms with the vision of chapter 7 in the earlier book. In his text, known as 4 Ezra, he described a vision of a monstrous eagle, an obvious symbol for Rome. The vision was subsequently explained in that later work as follows: "The eagle that you saw coming up from the sea is the fourth kingdom that appeared in a vision to your brother Daniel. But it was not explained to him as I now explain to you. . . . The days are coming when a kingdom shall rise on earth, and it shall be more terrifying than all the kingdoms that have been before it" (4 Ezra 12:11–13). According to this later author, the fourth kingdom in Daniel's vision was not the Hellenistic kingdom of Antiochus IV. Rather, it was the empire of Rome.

While the Seleucids and the Ptolemies were busy trying to destroy one another, Rome was gathering power in the West. The incessant wars between the Hellenistic dynasties contributed significantly to the downfall of each. The very fact that the Maccabean revolt was able to succeed clearly demonstrates the weakness of the Seleucid Empire in the second century CE. Contrast that to its early years when it looked to be the most significant of all the Hellenistic kingdoms. Following the battle of Ipsus (301 BCE), Seleucus controlled what is now eastern Turkey, Syria, Iraq, Armenia, southern Azerbaijan, Iran, Afghanistan, Pakistan, southern Uzbekistan, and Kyrgystan. But, by the conclusion of the Maccabean revolt, the Seleucids ruled only Syria.

The Ptolemaic Empire did not fare any better. Following Ipsus, Ptolemy controlled a sizeable territory starting with what is now eastern Libya, continuing counter-clockwise around the Mediterranean all the way to the modern-day southeastern Turkey, and ending with Cyprus. Although the Ptolemaic Empire did not shrink as dramatically as the Seleucid kingdom, by the middle of the second century BCE, the Ptolemies held Egypt alone. Years of feuding between the once great powers took their inevitable toll.

By the late first century BCE, Rome would control the entirety of the eastern Mediterranean (as well as Gaul and Spain in the West). But Rome's influence had also been felt in the East much earlier than that. For example, in the 190s BCE, the Roman military responded to an incursion by the Seleucid ruler Antiochus III into mainland Greece.[32] Rome drove Antiochus III out of Europe, followed him across the Hellespont into Asia and decisively defeated him at the city of Magnesia near Mt. Sipylus (near present-day Izmir, Turkey). But, after Antiochus's defeat, the Romans did not stay in Asia. Instead, they chose to return home. This was typical of Roman dealings in the East. Rome would intervene in the affairs of the Seleucids, the Ptolemies, and the Antigonids (the dynasty that came to dominate Macedon and Greece), when it suited Roman interests. That intervention was at times diplomatic and at times military. But, if the latter, the Romans chose not to linger. They preferred to remain in Italy.

But things changed in the mid–second century BCE. After several attempts to check the expansionist ambitions of the Antigonids, Rome moved east to stay; in 148 BCE, Macedon became a tribute-paying province of Rome, ruled by a Roman governor. Shortly thereafter, in 133 BCE, the Attalid ruler of Pergamum, Attalus III, died. Although Pergamum had successfully controlled northeastern Asia Minor for over a century, at his death Attalus bequeathed his realm to Rome.[33] Suddenly, Rome was in Asia. It did not take long for Rome to subdue its weakened Seleucid and Ptolemaic rivals. Within little more than a century, Rome would control the entire eastern Mediterranean.[34]

It is important to note here that when Rome took political control of the eastern Mediterranean world, that part of the empire retained its Hellenistic culture. While in western provinces like Gaul or Hispania (modern-day France and Spain), native peoples were expected to adapt to the Roman way of life, in the East, it was the Romans who adapted to Hellenism. The Greek language remained the language of choice, as evidenced by the fact that the whole of the New Testament—including Paul's letter to the Romans!—was composed in Greek. Homer continued to be taught, as did Plato and Aristotle. For some reason, the Romans were not threatened by the hellenization of the East. Rather, they embraced it.

---

32. The Aetolian League, an alliance of Greek city-states, requested aid from Antiochus against Rome. It is likely, at this point, that Antiochus thought his kingdom to be as powerful as Rome and he probably figured that if he drove Rome out of Greece, he could rule the East. Obviously, he was mistaken.

33. Attalus III had no son to succeed him and it is possible that he was trying to prevent a struggle for the throne.

34. Beginning in 63 BCE, Judea was ruled by Rome. Following Octavian's victory over the alliance of Marc Antony and Cleopatra (the last ruler of the Ptolemaic dynasty) at the Battle of Actium (31 BCE), Rome annexed Egypt.

Roman Rule in Judea

Roman authority arrived in Judea in the person of the general Gnaeus Pompey in 63 BCE. The original purpose of Pompey's military campaign to the East was to suppress unrest in Asia Minor. But, having achieved that goal, he did not immediately return to Rome. Instead, he headed south along the Mediterranean coast, defeated the last Seleucid ruler, Antiochus XIII "Asiaticus," and established Syria as a Roman province. Meanwhile, further to the south in Jerusalem, a struggle for leadership had been underway between two Hasmonean brothers, Hyrcanus II and Aristobulus II, each claiming the right to rule. Both appealed to Pompey for support. Pompey backed Hyrcanus II; however, he refused him the title of king. Instead, he allowed him to assume only the titles of High Priest and Ethnarch ("ruler of a people"). By so doing, Pompey supported the right of Hyrcanus to manage the affairs of Judea but, at the same time, he made it abundantly clear that Judea was now firmly under the control of Rome. Although Hyrcanus was allowed to rule locally, he was also expected to send tribute to the Romans and, if necessary, to answer to the Roman provincial governor of Syria.

Unfortunately, a succession of corrupt Roman governors in Syria fomented anti-Roman sentiment in Judea, which in turn led to an extended period of political instability there. Several attempts were made to reestablish Hasmonean independence but each was quashed by the Romans. Meanwhile, across the Mediterranean, power struggles among the leaders of the Roman Republic broke out—first between Pompey and Julius Caesar and then later, after Caesar was assassinated (44 BCE), between Octavian (Caesar's heir and nephew) and Mark Antony.[35] These power struggles held Rome's attention for almost two decades. For better or worse, the infighting among Roman leaders left a great deal of room in Judea for individuals or factions to maneuver politically.

When the strife among the Roman leaders ultimately reached its end in 31 BCE, Octavian emerged as the uncontested Roman leader.[36] Shortly after

35. Pompey was defeated by Julius Caesar at the Battle of Pharsalus in central Greece. Pompey fled to Egypt where he sought refuge but he was assassinated immediately upon his arrival there in 48 BCE. Following Julius Caesar's assassination in 44 BCE, Octavian and Antony together defeated Caesar's murderers, Brutus and Cassius, at Philippi in 42 BCE. Following Philippi, Antony allied himself with Cleopatra VIII of Egypt and took control of the eastern Mediterranean.

36. Octavian ultimately triumphed over Antony and Cleopatra at Actium off the western coast of Greece in 31 BCE.

Antony's defeat, Cleopatra—the last Ptolemaic ruler and Antony's ally—committed suicide (as did Antony). Consequently, Egypt, as well as virtually all of the Mediterranean, was now under Rome's control. Octavian was soon to be named Augustus, Rome's first emperor. Meanwhile, in Judea, Herod, the son of Antipater (a former official to Hyrcanus II), was appointed king by the Romans and commissioned to rule Judea in their stead. But, despite his appointment, he was not in control of Judea at that time. Rather, it was being governed by Antigonus, the son of Aristobulus II.[37] The Romans expected Herod to take control of the territory himself. He succeeded in capturing the city of Jerusalem in 37 BCE. From then until his death in 4 BCE, Herod governed Judea on Rome's behalf. It was at the end of Herod's rule that Jesus of Nazareth was probably born.[38]

Little got in the way of Herod's ambition. Anyone that he perceived as a threat to his rule was dealt with severely. This included Mariamne, his third wife, whom he executed in 29 BCE. Toward the end of his reign, he also executed a number of Pharisees who, according to Josephus, had "corrupted some of the people at court" (*Jewish Antiquities* 17.44).[39] Herod also killed two of his sons, Alexander and Aristobulus, sons that he had with Mariamne, on the charge that they were plotting his overthrow. This act allegedly prompted the emperor Augustus to quip—punning on the Greek words "son" (*huios*) and "pig" (*hus*)—"it was better to be Herod's pig (*hus*) than his son (*huios*)."[40] In other words, Herod, as a Jew, would not kill a pig (since the eating of pork was forbidden), but he obviously had no qualms about slaughtering his own children.

Despite his reputation for brutality, Herod was nonetheless a relatively

---

37. The history surrounding Herod's rise to power is complex. Herod's father, Antipater, who had served Julius Caesar in Egypt, consolidated power in Judea and, with Rome's support, became its de facto ruler. He appointed his son Herod to rule Galilee. Antipater, however, was assassinated in 43 BCE and shortly thereafter anarchy broke out. During this time, Antigonus, the nephew of Hyrcanus (the last Hasmonean king of Judea) and son of Aristobulus II (the rival of Hyrcanus II), formed an alliance with the Parthians, Rome's eastern rival. With Parthian backing, Antigonus seized power. Herod fled to Rome. There he was appointed ruler of Judea by the Roman senate (in either 40 or 39 BCE—ancient sources differ).

38. Herod is named as the ruler at (or shortly before) the time of Jesus's birth in Matthew 2 and in Luke 1:5. The Herod mentioned elsewhere in the Gospels is a different person, Herod Antipas, the son of Herod; Antipas ruled a portion of the earlier Herod's kingdom after his death.

39. While it is unclear exactly what the Pharisees' activities had been, it is likely that they were plotting an overthrow of the aging ruler.

40. The remark is preserved in Latin by Macrobius, *Sat.* 2.4.11 (although the pun does not work in that language): *Melior est Herodis porcum esse quam filium.*

capable leader. During his reign, Judea thrived economically. Unemployment was low, in part because of Herod's many building projects. These included the transformation of the coastal town, Strato's Tower, into a Hellenistic city, a city that he renamed Caesarea in honor of Caesar Augustus. In Caesarea, Herod constructed a theater, hippodrome, an imperial temple (dedicated to Augustus), an aqueduct that brought water from Mount Carmel some 20 miles to the north, and an artificial deepwater harbor. Herod also constructed massive palace-fortresses at Herodium (south of Jerusalem), Masada, and Jerusalem.

In Jerusalem itself Herod built a theater, an amphitheater, and a hippodrome. Most significantly, he completely rebuilt the Jerusalem temple. The temple's construction took over forty years and resulted in a magnificent structure that, unfortunately, would not survive the Jewish revolt of 66–73 CE.[41] A later Jewish text claimed that "he who has not seen the Temple of Herod has never seen a beautiful building" (b. B. Bat. 4a). Because of Herod's many construction projects in his capital, Jerusalem gained a significant reputation throughout the empire. The Roman author Pliny the Elder claimed that it was "easily the most outstanding city in the East" (*Natural History* 5.70).

Herod respected Jewish sensibilities within his territory, for the most part. When constructing the temple, for example, he employed priests as masons and carpenters since it was not lawful for non-priests to enter the temple itself. Nevertheless, he came into conflict with religious leaders over various matters, particularly toward the end of his reign. Some felt that Herod's assimilation to pagan culture was excessive. As Herod's health declined, two religious leaders convinced some of the young men of Jerusalem to tear down a golden eagle that Herod had installed over one of the temple gates. The leaders insisted that the eagle, as an image of a living creature, represented a violation of Jewish law.[42] After the young men tore down and destroyed the eagle, the perpetrators were arrested and taken to Herod. Outraged by the act, Herod had the leaders and some of the participants burned alive. Furthermore, he deposed the high priest, presumably for allowing the incident to occur.

When Herod died (4 BCE), his kingdom fell into chaos. Herod had stipulated in his will that his sons, Archelaus, Herod Antipas, and Philip, should inherit his realm—Archelaus as king, Antipas as tetrarch (literally, "ruler of a fourth") over Galilee and Perea (a strip of land to the east of the Jordan River),

---

41. John 2:20 claims that construction took forty-six years. It is not known if the author of that Gospel had accurate information but forty-six years is at least a reasonable approximation.

42. The offensiveness of the eagle may have been compounded by the fact that the eagle was a well-known symbol of Roman power (although it is unclear whether Herod intended it as such).

and Philip as tetrarch of the territories northeast of the Sea of Galilee. But, before any of them could take power, Herod's will had to be ratified by the Romans. In the meantime, the people of Jerusalem, recognizing that Archelaus was in line to be named king, demanded that he immediately lower taxes, release prisoners, and reinstate the high priest who had been deposed by his father following the golden eagle incident. But since Archelaus did not yet have Rome's blessing, he was powerless to do anything. Although he appeared sympathetic to the demands, he made no commitments.

At the festival of Passover, the crowd turned violent. Clashes between the people and police led Archelaus to send troops to the temple to reestablish order. The ensuing fracas resulted in a large number of deaths; according to Josephus, some three thousand people were killed (*Jewish Antiquities* 17.200–218; *Jewish War* 2.4–13). Leaving this volatile situation in the hands of Philip—his half brother, Archelaus set sail for Rome. There he attempted to convince Augustus to appoint him king in his father's place. Meanwhile, the crisis in Jerusalem intensified. Sabinus, a Roman official of the Syrian province, arrived at Jerusalem with troops to seize Herod's treasury and to occupy his strongholds. Sabinus's actions aggravated an already tense situation. At the Jewish festival of Pentecost (*Shavu'ot*), a festival that took place fifty days after Passover, a large group of Jews laid siege to Sabinus and his troops, trapping them in Herod's palace-fortress in Jerusalem. While the Romans were stuck there, unrest broke out in several places throughout Judea.

In the city of Sepphoris (in Galilee), the son of a former revolutionary named Judas seized a royal armory and took control of the surrounding area. In Perea (the territory east of the Jordan River), one of Herod's slaves, a certain Simon, proclaimed himself king. He and his followers burned Herod's winter palace at Jericho and plundered the surrounding territory. At the same time, elsewhere, a shepherd named Athronges proclaimed himself king. Accompanied by his four brothers and a significant number of followers, he set out to kill both Romans and Herodian allies. Josephus aptly summed up the situation: "Judea was filled with brigandage" (*Jewish Antiquities* 17.285). Order was restored only with the arrival of two Roman legions led by Varus, the Roman governor of Syria. Varus freed Sabinus and his besieged troops and then set about quashing the revolts. After restoring order in most areas, Varus crucified about two thousand rebels (*Jewish Antiquities* 17.295).

Meanwhile in Rome, arguments were made for and against Archelaus as king in Judea. Antipas, his brother, argued that Archelaus alone should rule since Herod's earlier will had left the kingdom in its entirety to him. A man named Nicholas of Damascus also argued in Archelaus's favor. But another delegation from Judea argued to the contrary. They asserted that none of Herod's sons should rule; Judea should instead be joined to the Roman province of Syria. In the end, Augustus divided Herod's territory closely along the lines laid out in Herod's will. But he did not give Archelaus the title of king. Instead, he made him tetrarch, the same title that he gave Herod Antipas and Philip. As a result, none of Herod's sons had authority over the others.

Of Herod's three sons, Philip seems to have been the most effective. He was the only one of the three to reign until his death (33/34 CE). He was also the only successor granted the coveted right to mint coins. He rebuilt the city of Paneas and renamed it Caesarea after the emperor.[43] Although Antipas did not rule to the end of his life, nevertheless, of the three tetrarchs, he reigned the longest (4 BCE–39 CE). Like his father, he was known for his construction projects. Among them, he rebuilt the city of Sepphoris (near Nazareth) and founded a new capital on the western shore of the Sea of Galilee. He named the capital Tiberias in honor of the emperor Tiberius, Augustus's successor.[44]

Antipas is probably best remembered for executing John the Baptist, an apocalyptic preacher who appears in all four New Testament Gospels as well as in one of Josephus's writings. The reason that John was executed is unclear. According to the Gospels, Antipas imprisoned him because he had condemned Antipas's marriage to Herodias, his brother's wife (Mark 6:17–19; cf. Matt 14:2–3; Luke 3:19).[45] The Gospels claimed that Antipas later executed him reluctantly because he had foolishly promised his daughter whatever she wanted ("even half my kingdom") after she had danced for him at a banquet. At the instigation of her mother, his daughter requested John's head (Mark 6:22–28; cf. Matt 14:6–11). Josephus, however, said nothing about the banquet. Instead, he indicated that Antipas was afraid that John's preaching was fomenting insurrection (*Jewish Antiquities* 18.116–18).[46]

43. This is the Caesarea Philippi mentioned in Mark 8:27 and Matt 16:13.

44. Augustus reigned until his death in 14 CE. He was succeeded by his adopted son Tiberius who ruled until 37 CE.

45. There is some confusion in Mark's and Matthew's accounts for they both claim that Antipas (called simply "Herod" in each narrative) had married his brother Philip's wife. In fact, Antipas married his half brother Herod II's wife. Her daughter, Salome, was Philip's wife.

46. Some combination of the two is possible. For example, John's preaching of a coming judgment may have "made some people think that they might lend God a hand and strike the first blow against immoral rulers. . . . If we combine Antipas' fear of insurrection (Josephus) and John's prediction of a dramatic future event that would transform the present order (the Gospels), we find a perfectly good reason for the execution. If John criticized Antipas' marriage, Antipas would have been all the readier to strike, and Herodias may have urged him on" (E. P. Sanders, *The Historical Figure of Jesus* [London: Penguin, 1993], 93).

Herod's son Archelaus was the least successful of the three tetrarchs; he ruled only ten years (4 BCE–6 CE), possibly because his territory was the most difficult to govern (in that it contained the capital). But it is also possible that his earlier act of sending troops against his would-be subjects predestined his rule to fail from its start. Unfortunately, we know very little about his administration. However, we do know that the people of Samaria and Judea (here meaning not all of Herod's territory but only the area south of Samaria) eventually banded together to complain about Archelaus to Augustus. They accused him of cruelty and tyranny. Surprisingly, Augustus acceded to their demands. He deposed Archelaus and banished him to Gaul. However, Augustus did not replace Archelaus with another from Herod's line nor did he give his territory to one of the other tetrarchs. Instead he placed Archelaus's territory under the supervision of the province of Syria. This meant that, henceforth, a military officer (called a prefect) would supervise the region.[47]

One may recall that some of Herod's former subjects had requested this kind of arrangement from Augustus as he was considering a succession plan; the Judean delegation believed that the people would be governed more fairly. Unfortunately, the military governorship did not work to the people's advantage. First, in order to assess the amount to be charged in taxes, the governor of the province of Syria, Quirinius, carried out a census.[48] Jewish opposition to it was immediate and passionate. A certain Judas, together with a Pharisee named Saddok, began an armed revolt, claiming that the census "carried with it a status amounting to downright slavery . . . and [they] appealed to the nation to make a bid for independence . . . and that Heaven would be their zealous helper to no lesser end than the furthering of their enterprise until it succeeded—all the more if with high devotion in their hearts they did not shrink from the bloodshed that might be necessary" (Josephus, *Jewish Antiquities* 18.4–5). Although Josephus does not tell us much more about the activities of Judas or Saddok, the book of Acts indicates that the armed revolt led by this individual ultimately failed (5:37).

The second reason that the military governorship did not benefit the people also had to do with taxes. Taxes in Archelaus's former territory increased significantly. Those taxes that the people had previously paid to Archelaus (and Herod before him) were increased and, since the people were now inhabitants of a Roman province, they were furthermore responsible for paying an annual

---

47. The prefect's residence was not in Jerusalem but rather in Caesarea, on the coast.

48. This is almost certainly the census mentioned in Luke 2:1–3, although Luke is mistaken about its timing and scope.

head tax (a *tributum capitis* in Latin).[49] Resentment over taxes likely lay behind the question posed to Jesus: "Should one pay taxes to Caesar?" (Mark 12:14; cf. Matt 22:17; Luke 20:22).

We know very little about the first four military governors who ruled over the former territory of Archelaus. But we know a fair amount about the fifth, Pontius Pilate. The Gospels, Josephus, and the Jewish philosopher Philo narrate several events from his reign. From what we can learn from these sources, Pilate went out of his way to offend the Jews that he ruled. For example, previous military governors had prevented their troops from entering Jerusalem with standards that depicted the emperor on medallions because, as Josephus claims, "our law forbids the making of images." Pilate, however, took "a bold step in subversion of Jewish practices, by introducing into the city busts of the emperor that were attached to the military standards" (*Jewish Antiquities* 18.55). At another time, Pilate confiscated funds from the temple to construct a new aqueduct for Jerusalem.[50] When the people gathered to complain, he dispatched soldiers—dressed as civilians—into the crowds to beat the protesters with clubs (Josephus, *Jewish War* 2.175–77; *Jewish Antiquities* 18.60–62).

The Gospel of Mark suggests that there was armed resistance among the Jews under Pilate. In connection with an outlaw named Barabbas, the Gospel mentioned "rebels in prison" and an "insurrection" that had occurred, although no further details were given (Mark 15:7; cf. Luke 23:19). The Gospel of Luke referred to "the Galileans whose blood Pilate had mingled with their sacrifices" but, like Mark in the earlier passage, Luke gave no further details (13:1). Could Luke's statement have been a reference to Pilate's brutal response to a revolt?[51] Revolutionary activity during his tenure as prefect

49. The Roman historian Tacitus gave us a piece of interesting information that confirms that the burden of the taxes was indeed significant. He relates that when Germanicus, the emperor Tiberius's adopted son, was in the area, "Syria and Judea, exhausted by their burdens, [pressed] for a diminution of the tribute" (*Ann.* 2.42.5).

50. Ancient temples, including the Jerusalem temple, frequently functioned as banks, that is, secure places (protected by the deity) where one could deposit valuables.

51. Pilate's reaction to an armed Samaritan group, intent on recovering sacred vessels allegedly hidden at Mount Gerizim by Moses, is telling. Although our source gives no evidence of outright revolutionary activity, Pilate nonetheless executed the ringleaders (Josephus, *Ant.* 18.85–89). Pilate's reaction in this case, however, cost him his job, for the Samaritans appealed to the Syrian governor who ordered Pilate to Rome for trial. It is unclear what happened to Pilate following that. The fourth-century Christian historian Eusebius claims that Pilate was banished to Gaul where he ultimately committed suicide (*Hist. eccl.* 2.7) but there are no earlier sources that report his fate.

would help to explain Pilate's swift crucifixion of Jesus of Nazareth, the "king of the Jews."[52]

Summary and Conclusions

This chapter began with a discussion of Alexander's conquest and the events that followed his untimely death. Alexander's dream of a single, unified world was never politically realized by any of his inner circle; for decades, many struggled to gain control over the entirety of his realm, but to no avail. The heirs of Alexander's would-be successors continued their fathers' struggles as did the generations that followed them. After centuries of battle, the various kingdoms that emerged out of Alexander's realm eventually wore each other out, making way for Rome to pick up the pieces. Nevertheless, although political unity failed, Alexander's dream of the cultural unity of the East largely succeeded. The empires that dominated the eastern Mediterranean world in the third and second centuries BCE—the Ptolemies, the Seleucids, the Attalids, and the Antigonids—were all *Hellenistic* kingdoms. The hellenization was so thorough that the eastern Mediterranean remained largely hellenized for a millennium, until the Muslim conquest in the seventh century CE.

We next turned to the Jewish reaction to hellenization, focusing on two different phenomena. The first was the production of the Septuagint, a Greek translation of the Hebrew Scriptures. The production of the Septuagint was almost certainly motivated by diaspora Jews who could no longer read the Scriptures in Hebrew; nevertheless they wished to remain connected to their cultural and religious heritage. Although we do not know much about the process, it probably began in the third century BCE, continued for many years, and was more or less completed by the late second century BCE. Although the translations made the Scriptures available to diaspora Jews, they also made them available to pagans, some of whom showed interest. Furthermore, the translation of the Scriptures into Greek would, many years later, ease the Jesus movement's entrance into the pagan cities of the Roman Empire.

The second Jewish response to hellenization that we considered centered on the forced hellenization of the Judean Jews in the second century BCE. The actions of the Seleucid ruler Antiochus IV showed us that although Judaism by and large accepted hellenization, most Jews were unwilling to hellenize

---

52. That Jesus was accused of sedition as "king of the Jews" appears in Mark 15:26, Matt 27:37, Luke 23:38, and John 19:21.

to the point of abandoning their own cultural and religious traditions. The forced hellenization of Judea ultimately had two significant results, each of which would eventually contribute to a change in the landscape of the eastern Mediterranean. First, the attempt to force hellenization politically backfired on Antiochus. It gave rise to an armed insurrection, the Maccabean revolt, that ultimately enabled Judea to break free of Seleucid control. Second, Antiochus's actions stimulated the rise of apocalyptic thinking, a Jewish worldview that subsequently influenced the religious thinking of the Judeans during Roman times, Judeans that included John the Baptist and Jesus of Nazareth.

Finally, we turned to Rome's conquest of the eastern Mediterranean and, in particular, Roman rule of Judea. Although Rome had initially been content to influence eastern events from afar, Antigonid actions on the Greek peninsula in the mid–second century BCE finally convinced Rome that it would be best to establish a Roman province in Greece. Shortly thereafter, Rome moved into Asia. In 64 BCE, the Seleucid Empire breathed its last as the Roman general Pompey established Syria as a Roman province. A few decades later, Rome took over what remained of the Ptolemaic Empire, when Octavian defeated Antony and his ally, Cleopatra, the last Ptolemaic ruler, at Actium.

Unlike in Syria, Egypt, and many other of its conquered territories, Rome governed Judea by means of a local client king, Herod. Although brutal at times, Herod ruled effectively. At his death, however, the landscape changed. Herod's realm was divided among three of his sons, none of whom had supreme power. Herod's sons Antipas and Philip ruled successfully, at least from the standpoint of the Romans. The third son, Archelaus, charged with governing Jerusalem and its environs, was, however, unsuccessful. Within ten years, his subjects had complained directly to the emperor who, surprisingly, acceded to their request to depose Archelaus. But instead of replacing Archelaus with another client ruler (or attaching his territory to that of Antipas or Philip), Augustus put it under military rule; its prefect was answerable to the governor of the province of Syria. We know almost nothing of the first four prefects who took power, but we have considerable information about the fifth, Pontius Pilate. Pilate's deliberate antagonizing of his Jewish subjects gave rise to unrest among the population. It was under this prefect that Jesus was executed. We will explore Jesus's teachings and activities as well as the possible reasons for his execution in the chapter that follows.

CHAPTER 2

The Early Years of the Jesus Movement

This chapter concerns both the ministry of Jesus and that of his disciples right after Jesus's death. Unfortunately, uncovering accurate information about either is complicated. On the one hand, the sources that focus on the teachings and actions of Jesus are neither early nor are they unbiased. On the other hand, only one document recounts the period of time shortly following Jesus's death; but that text—the book of Acts—was written six to nine decades after the events that it narrates. Furthermore, Acts clearly presents an idealized account of what happened. Because of these difficulties, before attempting any historical statements, we must address some methodological issues.

Looking for the Historical Jesus

What can we know about the life and ministry of Jesus of Nazareth? To many, this may sound like an odd question; after all, the New Testament contains four different accounts of Jesus's life and ministry. It would seem that these four accounts—the Gospels of Matthew, Mark, Luke, and John—would tell us all that we need to know about Jesus. Unfortunately, although the task may look simple, it is not. Significant problems attend any attempt to use the Gospels to reconstruct the life, activities, and teachings of Jesus. Particularly notable are the inconsistencies among the narratives. Three of the accounts, the so-called Synoptic Gospels (the Gospels of Matthew, Mark, and Luke), look fairly similar to one another. They represent, for the most part, variations on one narrative. But the fourth narrative, the Gospel of John, seems to tell a rather different story.

According to the story shared by the Synoptic Gospels, not long after his baptism in the Jordan River (a ritual performed by John the Baptist), Jesus began to preach throughout the area of Galilee. There he preached about the kingdom of God.[1] Jesus's preaching was terse; he taught using short sayings and brief parables. He also healed and exorcised (i.e., cast out) demons. After less than a year, Jesus traveled south to Jerusalem for the festival of Passover. While in that city, he entered the temple, turned over the tables of the money changers and the seats of the dove sellers, and accused them of making the temple a "den of bandits." Shortly thereafter, Jesus was arrested and condemned to death by the Roman prefect, Pilate.

On the other hand, according to John's Gospel, even though Jesus crossed paths with John the Baptist, there is no specific mention of his being baptized. The fourth Gospel tells us that Jesus preached not only in Galilee; he traveled back and forth a number of times between Galilee and Jerusalem. Furthermore, he almost never talked about the kingdom of God.[2] Rather, he spoke primarily about himself using metaphorical language of a kind not found in the other Gospels. He referred to himself as "the bread of life," "the light of the world," "the good shepherd," "the resurrection and the life," "the way, and the truth, and the life," and "the true vine."[3] The Jesus of John's Gospel did not teach using parables or short sayings; instead he delivered long monologues. Although he healed, he did not exorcise. Finally, as the author of John's Gospel tells the story, Jesus's disruptive action in the temple happened at the beginning of his ministry, not at its end.

Understanding the Sources

Overall, scholars are convinced that the portrait of Jesus that appears in the Synoptic Gospels represents the historical Jesus better than what is found in John's Gospel. However, to conclude that the Gospel of John gives the least historically reliable information about the historical Jesus does not thereby automatically mean that Matthew, Mark, and Luke provide us with an accurate portrait. A significant number of inconsistencies appear among these three

1. Matthew's Gospel rarely uses the phrase "kingdom of God." Rather, in that Gospel, Jesus speaks about the "kingdom of heaven." It is likely that the author's Jewish piety led him to refer to the deity indirectly. Regardless, the phrases are equivalent.

2. Jesus mentions the kingdom of God in John's Gospel only twice (at 3:3 and 3:5). Compare that to Luke's Gospel where the kingdom of God is mentioned thirty-two times.

3. For "the bread of life," see John 6:35 and 6:48; for "the light of the world," see 8:12 and 9:5; for "the good shepherd," see 10:11 and 14; for "the resurrection and the life," see 11:25; for "the way, and the truth, and the life," see 14:6; and for "the true vine," see 15:1.

Gospels. A few of the many examples that could be mentioned include the following:

1. In the Gospel of Matthew, Jesus insists on the continuing relevance of the Jewish law (i.e., the Torah).[4] This means that followers of Jesus were expected to, among other things, avoid foods that were ritually unclean (i.e., not kosher).[5] But, in Mark's Gospel, Jesus expressly overturns the food laws: "he declared all foods clean" (Mark 7:19).[6]
2. The Gospel of Matthew tells us that Jesus's father was a carpenter (Matt 13:55). But according to Mark's Gospel, it was Jesus who was the carpenter (Mark 6:3); no human father is even mentioned by Mark.
3. Both the Gospels of Matthew and Luke trace Jesus's ancestry; Matthew begins his genealogy with Abraham (Matt 1:1–16) while Luke traces Jesus's lineage back to Adam (Luke 3:23–38). While there is agreement or near agreement with regard to Jesus's ancestors from Abraham to David, from David on—a span of some 1,000 years—the genealogies do not match. They are not even close.
4. The Gospel of Luke indicates that Jesus and John the Baptist were relatives (1:36). The authors of the Gospels of Mark and Matthew, however, know nothing about this family connection.
5. In the Gospel of Mark, Jesus announces the imminent end of the age. In the other Synoptic Gospels, the end is envisioned as further in the future.[7] This is especially the case in Luke's Gospel. There, Jesus does not expect the end for many years.

Obviously, some of these inconsistencies are more important than others. But many of them—such as Jesus's view regarding Torah observance—are ex-

4. In Matt 5:18, Jesus says, "For truly I tell you, until heaven and earth pass away, not one letter, not one stroke of a letter, will pass from the law."

5. The biblical regulations on acceptable and unacceptable food are found in Lev 11 and Deut 14:3–21.

6. It is telling that in the parallel passage in Matthew (15:17), the phrase "thus declaring all foods clean" is omitted because, as already noted, Matthew believed in the continuing relevance of the Jewish law.

7. Compare Mark 13:1–37 to Matt 24:1–25:13 and Luke 21:5–36. Note that Matthew follows Jesus's apocalyptic discourse with two parables that speak of the delay of a master and a bridegroom. Both of these parables are used by Matthew to explain the delay of Jesus's return. Note also that Luke changes the meaning of Mark's desolating sacrilege (13:14), a sign of the end-time's imminence in Mark's Gospel, to refer to *Jerusalem's* end (21:20; cf. 21:24), not the end of the world.

tremely significant. Regardless, the fact that there are so many inconsistencies tells us that we cannot simply accept our sources at face value.

At the same time, we should not conclude from the inconsistencies that *all* of the material in these Gospels is historically unreliable. Indeed, the Gospels of Matthew, Mark, and Luke remain our best sources of information regarding the historical Jesus.[8] But accurate historical information seems to be interspersed with other material. How do we determine which is which? In order to answer that question, we need to understand a few things about the composition of the Synoptic Gospels.

Who Wrote the Gospels?

Unfortunately, we do not know who wrote any of the Gospels.[9] We can, however, eliminate some candidates. People from Jesus's inner circle almost certainly did not compose them. Although many readers assume that each Gospel gives eyewitness testimony from one of Jesus's original followers, three of the Gospels make no such claim. Nor do they identify their authors. The exception is the Gospel of John. At its very end, the assertion is made that the text was written by "the disciple that Jesus loved" (21:20, 24), a nameless character who appears in several other places in the Gospel. Nevertheless, the section in which this claim appears, chapter 21, was probably not part of the original Gospel; it was added later. However, even though the Gospels do not claim to have been composed by eyewitnesses, the lack of such a claim does not alone preclude that possibility. But, evidence from within the Gospels themselves

8. Virtually all of the information about Jesus from Greco-Roman authors is either late or paltry. The writings of the Jewish author Josephus provide a few references to Jesus. Unfortunately, the most noteworthy passage, the so-called *Testimonium Flavianum* (*Ant.* 18.3.3), exhibits signs of significant Christian redaction; we cannot be sure what came from the pen of Josephus and what came from the later hand. Although several attempts have been made to restore Josephus's original wording, no single reconstruction has been able to convince the majority of scholars. Although there are noncanonical Gospels, they are also late, from the second and third centuries. The exception is the Gospel of Thomas, which seems to contain some early material (although its final form is late). For an overview of the passages in Josephus and later pagan authors, see John P. Meier, *The Roots of the Problem and the Person,* vol. 1 of *A Marginal Jew: Rethinking the Historical Jesus,* ABRL (New York: Doubleday, 1991), 56–111.

9. Somewhere along the line, the four Gospels were credited to people named Matthew, Mark, Luke, and John. Those attributions are probably from the second century. The likelihood that the Gospels originally circulated without these names attached is suggested by the fact that some fourth-century manuscripts of Mark's Gospel are not labeled "According to Mark."

suggests otherwise. Indeed, we can be certain that the Synoptic Gospels (and possibly John's Gospel as well) are literarily related to one another.

Due to the close similarities that exist among the Synoptic Gospels, scholars have long suspected that some of the Gospel writers had access to one or more of the other Gospels when composing their texts. By the end of the nineteenth century, most had come to the conclusion that Mark was the earliest Gospel written and that the authors of Matthew and Luke each used Mark as one of their primary sources. Since an eyewitness would hardly need to depend on literary sources to tell his story, scholars were convinced that the Gospels of Matthew and Luke were not eyewitness accounts.[10] Of the three clearly interdependent (Synoptic) Gospels, this leaves only the possibility that the earliest Gospel, Mark, represents a first-hand report. But there are a number of problems with that hypothesis, not the least of which is the fact that none of the Gospels mention a follower of Jesus named Mark.

Why Were the Gospels Written?

Did the earliest Gospel writer (the author of the Gospel of Mark) intend to write a biography of Jesus? If we are speaking of biography as we currently understand it, the answer would be no.[11] The author of Mark's Gospel showed virtually no interest in the kinds of things that we would look for in a biography. For example, little is revealed to the reader about Jesus's immediate family;

10. The author of the Gospel of Luke claims that he was dependent on eyewitness accounts when he wrote his Gospel (Luke 1:2). Such an assertion suggests (although it does not prove) that the author himself was not an eyewitness.

11. From the standpoint of the ancients, Mark's Gospel would probably have been considered a biography. But our notion of biography differs significantly. We believe a biography should provide a complete, historically accurate account of an individual's entire life (insofar as that is possible). Ancient biographies, however, were more concerned with the "essence" and the "character" of the individual. Historical matters were secondary. In his parallel lives of Alexander and Caesar, the ancient writer Plutarch warned his readers, "I shall make no other preface than to entreat my readers, in case I do not tell of all the famous actions of these men, nor even speak exhaustively at all in each particular case, . . . not to complain. For it is not Histories (*historiai*) that I am writing, but Lives (*bioi*). . . . Accordingly, just as painters get the likenesses in their portraits from the face and the expression of the eyes, wherein the character shows itself, but make very little account of the other parts of the body, so I must be permitted to devote myself rather to the signs of the soul in men, and by means of these to portray the life of each, leaving to others the description of their great contests" (*Alex.* 1.2, 3 [Perrin]). For more on the difference between ancient biography and history, see Charles H. Talbert, "Once Again: Gospel Genre," *Semeia* 43 (1988): 53–74.

we hear absolutely nothing about his birth, his ancestry, or his childhood.[12] Rather, Jesus first appears on the scene as an adult: "In those days Jesus came from Nazareth of Galilee and was baptized by John in the Jordan" (1:9). Furthermore, we learn nothing about important people or events that may have led Jesus to leave behind his former life (as a carpenter; cf. 6:3) in order to preach the kingdom of God.

What then was the writer's purpose? A careful reading of the Gospel of Mark makes it clear that the author was focused on proclaiming the "good news" about Jesus Christ, the Son of God, who was destined to suffer an ignominious death and thereafter be raised from the dead.[13] In short, Mark's motivation was theological, not biographical (at least as we currently understand the word). Although Matthew and Luke added some information to what they had received from Mark in order to present a more complete narrative (such as a birth story and a genealogy), nevertheless, each of them, like Mark, focused on conveying to his audience not the history *of* but the "good news" *about* Jesus. It is noteworthy that the distinction between history and the proclamation of the "good news" was recognized as early as the third century by the great Christian theologian, Origen. He claimed that the authors of the Gospels "sometimes altered things which, from the eye of history, occurred otherwise." Origen was untroubled by this conclusion because, he claimed, "the spiritual truth was often preserved, one might say, in the material falsehood" (*Commentary on John* 10.2.4).

When Were the Gospels Written?

Although the precise dating of any Gospel is difficult, we can be relatively certain that none of them were written during Jesus's time. This is because

---

12. The little bit of information that we are given comes from chapters 3 and 6. In the former, we hear that Jesus's family came to take him away from Capernaum (and presumably back to Nazareth) because they thought that he was out of his mind (3:21). In chapter 6, when Jesus visited his native village of Nazareth, we get a bit more information: we are told that Jesus was a carpenter, the son of Mary, with brothers named James, Joses, Judas, and Simon. He also had some sisters, whom the author does not name (6:3).

13. The Greek term for "good news" is *euangelion*, which is usually translated "gospel." The term appears in Mark's Gospel and also Paul's letters, written earlier (in the 50s). Both Mark and Paul used the term to proclaim the "good news" about Jesus's death and resurrection. However, because Mark connected the term to his narrative about Jesus (Mark 1:1), the other three narratives about Jesus—those of Matthew, Luke, and John—were also later labeled "gospels."

we find material scattered throughout the Gospels that clearly comes from a time following Jesus's death (as we will shortly see).[14] But, how long after Jesus's death were the Gospels written? There are reasons to believe that the earliest Gospel, the Gospel of Mark, was written decades after Jesus's death. Indeed, even ancient commentators made this assumption.[15] But our most significant evidence for a late dating of the Gospel comes from Mark 13 where Jesus delivers an extended prediction about the destruction of the temple and the end of time. Scholars are convinced that a number of things in this chapter allude to the Jewish revolt against Rome, a revolt that began in 66 CE. Four years later, after an extended siege of Jerusalem, Roman troops broke through its walls, destroyed much of the city (including the temple), and slaughtered its inhabitants.

The clearest allusion to the revolt appears in Mark 13:14, where Jesus refers to a "desolating sacrilege." "Desolating sacrilege" is a phrase that originally appeared in the book of Daniel; there it pointed to the desecration of the Jerusalem temple by Antiochus IV in the second century BCE (Dan 9:27, 11:31, and 12:11). By alluding to that earlier action, Mark's Gospel obviously refers to some other defiling action in the Jerusalem temple. Although there is consensus that this "desolating sacrilege" was connected to the Jewish revolt, scholars are divided as to its precise reference. Some believe that the phrase pointed to the Roman general Titus's destruction of the temple in 70 after his troops entered Jerusalem.[16] Others argue that it referred to the Jewish Zealots' bloody purge of aristocrats and temple officials after they had gained control of the temple in 67–68 CE.

Regardless, we can be fairly certain that Mark's Gospel was written either during the course of the Jewish revolt or shortly after it. A reasonable

14. It seems that early Christians did not distinguish between things spoken by Jesus before his death and sayings attributed to the risen Jesus. That is to say, the early assemblies believed that the risen Jesus was in some way present with them (consider Jesus's statement in Matt 18:20: "Where two or three are gathered in my name, I am there among them"). Some sayings by a prophet that were spoken in the name of Jesus would have therefore likely found their way into the Gospels.

15. Papias, a second-century bishop of Hieropolis in Phrygia (Hieropolis is near present-day Denizli, in western Turkey), attributed the Gospel to a later disciple of Peter, who wrote down Peter's recollections of his time with Jesus.

16. These scholars would consequently understand Jesus's prediction of the temple's destruction in 13:1–2 as *vaticinium ex eventu*, a Latin phrase that means a prophecy after the fact. In other words, the historical Jesus did not himself predict the temple's end; instead, the Gospel's author attempted, at a later time, to make sense of the temple's destruction by showing that it had fulfilled a prophecy made by Jesus.

approximation would be 70 CE, give or take several years either way. In other words, it would have been written more than a generation after Jesus's time. Although the other Synoptic Gospels, those of Matthew and Luke, cannot be precisely dated, they must have been later than that since both were dependent on Mark's Gospel. It is therefore unlikely that either could have been written before 80 CE but it is quite possible that they could have been written considerably later than that.

Besides the Synoptic Gospels, we have access to one other early document focused on the sayings and deeds of Jesus. This text, like Mark's Gospel, was also used by the authors of the Gospels of Matthew and Luke. Although there are no surviving ancient copies of the document, scholars have been able to reconstruct it, at least in part, from corresponding passages in Matthew and Luke. Since the original name of the document remains unknown, for the sake of convenience, scholars refer to it as Q.[17] Q consists primarily of sayings by Jesus.[18] Unfortunately, attaching a date to Q is difficult. Most scholars prefer a range from 50 to 70 CE. But, even if we assume the earliest date (50), the sayings in this document follow Jesus's death by a couple of decades. Regardless, the sayings in Q provide valuable information for the reconstruction of a portrait of the historical Jesus.[19]

Our brief survey of our best source material (the Synoptic Gospels and Q) strongly suggests that these texts provide a less-than-precise picture of the historical Jesus. For one thing, although we have no reliable information about the authors of the texts, we can be fairly certain that they were not associates of Jesus. Rather, they gathered their material from later sources, whether oral or written. Second, the Gospels were not created as biographies (as we understand the term). They were instead intended to announce the "good news" *about* Jesus. This itself is telling; while the historical Jesus pro-

17. The label Q has been in use since the nineteenth century. It probably was derived from the German word *Quelle,* meaning "source."

18. Although Q refers to Jesus's abilities as a healer and an exorcist, the emphasis of the document is on Jesus's teachings. There is only one healing miracle in Q, that of the centurion's servant (Matt 8:5–13//Luke 7:1–10). Although Jesus does not explicitly exorcise in the document, Q nevertheless records the accusation that Jesus casts out demons by the power of Beelzebul, i.e., Satan (Matt 12:27–28//Luke 11:19–20).

19. It is important to note that the existence of Q (or the Q community) is not accepted by all scholars. No physical Q document has ever been discovered. Rather, Q has been reconstructed based on close similarities in the Gospels of Matthew and Luke (where there exists no corresponding Markan passage). For an accessible introduction to Q, see John S. Kloppenborg, *Q: The Earliest Gospel, An Introduction to the Original Stories and Sayings of Jesus* (Louisville, KY: Westminster John Knox, 2008).

claimed the kingdom of God, the Gospels focused instead on Jesus himself and on the belief that he was the Messiah and the Son of God. Finally, the Gospels were not written during Jesus's lifetime. Indeed, the earliest of them (Mark) was probably composed four decades or so after his death. Even the Q text postdated Jesus's death by at least two decades, and probably more. Regardless, it is important to note once again that, despite these conclusions, the material in the Synoptic Gospels (including the Q material) is not totally devoid of historical information about Jesus. Rather, the authentic sayings and deeds of the historical Jesus need to be separated from other, later material.

Separating Layers of Tradition within a Text

As has already been noted, the Gospel writers were not primarily interested in constructing historically accurate biographies of Jesus. Rather, they were intent on communicating to their audiences what they saw as the *significance* of Jesus's words and deeds. This meant portraying Jesus in a way that would be meaningful to the particular time and situation of their readers. In order to do that, the Gospel writers often added their own interpretative glosses to the material that had been passed down to them. In fact, we can plainly see how Matthew and Luke edited the material that they received from Mark. However, sometimes the traditions received by the Gospel writers had already been altered; sometimes, several layers of tradition are found in a particular passage.

A good example of the layers that accumulated around a tradition as time went on can be seen in the earliest Gospel (Mark) in one of Jesus's parables— the so-called parable of the sower (Mark 4:1–20). The whole of the parable, as it appears in Mark's Gospel, consists of the setting (Jesus seated in a boat, preaching to the crowd on the shore), the parable spoken by Jesus, a short dialogue between Jesus and his disciples, and a later interpretation given only to Jesus's disciples. The earliest stratum is the parable itself:

[Jesus said,] "Listen! A sower went out to sow. And as he sowed, some seed fell on the path, and the birds came and ate it up. Other seed fell on rocky ground, where it did not have much soil . . . and since it had no root, it withered away. Other seed fell among thorns, and the thorns grew up and choked it, and it yielded no grain. Other seed fell into good soil and brought forth grain, growing up and increasing and yielding thirty and sixty and a hundredfold." And he said, "Let anyone with ears to hear listen!" (4:3-9).[20]

The next layer consists of the interpretation of the parable. As mentioned above, shortly after telling the parable, Jesus explained it to his disciples:

The sower sows the word. These are the ones on the path where the word is sown: when they hear, Satan immediately comes and takes away the word that is sown in them. And these are the ones sown on rocky ground: when they hear the word, they immediately receive it with joy. But they have no root, and endure only for a while; then, when trouble or persecution arises on account of the word, immediately they fall away. And others are those sown among the thorns: these are the ones who hear the word, but the cares of the world, and the lure of wealth, and the desire for other things come in and choke the word, and it yields nothing. And these are the ones sown on the good soil: they hear the word and accept it and bear fruit, thirty and sixty and a hundredfold. (Mark 4:14-20)

But, how do we know that this explanation did not come from the historical Jesus himself? How do we know that it came from a later time?

First of all, we have evidence that the parable circulated in some places without the explanation that appears in Mark 4:14-20. The Gospel of Thomas, for example, contains an independent version of the parable of the sower without the allegorical explanation.[21] Furthermore, some later Christian writers, Justin Martyr (second century CE) and the author of the *Clementine Recognitions* (probably third century CE), interpret the parable in a way that suggests that it circulated in some places without the explanation.[22] But does that

20. I have replaced the phrase "and it sprang up quickly, since it had no depth of soil. And when the sun rose, it was scorched" with an ellipsis because it may represent a later addition to the parable. See John Dominic Crossan, *In Parables: The Challenge of the Historical Jesus* (San Francisco: Harper & Row, 1973), 39-41.

21. There is much about the Gospel of Thomas that is disputed, including the question of whether or not it was dependent on the canonical gospels. It is likely that the 114 sayings in the *Gospel* were compiled over a period of time and that, as a result, some of its sayings were dependent on the canonical gospels while others were not. Regardless, the Gospel of Thomas's version of the parable of the sower seems not to have been dependent on the parable in any of the canonical gospels. See Stephen J. Patterson, *The Gospel of Thomas and Jesus*, Foundations and Facets (Sonoma, CA: Polebridge Press, 1993), 22-23.

22. These writers "do not understand the parable . . . as a challenge to self-examination on the part of the audience [as later interpretation in vv. 14-20 would suggest], but as an

necessarily mean that the explanation was added later? Is it not possible that originally there was an explanation and texts like the Gospel of Thomas deleted it? Although the latter alternative is possible, it is not as likely for the simple reason that we can easily understand why someone would add an explanation (it helps clarify the meaning of the parable) but it is difficult to explain why someone would remove it, thereby rendering the parable less clear.

Second, some of the terms in the explanation do not seem to fit Jesus's time. Most significant is the term "word," found in several places in the explanation; it appears first in the phrase "the sower sows the word." "Word" functions here as the equivalent for the message of the gospel. Nowhere else in the Gospel of Mark do we see Jesus use the term with a similar meaning. This tells us that "word" was probably not employed by the *historical* Jesus in such a way. But "word" was used in this manner by those who came after Jesus. For example, Paul, writing two decades after Jesus's death, commended the Thessalonian community because, "in spite of persecution you received the *word* with joy" (1 Thess 1:6). The letter of James, certainly written no earlier than Paul's letter, also encouraged its recipients to "welcome with meekness the implanted *word* that has the power to save your souls" (Jas 1:21).[23] In both of these examples, "word" functions as the equivalent to "the Gospel message," just as in the interpretation of the parable.[24]

Third, there are metaphorical expressions in the parable's explanation that Jesus does not use elsewhere in the Gospels. However, we do find them in the literature of the later movement. These include the notion of the "word growing" (Acts 6:7; 12:24; 19:20; Col 1:6), and the idea of the word "bringing forth fruit" (Col 1:5–6; cf. Col 1:10); both expressions indicate the spread of the gospel.[25] For these three reasons, therefore, we can safely conclude that the parable's explanation did not come from the historical Jesus. It was instead added at a later time, likely before Mark's Gospel was composed. That is to say, Mark probably knew the parable with the explanation already attached to it; he did not attach it himself.[26]

---

encouragement to the . . . preacher not to be faint-hearted in his labours" (Joachim Jeremias, *The Parables of Jesus* [New York: Scribner's Sons, 1963], 150–51 n. 87).

23. It is unclear when James was written. Some have argued for the middle of the first century while others insist that it was written later, perhaps even as late as the mid–second century.

24. "Word" also appears as the equivalent of the Gospel message in Gal 6:6 and Col 4:3.

25. At times the English translations hide the similarity. For example, whereas both Acts 6:7 and 12:24 literally speak of the word "growing," the NRSV translates the former by saying that the word "spread" and the latter by claiming that the word "advanced."

26. It is probable that the allegorical interpretation (vv. 14–20) was not added by Mark

But this is not the only late addition to this brief story. There is a third layer that is chronologically even later. It consists of the setting of the story and the dialogue. Both come from the author of Mark's Gospel. The setting, that is, the scene that opens the section, appears prior to Jesus's recitation of the parable: "Again he began to teach beside the lake. Such a very large crowd gathered around him that he got into a boat on the lake and sat there, while the whole crowd was beside the lake on the land. He began to teach them many things in parables, and in his teaching he said to them . . ." (Mark 4:1–2). The setting of this important scene by the lake (i.e., the Sea of Galilee) almost certainly came from the pen of Mark. It reflects the author's interest in the lake, a geographic feature that plays a prominent and symbolic role throughout the first half of the Gospel (1:16; 2:13; 3:7–9; 4:35–41; 5:21; 6:31–33; 6:45–52; 8:13–21).

The dialogue between Jesus and the disciples that appears between the parable and its explanation was also added by the author of the Gospel: "When [Jesus] was alone, those who were around him along with the twelve asked him about the parables. And he said to them, 'To you has been given the secret of the kingdom of God, but for those outside, everything comes in parables; in order that they may indeed look, but not perceive, and may indeed listen, but not understand; so that they may not turn again and be forgiven.' And he said to them, 'Do you not understand this parable? Then how will you understand all the parables?'" (Mark 4:10–13).

How do we know that the author of Mark's Gospel added this interchange between Jesus and his disciples? The most compelling reason is that the dialogue, which includes Jesus's rebuke of the disciples for their lack of understanding (4:10, 13), coheres with Mark's depiction of the disciples elsewhere in the Gospel. Throughout the Gospel, the disciples' inability to comprehend Jesus's message, despite having received privileged information, is highlighted (see, among other places, 4:35–41; 6:47–52; 7:17–22). Other reasons to suspect Markan authorship of the dialogue has to do with the language in the passage. The reference to "those around him" (4:10) and those "outside" (4:11) parallels language in the previous chapter where Jesus teaches his followers about his true family versus his biological one (Mark 3:31–34).[27]

We can, therefore, see in this brief passage from Mark's Gospel three sepa-

---

because the interpretation contains a significant number of words that are not found elsewhere in Mark's Gospel.

27. In 3:31, Jesus's family (who stand *outside*) do not understand his significance (cf. 3:20–21). This corresponds to the outsiders in 4:12 who have "eyes but do not see and ears but do not understand." "Those around him" in 3:32 and 3:34 represent his followers as do "those around" him in 4:10.

rate layers of tradition. The core story, <u>the parable itself (</u>in normal print below), <u>probably came from the historical Jesus.</u> To this was later added an interpretation to clarify the parable's meaning (underlined print below).[28] When Mark wrote his Gospel, he provided a setting—Jesus preaching from a boat to those on shore—as well as a brief dialogue between Jesus and his disciples (italicized print below):

[1]*Again he began to teach beside the lake. Such a very large crowd gathered around him that he got into a boat on the lake and sat there, while the whole crowd was beside the lake on the land.* [2]*He began to teach them many things in parables, and in his teaching he said to them:* [3]"Listen! A sower went out to sow. [4]And as he sowed, some seed fell on the path, and the birds came and ate it up. [5]Other seed fell on rocky ground, where it did not have much soil, and it sprang up quickly . . . and since it had no root, it withered away. [7]Other seed fell among thorns, and the thorns grew up and choked it, and it yielded no grain. [8]Other seed fell into good soil and brought forth grain, growing up and increasing and yielding thirty and sixty and a hundredfold." [9]And he said, "Let anyone with ears to hear listen!"

[10]*When he was alone, those who were around him along with the twelve asked him about the parables.* [11]*And he said to them, "To you has been given the secret of the kingdom of God, but for those outside, everything comes in parables;* [12]*in order that 'they may indeed look, but not perceive, and may indeed listen, but not understand; so that they may not turn again and be forgiven.'"* [13]*And he said to them, "Do you not understand this parable? Then how will you understand all the parables?* <u>[14]The sower sows the word.</u> <u>[15]These are the ones on the path where the word is sown: when they hear, Satan immediately comes and takes away the word that is sown in them.</u> <u>[16]And these are the ones sown on rocky ground: when they hear the word, they immediately receive it with joy.</u> <u>[17]But they have no root, and endure only for a while; then, when trouble or persecution arises on account of the word, immediately they fall away.</u> <u>[18]And others are those sown among the thorns: these are the ones who hear the word,</u> <u>[19]but the cares of the world, and the lure of wealth, and the desire for other things come in and choke the word, and it yields nothing.</u> <u>[20]And these are the ones sown on the good soil: they hear the word and accept it and bear fruit, thirty and sixty and a hundredfold."</u>

---

28. But the clarification of the parable's meaning also changes the meaning of the original parable. The interpretation makes the parable about true and false followers of Jesus. But the original parable seems to have been about perseverance in the face of repeated failure.

Like a snowball that grows as it is rolled along the ground, Jesus's simple story of a farmer scattering seed picked up additional material over time. Unfortunately, separating the earlier from the later material is often easier said than done. The academic quest for the historical Jesus has been long and contentious. And, indeed, despite its lengthy history, there are still many points about which scholars disagree. But there is agreement on certain things. Quite a few sayings and deeds can be traced, with some confidence, back to the historical Jesus.

What Can We Know about the Historical Jesus?

We know very little about Jesus's early life other than that he grew up in the small village of Nazareth in Galilee. At the time of his birth, the whole of Judea, including Galilee, was ruled by Herod the Great. But shortly after Jesus's birth, Herod died and Galilee came under the control of Antipas, Herod's son. Although Nazareth was a small village, probably containing only a couple hundred people, it lay within a few miles of the much larger Hellenistic city of Sepphoris. Consequently, it is possible that Jesus was exposed to some Hellenistic cultural ideas as he was growing up. Indeed, some scholars have even suggested that, although Aramaic was his first language, Jesus probably knew at least some Greek.

As an adult, Jesus was attracted to the message of John the Baptist. John, a Jewish ascetic and apocalyptic preacher, believed (as we would expect of an apocalyptic preacher) that the world was corrupted by the forces of evil. Furthermore, he proclaimed that it was destined to come under God's wrathful judgment in the near future. Luke's Gospel portrays John's preaching as follows:

> You brood of vipers! Who warned you to flee from the wrath to come? Bear fruits worthy of repentance. Do not begin to say to yourselves, "We have Abraham as our ancestor"; for I tell you, God is able from these stones to raise up children to Abraham. Even now the axe is lying at the root of the trees; every tree therefore that does not bear good fruit is cut down and thrown into the fire. . . . His winnowing fork is in his hand, to clear his threshing floor and to gather the wheat into his granary; but the chaff he will burn with unquenchable fire. (3:7–9, 17)

As this passage indicates, John warned his listeners to repent of their sins or face destruction by "the wrath to come."[29]

29. Cf. Luke 3:10–14, which adds: "And the crowds asked him, 'What then should we

But John did not only preach. He also baptized his followers. As both the writers of the Gospels and Josephus tell us, John's baptism was intended as a sign of the forgiveness of sins. The Gospel of Mark describes it as a "baptism of repentance for the forgiveness of sins" (1:4). Josephus tells us about John: "He exhorted the Jews to lead righteous lives, to practice justice toward their fellows and piety toward God, and so doing to join in baptism. . . . [Baptism] was a consecration of the body implying that the soul was already thoroughly cleansed by right behavior" (*Jewish Antiquities* 18.117).

At some point in his adult life, Jesus was baptized by John and likely became one of his followers.[30] It is unclear how much time Jesus spent with John. Regardless, at some point in time, Jesus struck out on his own.[31] We do not know what drove Jesus to begin his own ministry. Perhaps he came to think differently than did the Baptist. Or perhaps John's arrest by Herod Antipas left him no choice.[32] Jesus carried over many things from his teacher to his own ministry. Certainly baptism, which would eventually become the movement's initiatory rite, can be traced to John. Jesus's apocalyptic message also came from John. But other elements of Jesus's ministry were original to him.

Ultimately, we can see a number of significant differences between the actions of John and Jesus. John, for example, drew people to him at the Jordan; Jesus, however, did not stay in one place; he went to the people,

---

do?' In reply he said to them, 'Whoever has two coats must share with anyone who has none; and whoever has food must do likewise.' Even tax collectors came to be baptized, and they asked him, 'Teacher, what should we do?' He said to them, 'Collect no more than the amount prescribed for you.' Soldiers also asked him, 'And we, what should we do?' He said to them, 'Do not extort money from anyone by threats or false accusation, and be satisfied with your wages.'"

30. We can be relatively certain that Jesus was baptized by John. This is because most of the accounts in the Gospels try to deal in one way or another with the lesser figure (John) baptizing the greater. The Gospel of Matthew does this by having John object to baptizing Jesus. He only gives up his objection when Jesus reassures him, saying, "Let it be so now; for it is proper for us in this way to fulfill all righteousness." The Gospel of Luke tries to minimize the problem by taking John the Baptist out of the account. Jesus is baptized but nowhere does it say that John performed the baptism. The Gospel of John has no baptism account although the author seems aware of the story of Jesus's baptism (cf. John 1:33).

31. The first chapter of John's Gospel indicates that Jesus's first disciples were originally disciples of John (1:35–42). It is possible that Jesus, a follower of John, drew his first disciples from among John's ranks.

32. Mark shows Jesus beginning to preach after John was arrested (Mark 1:14–15). Both Matthew and Luke imply the same (Matt 4:12–17 and Luke 3:19–22). John, on the other hand, depicts John and Jesus carrying on their ministries at the same time.

wandering among the small towns and villages in Galilee.[33] John was an ascetic, but Jesus rejected John's practice of self-denial and preferred instead to enjoy meals in the company of others.[34] The contrast between the two is illustrated by an illuminating passage from Q, in which Jesus complains about the fickleness of those who would disparage both John and himself: "For John the Baptist has come eating no bread and drinking no wine, and you say, 'He has a demon'; the son of man [i.e., Jesus] has come eating and drinking, and you say, 'Look, a glutton and a drunkard, a friend of tax collectors and sinners!'" (Luke 7:33–34; cf. Matt 11:18–19). It was, however, not just Jesus's actions that set him apart from John. Some of their teachings also differed.

Although Jesus likely inherited the idea of "the kingdom of God" from his mentor, he nevertheless put his own spin on it. For John, the kingdom would bring about the end of the current age with a divine judgment. Presumably, it would be followed by a new age, the age of the kingdom of God. With this, it seems, Jesus did not disagree. However, unlike John, Jesus taught that, in some way, the kingdom was already present. Consider, for example, the parable in which Jesus compared the kingdom to the actions of a woman making bread: "To what should I compare the kingdom of God? It is like leaven that a woman took and hid in three measures of flour until all of it was leavened" (Luke 13:20–21; cf. Matt 13:33). It is important to note that Jesus did not simply compare the kingdom to the leaven itself. Rather he compared it to both the leaven and the process of the woman's hiding it in the flour. By means of this parable he thereby suggested that the kingdom was already present, albeit hidden. Eventually though it would be fully evident just as the three measures of flour would, at some point, be entirely leavened.

A similar parable is that of the mustard seed. The version from Mark's Gospel is as follows: "With what can we compare the kingdom of God, or what parable will we use for it? It is like a mustard seed, which, when sown upon the ground, is the smallest of all the seeds on earth; yet when it is sown it grows up and becomes the greatest of all shrubs, and puts forth large branches, so that the birds of the air can make nests in its shade" (Mark 4:30–32; cf. Matt 13:31–32; Luke 13:18–19; Gos. Thom. 20). This parable, like that of the leaven,

33. For reasons unknown, Jesus avoided the large cities. While he seems to have spent some time in the small town of Capernaum, there is no indication that he preached or healed in places like Sepphoris or Tiberias.

34. Indeed, the sharing of meals was an activity that his followers would continue long after their master's death.

suggested the presence of the kingdom in the here and now (although as a very tiny entity).[35] But the comparison of the kingdom to the mustard seed also provided an interesting twist to the message. The listener would likely have expected that "the smallest of all seeds" would grow into the largest of all *trees*. Indeed, this is what happens in Luke's later version of the parable.[36] But in this, the earliest version, the mustard seed instead grew into a large shrub, and a troublesome one at that (mustard plants were known for their invasive character). This parable therefore not only suggests the hidden presence of the kingdom, it also suggests that the final result could be surprising and unexpected.

A particularly interesting detail about the historical Jesus's ministry concerned his association with malefactors. In various places throughout the Gospels, Jesus was accused of consorting with "tax collectors and sinners." Who were these people? The tax collectors with whom Jesus fraternized were not, as we might expect, officials who gathered tribute for Rome. Rather, they were customs officers; those who collected duties on imports and exports. Such individuals could be readily found in places like Capernaum (where Jesus spent time), a town near the border of Antipas's territory. There, goods coming into Antipas's territory or leaving it would be taxed. Those who collected the tolls on such goods were typically considered dishonest. They were reputed to charge more than required and pocket the difference. Furthermore, they were thought to take advantage particularly of the peasantry, those who had the least to spare.

Who were the "sinners" with whom Jesus associated? Here the term "sinners" does not refer to people who occasionally transgressed the Torah. Instead, it points to those who were normally considered to be beyond redemption, those who might have been better labeled "the wicked."[37] An example of such a person appears in Jesus's parable of the prodigal son. In that story, an

35. Later Jewish rabbis would also use the mustard seed as an example of the tiniest of things (yBer. 8d; bBer. 31b).

36. "[Jesus] said therefore, 'What is the kingdom of God like? And to what should I compare it? It is like a mustard seed that someone took and sowed in the garden; it grew and became a tree, and the birds of the air made nests in its branches'" (Luke 13:18–19). Matthew's version, on the other hand, cannot seem to decide whether the final product is a bush or a tree: "[Jesus] put before them another parable: 'The kingdom of heaven is like a mustard seed that someone took and sowed in his field; it is the smallest of all the seeds, but when it has grown it is the greatest of shrubs and becomes a tree, so that the birds of the air come and make nests in its branches'" (Matt 13:31–32).

37. E. P. Sanders, *The Historical Figure of Jesus* (London: Penguin, 1993), 227–29.

impatient young man audaciously demanded his inheritance from his father while that parent was still alive. After the young man received it, he went abroad and "squandered his property in dissolute living" (Luke 15:13).

Why did Jesus associate with such unsavory people? It is usually assumed that he did so in order to bring about their repentance. But, there is a significant problem with this assumption; if Jesus intended to reform such wayward types, why would he have been criticized for it? One would have instead expected him to be lauded. How could anyone possibly object to the reformation of lost sinners or dishonest tax collectors? It is possible to eliminate this problem by supposing that Jesus, unlike his mentor John, did not focus on repentance. Although it is hard to believe that he would have objected to the repentance of these people, his focus lay elsewhere. It seems that he was more concerned with proclaiming God's love for those believed beyond redemption than he was with insisting on their repentance.[38]

The parable of the prodigal son, mentioned above, is instructive in this regard. As Jesus told the story, the dissolute son—in dire straits because he had squandered all the money—was desperate. He could not imagine that he could ever be reconciled with his father, given the enormity of his offense. But in his desperation, he dared to hope that his father would at least have enough compassion to hire him as a laborer:

> When [the son] had spent everything, a severe famine took place throughout that country, and he began to be in need. So he went and hired himself out to one of the citizens of that country, who sent him to his fields to feed the pigs. He would gladly have filled himself with the pods that the pigs were eating; and no one gave him anything. But when he came to himself he said, "How many of my father's hired hands have bread enough and to spare, but here I am dying of hunger! I will get up and go to my father, and I will say to him, 'Father, I have sinned against heaven and before you; I am no longer worthy to be called your son; treat me like one of your hired hands.'" (Luke 15:14–19)

Note that the son in this story shows little in the way of repentance. Rather, he seems solely focused on escaping the difficult situation that he had brought upon himself.

Having formulated his plan, he headed back to his former home. But as he approached, his father caught sight of him and responded in an unex-

---

38. Sanders, *Historical Figure*, 230–37.

pectedly gracious way: "But while [the son] was still far off, his father . . . ran and put his arms around him and kissed him." Before the son could finish his previously prepared speech, "The father said to his slaves, 'Quickly, bring out a robe—the best one—and put it on him; put a ring on his finger and sandals on his feet. And get the fatted calf and kill it, and let us eat and celebrate; for this son of mine was dead and is alive again; he was lost and is found!'" (Luke 15:20–24). Even before the son could ask for some kind of accommodation, his father granted him full forgiveness. Beyond his wildest expectation, he was brought back into the family. When the father's other son complained about the injustice of it all, the father responded: "this brother of yours was dead and has come to life; he was lost and has been found" (Luke 15:32).

In light of Jesus's association with unsavory company, one might easily conclude that his message was much more radical than that of John the Baptist. Jesus did not insist on sinners' repentance as his former mentor had done. He did not threaten the wicked with "unquenchable fire," fire that would accompany the end which was soon to arrive. Instead, Jesus ate and drank with tax collectors and sinners, those that others would have condemned as lost, those whose actions were beyond the pale. Furthermore, he told them that God loved them as the father had loved his prodigal son; they, like the son who was welcomed back into his father's family, would be welcomed into the kingdom.[39]

In addition to teaching about the kingdom and ministering to "tax collectors and sinners," Jesus was also a skilled exorcist.[40] That is to say, he had the ability to cure those who were thought to be demon-possessed. Consider, for instance, the story of Jesus's interaction with the man who "lived among the tombs." Because of his conduct, this unnamed man had been forced out of normal society; he was compelled to live on its periphery: "No one could restrain [this man] any more, even with a chain; for he had often been restrained with shackles and chains, but the chains he wrenched apart, and the shackles he broke in pieces; and no one had the strength to subdue him. Night and day among the tombs and on the mountains he was always howling and bruising himself with stones" (Mark 5:3–5). While in our time, we would probably

---

39. Cf. Sanders, *Historical Figure*, 233.

40. Jesus was not the only person of his time to be credited with the power to exorcise. The Jewish historian Josephus mentions a certain first-century Jew named Eleazar who could exorcize (*Ant.* 8.46–48); the New Testament book of Acts tells us of other Jewish exorcists, specifically, the seven sons of a priest named Sceva (Acts 19:13–14); and Philostratus, the biographer of the pagan philosopher Apollonius of Tyana (a contemporary of Jesus), claims that Apollonius himself could also cast out demons (Philostratus, *Life of Apollonius* 3.38; 4.20).

consider such an individual a victim of mental illness, people in Jesus's day would have traced the man's bizarre behavior to one or more demons that had taken him over. Demons were thought responsible for many of the ills that befell human beings. Once possessed by one or more of them, a person could lose all control of his or her thoughts and actions.

The only hope for such a possessed individual was an exorcist, someone who could drive the demon (or demons) out of him. We can see Jesus doing just that in the continuation of the above story:

> When [the man] saw Jesus from a distance, he ran and bowed down before him; and he shouted at the top of his voice, "What have you to do with me, Jesus, Son of the Most High God? I adjure you by God, do not torment me." For [Jesus] had said to him, "Come out of the man, you unclean spirit!" Then Jesus asked him, "What is your name?" He replied, "My name is Legion; for we are many." [The man] begged him earnestly not to send them out of the country. Now there on the hillside a great herd of swine was feeding; and the unclean spirits begged him, "Send us into the swine; let us enter them." So he gave them permission. And the unclean spirits came out and entered the swine; and the herd, numbering about two thousand, rushed down the steep bank into the lake, and were drowned in the lake. (Mark 5:6–13)

Although this is the most dramatic of all the exorcisms in the Gospels, it is only one of many mentioned. While this particular exorcism makes for a wonderful story, there are a number of oddities in it that render it historically suspect.[41] Consequently, this particular narrative probably represents a later, legendary (and highly exaggerated) tale meant to display Jesus's remarkable power over demons; perhaps it is an exaggerated account of an actual exorcism by Jesus.

Regardless of the historicity of this particular story, there are many references to Jesus exorcising in the Gospels. There is little doubt that Jesus was believed to have the ability to cast out demons. Even his detractors acknowledged his talent; they, however, claimed that his power to exorcise came from Beelzebul (i.e., Satan), the ruler of the demons.[42] Jesus, of course, rejected their

---

41. First, the exorcism presumably happened at Gerasa (modern-day Jerash, Jordan), a town nowhere near any body of water. Second, the behavior of the pigs is curious. Normally, when frightened, pigs do not run as a herd; instead, they scatter. Third, pigs are very good swimmers. See John P. Meier, *Mentor, Message, and Miracles*, vol. 2 of *A Marginal Jew: Rethinking the Historical Jesus*, ABRL (New York: Doubleday, 1994), 651–52, 666 n. 21.

42. "Beelzebul" is a variation on the name of the Canaanite deity, Baal-zebub, mentioned

interpretation. Instead, he countered: "If I cast out the demons by Beelzebul, by whom do your exorcists cast them out? Therefore they will be your judges. But if it is by the finger of God that I cast out the demons, then the kingdom of God has come to you" (Luke 11:19–20; cf. Matt 12:27–28). Jesus here insisted that his exorcisms were enacted by God working through him (i.e., "by the finger of God"), not by Satan. To the contrary, Jesus elsewhere asserted that his exorcisms were *defeating* Satan, one possessed person at a time; he was "tying up the strong man" (i.e., Satan) so that he could plunder his house (Mark 3:27; cf. Matt 12:29; Luke 11:22).

Jesus was also credited with the ability to heal. The Gospels tell of numerous cures of the blind, the lame, and the infirm. Jesus regarded these cures, like his exorcisms, as evidence of the presence of God's Kingdom. For example, when John sent his disciples to ask Jesus if he was "the one who is to come," he told them: "Go and tell John what you have seen and heard: the blind receive their sight, the lame walk, the lepers are cleansed, the deaf hear, the dead are raised, the poor have good news brought to them" (Luke 7:22; cf. Matt 11:4–5). At first glance, Jesus's response to John seems a bit enigmatic. But once we recognize that he was alluding to a couple of biblical prophecies from Isaiah, his answer makes much more sense.

The first of the prophecies foretells a coming age of blessedness: "Then the eyes of the blind shall be opened, and the ears of the deaf unstopped; then the lame shall leap like a deer, and the tongue of the speechless sing for joy" (Isa 35:5–6).[43] The second prophecy claims: "The spirit of the Lord God is upon me, because the Lord has anointed me; he has sent me to bring good news to the oppressed, to bind up the broken-hearted, to proclaim liberty to the captives, and release to the prisoners" (Isa 61:1). By alluding to these two scriptural passages, Jesus implicitly claimed that, by his healing actions, he had fulfilled ancient prophecy that foretold a new, utopian age. Jesus believed that this was the "kingdom" proclaimed by him and made visible in his acts of healing and exorcism.

---

in 2 Kgs 1:2–3, 6, 16. By Jesus's time, Beelzebul had come to mean Satan. We also find the term used in reference to Satan in the Jewish work *The Testament of Solomon*, a text composed sometime in the first few centuries CE.

43. This passage was originally focused on the end of Babylonian exile. But it was later interpreted as a reference to the coming age. Cf. the "Messianic Apocalypse" from the Dead Sea Scrolls: "The heavens and earth will listen to his Messiah . . . He who liberates captives, restores sight to the blind, straightens the bent . . . He will heal the wounded, and revive the dead and bring good news to the poor" (4Q521 frag. 2 II, 1, 8, 12). Cited in Geza Vermes, *The Authentic Gospel of Jesus* (London: Penguin, 2004), 199–200.

But Jesus did not think that he alone should proclaim the kingdom of God or that its presence could be perceived only in *his* activities. His disciples were also to announce the kingdom in their words and deeds: "He called the twelve and began to send them out two by two, and gave them authority over the unclean spirits. He ordered them to take nothing for their journey except a staff. . . . So they went out. . . . They cast out many demons, and anointed with oil many who were sick and cured them" (Mark 6:7–8, 12–13). According to one of the accounts in the Gospels, Jesus's disciples returned, amazed at their power, "Lord, in your name even the demons submit to us!" Jesus claimed, in response, that he had had a vision of Satan's demise, "I watched Satan fall from heaven like a flash of lightning" (Luke 10:17–18).[44]

While Jesus proclaimed the kingdom as a present-day reality, he anticipated that, at some point in the future, it would be fully realized. There are some indications that Jesus expected the future, fully realized kingdom of God to appear on earth as the earthly restoration of Israel. We see a hint of this in Jesus's singling out twelve disciples to correspond to the number of ancient Israel's tribes; Jesus claimed that his disciples would sit on thrones and judge those twelve tribes (Luke 22:30; cf. Matt 19:28). He apparently also anticipated that scattered Jewish exiles would return from the four corners of the earth when he said that "people [would] come from east and west, from north and south, and [would] eat in the kingdom of God" (Luke 13:29; cf. Matt 8:11). Based on this saying alone, it does not sound as if these returning exiles would eat together in some transcendent realm. Rather, Jesus seems to presume an earthly banquet, probably at Jerusalem. If Jesus did indeed expect the fully realized kingdom to be an earthly restoration of Israel, he would not have been the only one in ancient Judaism with such an expectation. We see something similar in a number of Jewish writings from the Roman period.[45]

But, on the other hand, there are also several sayings that point to the kingdom as appearing in heaven. In one saying, Jesus warns, "If your eye causes you to stumble, tear it out; it is better for you to enter the kingdom of God with one eye than to have two eyes and to be thrown into hell" (Mark 9:47). In another saying, Jesus predicts, "I tell you, on that night there will be two in one bed; one will be taken and the other left. There will be two women

44. Since this is only attested in Luke, some (or all) of it may not go back to the historical Jesus. The disciples' comment sounds late (i.e., it sounds like something from after Jesus's death when exorcisms would have been performed in Jesus's name). The vision of Satan's fall, however, sounds authentic.

45. E.g., the Psalms of Solomon, a Jewish writing from the first century BCE (17:21–28) and Sirach, an apocryphal text written more than a century earlier (36:13–16).

grinding meal together; one will be taken and the other left" (Luke 17:34–35; cf. Matt 24:40–41). In the first of these sayings, "entering" the kingdom is contrasted with being thrown into hell. This suggests that the location of the kingdom was the reverse of hell, that is, in heaven. In the second saying, being "taken" (versus being left) suggests the gathering of people somewhere other than earth; again, heaven seems most likely.

Unfortunately, given the two different and dissimilar scenarios implied by these various passages, it is not exactly clear what the historical Jesus had in mind when he spoke of the *coming* kingdom. Would the kingdom of God appear on a transformed earth? Did Jesus expect the restoration of an earthy Israel? Or would those who entered the kingdom travel to heaven, the abode of the deity? It is unclear. Perhaps Jesus was more concerned with announcing the kingdom than accurately describing it. Or, as is more likely, he did not noticeably distinguish between existence on a renewed earth and existence with the deity in heaven. Other apocalyptic writers have also—at least from our perspective—muddied the distinction. The author of the book of Revelation, for example, envisioned the descent of the heavenly Jerusalem to the earth; there humans would dwell following the final judgment. However, he also described God dwelling in this heavenly/earthly Jerusalem (Rev 21–22). Perhaps Jesus thought along such lines. But whatever his understanding of the nature of the future kingdom, we can be certain that he believed that it would come soon: "Truly I tell you," he warned his disciples, "this generation will not pass away until all these things have taken place" (Mark 13:30).

Jesus's ministry was short-lived. The Synoptic Gospels imply that it lasted less than a year; the Gospel of John indicates that it lasted two to three years. Regardless, after some period of time wandering throughout Galilee, Jesus and his disciples traveled south to Jerusalem to celebrate Passover. While there, Jesus caused a disturbance in the temple, a disturbance typically described as a "cleansing." The Gospel of Mark describes this event as follows: "And he entered the temple and began to drive out those who were selling and those who were buying in the temple, and he overturned the tables of the money changers and the seats of those who sold doves; and he would not allow anyone to carry anything through the temple" (Mark 11:15–16).

The motivation and intended meaning of Jesus's action is uncertain. Scholars have interpreted it in a number of different ways: some have suggested that Jesus was protesting the merchants' exploitation of the impoverished population.[46] Another interpretation understands Jesus's act as a critique of the

---

46. Such an interpretation is supported by Jesus's accompanying comments: "Is it not

temple's sacrificial system. Other scholars believe that Jesus was performing a symbolic destruction of the temple in anticipation of a new structure built by God.[47] Still others argue that Jesus was making a political protest against the collaboration of the priestly aristocracy with the Romans. Finally, it has even been suggested that Jesus's action in the temple represented a kind of architectural protest: when Herod remodeled the temple, he moved the vendors from outside the temple mount to a place in the temple's outer court; Jesus thought that even the outer court was sacred space and it should have been reserved for prayer and teaching, not commerce.[48] A number of these interpretations are viable possibilities. Consequently, it is difficult to be sure of Jesus's intent.

Regardless, Jesus's temple action during Passover alarmed both Roman and Jewish authorities. Since the festival of Passover commemorated Israel's liberation from her Egyptian oppressors, it was a time that Jews were particularly sensitive to their subjugation by the Romans. Add to that the fact that thousands of Jewish pilgrims were normally in Jerusalem for the festival and it becomes understandable how trouble could, and sometimes did, break out at that time. We have already noted the violence that broke out in the temple precincts at Passover following Herod's death. Josephus recounts another riot that broke out at Passover several decades later when a Roman soldier on the walls overlooking the temple made a rude gesture to those inside (*Jewish War* 2.224–27). Consequently, both Jewish and Roman leaders were on alert during the festival.[49]

The Jewish high priest, possibly fearing an insurrection, sent his troops to secretly arrest Jesus, who was subsequently turned over to the Romans. The Roman prefect, Pontius Pilate, charged him with sedition and ordered that he be executed. Jesus was quickly taken outside of the city and crucified. His crucifixion occurred on a Friday, although we cannot be certain of the year (30 CE is a reasonable estimate).[50]

written, 'My house shall be called a house of prayer for all the nations'? But you have made it a den of robbers'" (Mark 11:17). But, many scholars believe that those comments were added later.

47. E.g., Sanders, *Historical Figure*, 249–62.

48. Adela Yarbro Collins, *Mark: A Commentary*, Hermeneia (Minneapolis: Fortress, 2007), 527–29.

49. Because unrest could occur during Passover, the Roman prefect, who normally resided at Caesarea, traveled to Jerusalem for the festival. He brought with him an extra body of soldiers who could, if needed, step in to quell any disturbances.

50. Although, on the surface, it would seem a simple matter to determine the year of Jesus's death, there are significant difficulties. One major problem has to do with the chronological inconsistency between the synoptic accounts versus that of John; the Synoptic Gospels depict Jesus crucified on Passover while John's Gospel puts it on the day of preparation (i.e.,

Jesus and Judaism

It is important to recognize, contrary to much popular opinion, that all of Jesus's teaching and actions were performed in a Jewish context. Jesus, of course, was a Jew, as were his followers, those he healed and exorcised, and those to whom he preached. While it is often presumed that Jesus stood against the Judaism of his day—particularly against law observance—such an assumption is, quite simply, incorrect. It is true that sometimes his understanding of Jewish law differed from that of other Jews of his time. For example, according to Mark 7:1–23, Jesus felt no ritual compulsion to wash his hands before eating. In this matter he differed from the Pharisees. However, whether or not one washed one's hands before a meal was a matter of *interpreting* the law, not overturning it.[51] Other Jews would have sided with Jesus in this controversy.[52]

A similar conclusion can be drawn about Jesus's Sabbath healings. As far as we can tell, Jesus did not believe that healing on the Sabbath was tantamount to abolishing Sabbath observance. Rather, the issue for Jesus, as for other Jews of the time, focused on determining which activities could be performed on the Sabbath and which could not. While some Jews would have objected to Sabbath healings, other Jews would not have. Indeed, Jesus's dictum, "The Sabbath was made for humankind, and not humankind for the Sabbath" (Mark 2:27) sounds remarkably like the later rabbinic claim, "The Sabbath is delivered up to you, and not you to the Sabbath."[53] On the whole, it is safe to say that Jesus's behavior did not fall outside the bounds of the Judaism of his day. This makes it all the more remarkable that the movement begun by Jesus would come to be dominated by non-Jews within less than a century.

---

the day before Passover). Another problem has to do with the synchronization of the solar and the lunar calendar (the latter was used to determine the dates of Jewish festivals). In order to keep them somewhat in sync, every now and then an extra year was added to the lunar calendar. Unfortunately, we do not know when these years were added. It probably did not happen regularly but as it was felt necessary. Assuming that the chronology of the synoptic accounts is accurate, one scholar has argued that 14 Nisan (the date of Passover) would likely have fallen on a Friday in either 30 or 33 CE. For a more complete discussion, see Meier, *Roots of the Problem*, 401–2.

51. It is important to note here that the parenthetical comment in Mark 7:19 ("thus he declared all foods clean"), where Jesus seems to be overturning Jewish dietary laws, comes not from the historical Jesus but from the early church, possibly from the author of the Gospel himself.

52. For a helpful discussion of this passage, see Sanders, *Historical Figure*, 218–21.

53. Mekilta on Exod 31:14, cited in Geza Vermes, *The Authentic Gospel of Jesus* (London: Penguin, 2003), 45.

How Did Jesus Understand His Role?

Another question worth asking has to do with Jesus's understanding of his role. Or to put it another way, who did Jesus think that he was? One way to approach this question is to look at some of the more important titles that we find tied to him in the Synoptic Gospels and to ask which of them originated with Jesus. The most significant of these include "Christ" (i.e., "Messiah"),[54] "Son of God," and "Son of Man." Of these titles, we can quickly eliminate "Son of God" as originating with the historical Jesus. Jesus does not use the title in reference to himself in the Synoptic Gospels.[55]

The next title to be considered is "Son of Man." It appears dozens of times in the Gospels but it does not always mean the same thing. In some places, for example, it functions as a circumlocution for "I" (in the same way that a person today might refer to him or herself as "yours truly").[56] In other places, however, it points to an end-time heavenly figure. When used in the former manner, as another way of referring to oneself, son of man does not function as a title per se (consequently, I have not capitalized it). When Jesus used the phrase in this manner, he did not make any kind of extraordinary claim for himself. Consider the saying, "Foxes have holes, and birds of the air have nests; but the son of man has nowhere to lay his head" (Luke 9:58; Matt 8:20). This saying originally meant something like, "animals have places to sleep but I do not."[57]

Elsewhere in the Gospels, however, Son of Man does function as a title, specifically a title for an end-time heavenly figure (in cases where it does function as a title, I will capitalize it). Such a use of Son of Man was derived from the apocalyptic book of Daniel. As we saw in the previous chapter, according to one of the visions in that book, at the end of time, the deity would hand over power to "one like a Son of Man" (7:13–14). The Daniel passage was very influential in later apocalyptic speculation. We see references to an end-time

54. The term *messiah* is a transliteration of the Hebrew word *mashiah* (Aramaic: *mashiha*). It means "anointed one." The Greek for this is *christos*. Therefore Christ = Messiah.

55. In Matt 16:16, Peter does use it in reference to Jesus and Jesus seems to acknowledge the title. However, this passage does not go back to the historical Jesus. Rather, it is a Matthean expansion of Mark 8:27–30. It is likely that the "Son of God" title arose among Jesus's followers shortly after his death.

56. This is an idiomatic meaning that makes sense only in Aramaic, Jesus's original language.

57. For a concise and informative discussion of the "son of man" phrase, see Vermes, *Authentic Gospel*, 234–36.

Son of Man not only in the New Testament, but also in a first-century CE Jewish writing, the *Similitudes of Enoch*. There the Son of Man functions as the end-time judge.[58]

A good example of the titular use of the Son of Man (i.e., as a heavenly figure) appears in the Gospels in an end-time prediction attributed to Jesus: "In those days, after that suffering, the sun will be darkened, and the moon will not give its light, and the stars will be falling from heaven, and the powers in the heavens will be shaken. And then the Son of Man will be seen coming in clouds with great power and glory" (Mark 13:24–26; cf. Matt 24:29–30; Luke 21:25–27). Unfortunately, there are two problems connected with this kind of Son of Man reference in the Gospels. The first has to do with the identification of the Son of Man figure and the second has to do with the dating of these passages: are they early (i.e., from Jesus himself) or late (from the later movement)?

First, assuming for the moment that the passages in which the Son of Man functions as a title were indeed spoken by the historical Jesus, to whom was he referring? Note that in the Markan passage, quoted above, Jesus spoke of the Son of Man "coming in the clouds with great power and glory" as if he were *someone else*. This is characteristic of Jesus's use of the title; nowhere in the Gospels does he explicitly identify *himself* with that heavenly personage.[59] Some scholars, as a result, have suggested that the historical Jesus did indeed foretell the coming of the cloud-riding Son of Man at the end of time but he was predicting the arrival of someone else. It was only after his death that his followers decided that those references were meant to point to Jesus.

Other scholars, however, believe that the sayings focused on the end-time

---

58. *The Similitudes of Enoch* later became part of *1 Enoch*. For the Son of Man as judge, see *1 Enoch* 46, 48, and 69.

59. Texts such as Mark 14:41 and 14:61–63 are worth noting. In the former ("The hour has come; the Son of Man is betrayed into the hands of sinners"), "son of man"—despite its capitalization in the NRSV translation—can easily be read as a circumlocution for "I." That is to say, it could be interpreted as Jesus simply declaring, "I am betrayed into the hands of sinners." If that is the proper way to read the sentence (and I believe that it is), then Jesus here does not identify himself with the heavenly Son of Man. The latter text ("Again the high priest asked him, 'Are you the Messiah, the Son of the Blessed One?' Jesus said, 'I am; and "you will see the Son of Man seated at the right hand of the Power," and "coming with the clouds of heaven"'"), is as close as we can come to Jesus identifying himself with the heavenly Son of Man. However, the identification is implicit rather than explicit and is only possible if the Son of Man is understood to be identical to the Messiah. Based upon everything else that we see in Mark's Gospel, it is not clear that such an identification can be assumed. One could read the passage as Jesus simply warning the high priest of the imminence of the end.

Son of Man were not spoken by the historical Jesus. Rather, they came from the later movement, following Jesus's death, when his disciples identified him with the heavenly figure. Regardless, given these problems, we cannot simply assume that Jesus spoke about himself as the heavenly Son of Man expected at the end of time. All we can claim with any certainty is that the historical Jesus sometimes used the phrase *son of man* (but not the title) as another way of talking about himself. When he used the expression in this way, he made no extraordinary claims for his position but instead simply spoke of himself as a human being.[60]

What about the title *Messiah* (*Christ*)? This title was ubiquitous in early Christianity. It appears hundreds of times in the New Testament, in every writing except one.[61] But does it go back to the historical Jesus? Or did the later writers ascribe the title to him? In the Gospels, although other characters (such as his disciples) claimed that Jesus was the Messiah, he himself did not. The exception comes in his trial before the council and, in that case, it appears in only one Gospel, the Gospel of Mark. There, when asked by the high priest, "Are you the Christ?" Jesus answers affirmatively (Mark 14:61–62). In the corresponding passage in Luke's Gospel. Jesus evades the question (22:67) and in Matthew's Gospel, he seems to deny it (Matt 26:64).[62]

So we do not have strong evidence that Jesus claimed this title for himself. But, assuming for the moment that he did, what would he have been asserting? The term *messiah* literally means someone who had been anointed. In ancient Judaism, this figure would most likely have been a king.[63] In the Psalms of Solomon, mentioned earlier, the anticipated "Lord Messiah" is understood in such a fashion. He is labeled the son of David (David was the founder of the

---

60. While it is not impossible that the historical Jesus claimed to be the end-time, heavenly, Son of Man, it seems unlikely to me for two reasons: first, the historical Jesus did not lay claim to other exalted titles such as "Son of God" or, as we will see, "Messiah," and, second, in the Gospels he nowhere explicitly claims to be the heavenly Son of Man. The closest he comes is in Mark 14:61–63 but there, as demonstrated before, the identification is not explicit. Furthermore, the dialogue in Mark 14:61–63 is unlikely to be historical. See below, note 62.

61. "Christ" does not appear in 3 John, although some translations include it in verse 7. The Greek text there speaks only of "the name." For the sake of clarity, translators sometimes insert "Christ."

62. It should be pointed out that the dialogue during the trial is almost certainly not historical. According to the Gospels themselves, none of Jesus's followers were there. Rather, the dialogues were probably created later by the Gospel writers who tried to imagine what had gone on.

63. It should, however, be pointed out that others beside the king were also anointed. For example, prophets were sometimes anointed.

royal dynasty) and the future ruler of Israel. As such he was expected to purge Jerusalem of non-Jews and redistribute to the tribes of Israel the lands that had been assigned to them in ancient times (17:21–32). Would Jesus have considered himself to be such a kingly figure? Although he spoke of a kingdom, Jesus nowhere explicitly claimed kingship. Indeed, when he spoke of leadership, he redefined it in a radical way: "The greatest among you must become like the youngest, and the leader like one who serves. For who is greater, the one who is at the table or the one who serves? Is it not the one at the table? But I am among you as one who serves" (Luke 22:26–27; cf. Matt 20:25–27; Mark 10:43–45). By describing himself as one who serves, Jesus depicted his role in a quite different way than we see, for example, in the Psalms of Solomon. So if Jesus claimed to be the Christ, the Messiah of Israel, he certainly had a different notion of the part than did others of his time.

Nevertheless, even if Jesus himself did not overtly claim the title "Messiah," there are good reasons to suppose that the title can be traced back to his time. First, since there is no evidence for the idea of a suffering messiah prior to Christianity, it is hard to imagine that Jesus's disciples would have attributed the title to him *after* his death. Second, whether or not Jesus actually embraced the title "Messiah," he almost certainly raised messianic expectations among some. If the story of Jesus's entrance into Jerusalem found in the Gospels is a reflection of history (rather than a later creation), then he was clearly viewed by some as a royal messiah. In the words of one scholar, "Jewish pilgrims hailed Jesus as messiah in Jerusalem. Pilate killed him as a messianic pretender—not . . . because *Jesus* thought he was messiah (would Pilate have cared about Jesus's self-identity?), but because others thought and proclaimed that he was."[64] Perhaps Jesus's talk of the kingdom suggested to his followers that he must be its king, that is, the messiah. But regardless of the opinion of his followers, Jesus's enemies certainly understood him in these terms (although they viewed him as a *false* messiah). This is made obvious by the fact that Jesus was executed by the Romans as a royal pretender; the inscription on the cross read "the king of the Jews" (Mark 15:26; Matt 27:37; Luke 23:38; John 19:19).

In sum, of the most common titles attributed to Jesus in the Synoptic Gospels, "Son of God," "Son of Man," and "Messiah" or "Christ," we can assume the following. First, the title "Son of God" was probably not claimed by Jesus. Rather, it was attributed to him after his death. Second, while Jesus used the phrase "son of man" in reference to himself, he probably meant it not in a titular sense but as a circumlocution for "I," much as one might

64. Paula Fredriksen, *Jesus of Nazareth: King of the Jews* (New York: Vintage, 1999), 234.

today use "yours truly" to speak of oneself. Although in the Synoptic Gospels Jesus spoke of the end-time, heavenly "Son of Man," in those passages (assuming that they accurately reflect the sayings of the historical Jesus), he never explicitly connected that figure with himself. Third, although Jesus likely did not use the title "Messiah" or "Christ" as a self-designation, others of his time (e.g., his followers and his opponents) may have thought of him in those terms.

What then can we conclude about Jesus's understanding of his role? Unfortunately, this is an extremely difficult question to answer. However, because the historical Jesus focused on proclaiming the kingdom rather than talking about himself, we can reasonably conclude that Jesus understood his role as the herald of God's kingdom. He both taught about the kingdom and he saw his activities connected to it; he viewed his exorcisms and healings as the manifestation of the kingdom of God in his time. Although Jesus's action in the temple shortly before his death was probably meant as either a symbolic act or some kind of protest, we can no longer know exactly what he meant by it.

The Disciples Gather after Jesus's Death

What happened after Jesus's death? What caused his disciples to continue the movement of their former master? Unfortunately, we have very little information about the earliest years of the movement. The book of Acts, written by the same author that penned the Gospel of Luke, provides us with some material. Unfortunately, since the account in Acts comes from a much later time than the events that it describes (50–90 years), it is unclear how much reliable information its author possessed.[65] Furthermore, the Acts account clearly idealized the movement's beginnings. Consequently, we must acknowledge that the months and years immediately following Jesus's death remain in the shadows. The best that we can do is make some educated guesses about the thoughts and actions of Jesus's original followers.

Jesus's disciples likely fled at the time of his arrest and went into hiding.[66]

---

65. Although the book of Acts could have been written as early as the 80s, it is also possible that it was produced in the early second century, perhaps as late as 120 CE.

66. This much can be affirmed by Mark's Gospel. According to that text, all of Jesus's disciples except Peter fled at his arrest (14:50). They never returned (the Gospel originally ended at 16:8; the disciples appear in the secondary endings, added later). Shortly thereafter, Peter denied knowing Jesus and likewise departed from the story.

Since their leader had been executed as a messianic pretender, they probably also feared for their lives. It would not have been unusual for the Romans to execute anyone having anything to do with a movement that they considered seditious.[67] Nevertheless, after a short period of time, Jesus's disciples experienced their master's presence in some way and they determined that God had raised him from the dead.

The sense in which Jesus's followers experienced his presence after his death (i.e., his resurrection) is unclear. Our sources disagree. The accounts in the Gospels indicate that Jesus left his tomb and his disciples experienced him objectively, that is to say, they actually saw him with their own eyes.[68] However, an earlier account by Paul could suggest that Jesus was experienced by his followers in a vision (1 Cor 15:5–7).[69] Furthermore, several early hymns, embedded in New Testament letters, envision Jesus's resurrection not as a re-suscitation of Jesus's previously dead body (as we see in the Gospels) but as a kind of exaltation. That is to say, they depict Jesus as having been raised from the dead and taken directly to heaven. According to one of them:

67. For example, as mentioned in the previous chapter, the Roman leader Varus crucified two thousand people who had been involved in the revolts following Herod's death (Josephus, *Ant.* 17.295). Pontius Pilate also slaughtered the crowd that had followed a Samaritan prophet to Mount Gerizim to recover temple vessels allegedly left there by Moses (Josephus, *Ant.* 18.85–87). Closer to the time of the Jewish revolt, Josephus tells us of several revolutionary figures, among them an individual named Theudas and someone known only as "the Egyptian." Many among the crowds who followed these individuals were slaughtered by Roman leaders (Josephus, *Ant.* 20.97–99, 169–172; Josephus, *J. W.* 2.261–63).

68. There are some significant disagreements among these narratives. Mark's narrative contains no post-resurrection appearance of Jesus (note that the original Gospel ended at 16:8). The women who came to his tomb were simply told (by an unknown figure) that Jesus had been raised from the dead. The women fled, terrified, and failed to pass on that information (Mark 16:1–8). According to Matthew's story, Jesus appeared to the women after they had left the tomb. He later appeared to the eleven disciples, i.e., the twelve minus Judas (Matt 28:1–20). In Luke's story, Jesus appeared to two of his disciples who had left Jerusalem and were headed west to the town of Emmaus. The disciples at first did not recognize him although eventually they did. Later, Jesus appeared to the other disciples (Luke 24:1–53). John's Gospel contains four post-resurrection appearances. First, Jesus appeared to Mary Magdalene. Then he appeared to all of the disciples except Thomas, who happened to be gone at the time. Then he appeared to all of the disciples, including Thomas (John 20:1–29). Finally, Jesus appeared to all of the disciples while they were fishing in Galilee (John 21:1–14). The last appearance, however, occurs in an ending that is probably secondary.

69. In that account the verb "to appear" was used. Elsewhere it was sometimes used in connection with a vision. The same verb is used in the same passage to describe Paul's experience of the risen Jesus, which almost certainly happened in a vision.

> [Jesus] was revealed in flesh,
>> vindicated in spirit,
> He was seen by angels,
>> proclaimed among the nations,
> He was believed in throughout the world,
>> taken up in glory. (1 Tim 3:16)

The final line of this hymn points to Jesus's resurrection. By making the statement that he was "taken up in glory," the hymn does not claim that he was raised from the tomb to walk again on earth (as described by the Gospel narratives), but rather it suggests that he was "taken up in glory," presumably to heaven.[70] If Jesus was believed to have been raised directly from the dead to heaven, that belief in turn suggests that his disciples would have likely experienced his resurrection as a vision of a heavenly being. Unfortunately, we will never know for sure what they experienced. All we can say for sure is that they believed that God had in some way raised Jesus from the dead.

Regardless of their experience of the resurrection, Jesus's followers later gathered together in Jerusalem. There, they attempted to understand the true identity of their mentor and the meaning of his death and resurrection. Jesus was indeed, they concluded, the Messiah of Israel (i.e., the Christ); although he had been slain by his enemies, his resurrection indicated that he had been vindicated by the deity. Since Jesus had announced the kingdom of God to his followers, they determined that he was about to return in the near future to bring about the full manifestation of the kingdom.

It is important to remember that, like their teacher, Jesus's disciples originally functioned entirely within the context of Judaism. Like other Jews in Jerusalem, they would have prayed and sacrificed at the temple, followed Jewish dietary laws, rested on the Sabbath, and observed Jewish festivals. But they were probably not content to keep their ideas about Jesus's identity to themselves. Rather, they likely tried to convince their fellow Jerusalemites that Jesus was the long-awaited Messiah of Israel who would return soon to usher in the kingdom.

We get a bit more information about the Jerusalem community of Jesus followers from one of Paul's letters, written in the early 50s. In his letter to the Galatians, Paul provides us with the names of the community's leaders:

70. Other hymns that tell a similar story appear in Eph 4:8–10 and Phil 2:5–11 (specifically v. 9).

James, Peter (usually called Cephas by Paul), and John (Gal 2:9).[71] Obviously, as the Gospels tell us, Peter was one of the most prominent disciples of Jesus. James, Paul informs us, was the brother of Jesus (Gal 1:19).[72] John's identity, however, is not certain. It is possible (and perhaps likely) that John was the son of Zebedee, a disciple who played an important role in the Gospels.[73] From what we see elsewhere in Paul's letter, it seems as if the most powerful of the three was James.

Besides the assembly of Jesus followers in Jerusalem, led by Peter, James, and John, we have evidence of one other group of Jesus followers in the Jewish homeland. This group was likely not an urban assembly like the one in Jerusalem but a rural one, active in the area of Galilee where Jesus himself had preached. This is the community that produced Q, the document that the authors of Matthew and Luke used as a source for their Gospels.[74] The members of the Q community believed that they were carrying on the work of their former teacher. They took seriously the following instructions that Jesus delivered to his disciples:

> The harvest is plentiful, but the day laborers are few; therefore ask the Lord of the harvest to dispatch day laborers into his harvest. Be on your way! Look, I send you out like sheep in the midst of wolves. Carry no purse, nor knapsack, nor sandals, nor stick; and greet no one on the road. Into whatever house you enter, first say, "Peace to this house!" And if a son of peace be there, let your peace come upon him; but if not, let your peace return upon you. And at that house, remain, eating and drinking whatever they provide, for the day laborer is worthy of his wages. Do not move around

71. Both "Peter" and "Cephas" are nicknames, the former a Greek nickname and the latter Aramaic. Each is best translated, "Rocky." Peter's actual name was Simon.

72. The identification of James as one of the leaders of the Jerusalem assembly is curious. As we will see in a later chapter, the Gospel of Mark lists James as one of Jesus's four brothers. But that same Gospel also indicates that the members of Jesus's family were unsympathetic to his activities (Mark 3:21). Obviously, at some point in time, James joined the movement (whether before or after Jesus's death is not clear). According to 1 Cor 15:7, Jesus appeared to James after his death. Perhaps at this time, James became a follower.

73. Both James and John, the sons of Zebedee, are important figures in the Gospel accounts. Acts tells us (probably accurately) that James had been executed prior to this by Herod Agrippa, the ruler of Judea, who reigned between 37 and 44 (Acts 12:2).

74. Because Q mentions a number of very small villages in the area of Galilee, it is likely that this group was located there. Unfortunately, we have no idea what ultimately happened to this community. It may have disbanded or possibly even been destroyed during the Jewish revolt against the Romans (66–74 CE).

from house to house. And whatever town you enter and they take you in, eat what is set before you; And cure the sick there, and say to them, "The kingdom of God has reached unto you." (Q 10:2–9)[75]

This passage—which the members of the Q group may have viewed as their own commission from Jesus—suggests that the community was composed of itinerants who, like their founder, proclaimed the kingdom and healed the sick in the small Jewish towns and villages of Galilee. They presumably relied on the sympathetic rural populace to feed and shelter them much as Jesus had.

Curiously, this community did not refer to Jesus as the Messiah; neither that term nor "Christ" appears anywhere in Q (as that document has been reconstructed by scholars). The community did, however, expect Jesus to return to inaugurate the kingdom; they believed that he would appear as the heavenly "Son of Man." Exactly when Jesus, the Son of Man, was to return was not clear but the members of the community expected it in the very near future: "Know this: if the householder had known in which watch the robber was coming, he would not have let his house be dug into. You also must be ready, for the Son of Man is coming at an hour you do not expect" (Q 12:39–40). The Son of Man's arrival would be vivid and unmistakable. Elsewhere in the Q document we find the following saying: "If they say to you: 'Look he is in the wilderness,' do not go out; 'look, he is indoors,' do not follow. For as the lightning streaks out from Sunrise [i.e., the East] and flashes as far as Sunset [i.e., the West] so will be the Son of Man on his day" (Q 17:23–24). In the meantime, however, the members of the community were to expect rejection, harassment, and even persecution. But they were not to retaliate. Instead, as Jesus had instructed them, they were to love their enemies and pray for those who abused them (Q 6:27–28).

The Movement Outside Judea

It is no surprise that the followers of Jesus formed communities in Jerusalem and Galilee after their mentor's death. What is surprising is the movement's journey into areas *beyond* Jewish territory. Once things moved outside of Jewish territory, things began to change, sometimes dramatically. For example,

75. Note that the Q citations follow the chapter and verse numbers that appear in Luke's Gospel; in other words, Q 10:2–9 corresponds to Luke 10:2–9. All reconstructions and translations of Q are from Kloppenborg, Q, *The Earliest Gospel*, 123–44.

while the Jesus movement in the Jewish homeland was Torah-observant, such was not necessarily the case with Jesus followers in the larger Greco-Roman world because non-Jews were incorporated into the movement. We cannot be sure when non-Jews were initially welcomed into the assemblies of Jewish Jesus followers, but it must have happened shortly after Jesus's death. The book of Acts narrates two different stories that explain how non-Jews came to be in the movement.

The first story centers on a Roman centurion named Cornelius who lived in the Judean seaside town of Joppa (now Jaffa). Although Cornelius was a pagan, he was, according to Acts, "a devout man" as was his whole household. Directed by a vision from God, Cornelius summoned Peter to his house. Meanwhile, Peter had also experienced a vision but his was quite enigmatic. As the reader eventually finds out, Peter's vision had authorized him to take the message about Jesus to non-Jews. But, at this point in the story, Peter had not yet discovered the vision's meaning.

Regardless, upon arriving at Cornelius's house, Peter reluctantly began to preach. But once the members of Cornelius's household heard Peter's message, the Spirit fell upon them and they began to speak in tongues and praise God. In response, Peter baptized them, asking, "Can anyone withhold the water for baptizing these [non-Jewish] people who have received the Holy Spirit just as we [Jews] have?" (Acts 10:1–48). While this story is engaging, its historical accuracy is questionable.[76] Rather, it functions in Acts to justify the presence of non-Jews in the movement.

The second story tells of the exodus of Jesus followers from Jerusalem following the violent death of Stephen, who had been killed by a mob in that city: "Now those who were scattered because of the persecution that took place over Stephen traveled as far as Phoenicia, Cyprus, and Antioch, and they spoke the word to no one except Jews. But among them were some men of Cyprus and Cyrene who, on coming to Antioch, spoke to the [Greeks] also, proclaiming the Lord Jesus. The hand of the Lord was with them, and a great number became believers and turned to the Lord" (Acts 11:19–21).[77] From a historical perspective, this narrative sounds much more likely. Antioch was one of the largest cities of the Roman Empire, it was relatively close to Jeru-

---

76. Historically, the idea that Peter took the Gospel to gentiles makes little sense for, in the letter to the Galatians (written long before Acts), Paul claimed that "Peter had been entrusted [by God] with the Gospel for the circumcised" while he (i.e., Paul) "had been entrusted with the Gospel for the uncircumcised" (Gal 2:7). In other words, as Paul tells the story, Peter had a reputation for proselytizing Jews.

77. NRSV translation modified.

salem (approximately four hundred and fifty miles), and it had a large Jewish population. As a result, it would not be unexpected to find Jewish Jesus followers in that city (possibly as a result of persecution in Jerusalem or possibly for other reasons). But regardless of how or why non-Jews were brought into the movement, Antioch sounds like a probable location for it to have first happened. Not surprisingly, Antioch is also the city in which we find Paul, the self-proclaimed "apostle to the gentiles" (Rom 11:13), toward the middle of the first century CE (Gal 1:21; 2:11).

Without a doubt, Paul was one of the most interesting figures in the early years of the Jesus movement. We know from his own writings that he originally persecuted the movement with the purpose of extinguishing it (Gal 1:13). Although we cannot be sure of Paul's rationale for persecuting Jesus's followers, we know that, during the course of his activities, he had an experience that changed his life. Acts provides us with a dramatic account of that experience; three times Acts tells of a vision that Paul had while on a journey to round up members of the Jesus movement in Damascus (Acts 9:1–19; 22:1–16; 26:9–18). According to those accounts, Paul was struck down to the ground, challenged by the voice of Jesus, blinded, and then healed in Damascus by a person named Ananias, a man who subsequently baptized him.

But, the accounts in Acts are clearly a later novelistic interpretation of Paul's conversion. The apostle's own report is much less colorful. Indeed, it contains very few details. Paul simply says that:

> When God, who had set me apart before I was born and called me through his grace, was pleased to reveal his Son to me, so that I might proclaim him among the Gentiles, I did not confer with any human being, nor did I go up to Jerusalem to those who were already apostles before me, but I went away at once into Arabia, and afterwards I returned to Damascus. (Gal 1:15–17)

This account tells us nothing about the circumstances surrounding Paul's change of heart. In fact, although his life-changing experience is usually labeled a conversion, his own description of the experience would more appropriately be called a commission. Paul did not cease being a Jew; rather he saw his encounter as a commission to proclaim God's son to non-Jews.

Here it is important to note the fundamental distinction between Paul's understanding of Jesus's significance and that of the communities of Jesus followers that we have already looked at. Obviously, the Jerusalem community and the Q community understood Jesus's role as the leader of a Jewish movement. The community in Jerusalem almost certainly viewed Jesus as the *Jewish*

Messiah. The Q community saw Jesus as a Jewish teacher of wisdom (as well as a healer and exorcist) who, although unjustly killed, would soon return to usher in the kingdom. There is nothing in the Q document that suggests that non-Jews belonged to that community. Nor is there any indication that itinerants from that community reached out to gentiles. Paul, however, thought differently. He insisted that the movement open its doors to non-Jews. Most importantly, he insisted that non-Jews, once they had entered the community, remain non-Jews and *not* convert to Judaism.

But Paul not only focused on a different audience than did other Jewish Jesus followers, his teachings were also distinctive. Paul did not focus on the kingdom. In fact, he rarely mentioned it.[78] Nor did he show any great concern for Jesus's life or teachings. Although, like other Jesus followers, Paul expected the return of Jesus, nowhere in his letters did he refer to him as the Son of Man.[79] While Paul frequently called Jesus "Christ," that term sounds more like Jesus's second name in his letters than a title (i.e., Jesus Christ rather than Jesus, the Christ). For titles, Paul preferred Jesus as *Kyrios* ("Lord" or "Master") or Jesus as the Son of God, possibly because these terms would have made more sense to non-Jews.[80]

But it was not just terminology that was different. Paul's understanding of Jesus's role also differed from others in the movement. He understood Jesus's death to be the most significant aspect of his mission. The Q community, on the other hand, focused on Jesus's sayings; it attached no positive value to Jesus's death. From its perspective, such was the fate that awaited prophets.[81] It is likely that the Jerusalem community understood Jesus's death in a similar

78. Exceptions appear in 1 Cor 4:20, 6:9–10, 15:50, and Gal 5:21.

79. It should be noted, however, that the end-time scenario laid out in 1 Cor 15:23–28 is compatible with the expectations regarding the arrival of the Son of Man. The title is, however, missing.

80. This is not to assume that Paul invented these titles. "Lord" was also a title used by Jewish Jesus followers as evidenced by the fact that it is preserved in Aramaic (*Maran*). See 1 Cor 16:22 and Did. 10.6.

81. "Woe to you, Pharisees, for you love the best seat in the synagogues and salutations in the market places. Woe to you, for you are like graves which are not seen, and people walking over them do not know it. . . . Woe to you Pharisees, for you load people with burdens hard to bear, and you yourselves with your finger do not move them. Woe to you, for you build the memorials of the prophets, but your fathers killed them. So you are witnesses and you consent to the deeds of your fathers; for they killed them. . . . Therefore also Wisdom said, I will send them prophets and apostles, and some of them they will kill and persecute, so that the blood of all the prophets which has been shed from the foundation of the world may be required from this generation" (Q 11:43–44, 46–48, 49–50).

way. But, for Paul, Jesus's death was salvific. That is to say, Jesus died for the remission of others' sins.[82] Furthermore, Jesus had died for all, Jews and non-Jews alike. Indeed, for Paul, the oneness of God—a fundamental Jewish principle—demanded the inclusion of non-Jews in the movement *as* non-Jews (and *not* converts to Judaism). In his letter to the Romans, he asked the question: "Is God the God of Jews only? Is he not the God of Gentiles also?" His answer, of course, was, "Yes, of Gentiles also, since God is one" (Rom 3:29–30).[83]

It should come as no surprise that Paul's way of thinking came into conflict with other members of the Jesus movement. Things came to a head in Antioch, probably less than twenty years after Jesus's death. As a result of a controversy in that city over non-Jews in the community of Jesus followers, Paul traveled to Jerusalem where he met with the Jerusalem leaders (James, Peter, and John). Two accounts of the meeting are available, one in Acts and the other from Paul himself (Acts 15:1–21; Gal 2:1–10). The accounts largely agree but there are nonetheless a couple of significant (and irreconcilable) differences between them.[84]

What is clear from both accounts, however, is that a deal was struck between Paul and the leaders of the Jerusalem community. Unfortunately, at this point the sources diverge somewhat, but the things that we can be relatively sure were included in the agreement are as follows. First, the Jerusalem leaders assured Paul that his gentile converts would not have to undergo circumcision and live as Jews (Gal 2:3; Acts 15:19). Second, it was agreed that, from that point forward, Paul would focus his missionary efforts on non-Jews while the Jerusalem leaders would take responsibility for evangelizing Jews (Gal 2:9). Third, Paul would take up a collection of money from the believers in Antioch and

82. Paul almost certainly did not invent this idea. In 1 Cor 15:3–4, he claimed that he received it (i.e., it was taught to him). It is likely that such an idea was created in the assembly at Antioch.

83. As we will see in the following chapter, Paul here seems to be alluding to the *Shema*, a Jewish prayer based on Deut 6:4; this prayer was and still is an important prayer in Judaism. For a helpful discussion of Paul's use of the *Shema* in Rom 3:29–30, see Mark D. Nanos, *The Mystery of Romans: The Jewish Context of Paul's Letter* (Minneapolis: Fortress, 1996), 179–87.

84. Most notably, Acts tells of a letter (carried by Paul and Barnabas) to the Antioch community. In that letter, the leaders insisted that, although the non-Jewish members of the community did not need to convert to Judaism, they did need to "abstain from meat that has been sacrificed to idols and from blood and from what is strangled and from fornication" (Acts 15:29). Paul says nothing about this in his account of the meeting. Furthermore, he makes no mention of it when the issue of meat sacrificed to idols later comes up at Corinth. If this had been part of the agreement, it is surprising that he had not informed the Corinthians of it when he founded that community.

send it to the impoverished church in Jerusalem. The money may have been for famine relief (Gal 2:10).[85]

On the surface, it looked like the controversy was resolved, largely by keeping the non-Jewish believers separate from the Jewish believers (point two mentioned above). But, at the same time, the different parties involved in the agreement seem to have had somewhat different understandings of what they had agreed to. This lack of clarity is demonstrated by an incident that happened in Antioch shortly after the Jerusalem agreement had been concluded. We know about this incident only because Paul mentions it in his letter to the Galatians. Acts says nothing about it. Unfortunately, because of the brevity of Paul's account, there are many details that we remain uncertain about.

Nevertheless, we can be sure that, at some point after Paul returned to Antioch, Peter traveled there and stayed with the community for a period of time. While he was there, Peter participated in the ritual meal of the Antioch assembly (the Eucharist), with both Jewish and non-Jewish members of the community.[86] In other words, while in Antioch, Peter followed the assembly's normal practice. However, at some point during Peter's stay, some people from the Jerusalem community arrived, a group that Paul referred to as "certain people from James" (Gal 2:12). While this group was in Antioch, Peter—probably out of consideration for the conservative sensibilities of the "people from James"—changed his practice and ate the ritual meal only with the Jewish members of the community.[87] It seems that the other Jews in the community followed Peter and also separated from the non-Jews.[88]

85. There is evidence to suggest that at about this time there had been famine in Jerusalem and its environs. Acts 11:27–30 mentions a worldwide famine in response to which the Antioch church sent relief through Paul and Barnabas. While the account of the Antioch community's response to the famine comes *before* the narrative of the Jerusalem meeting, it is likely that the former represents a misplaced reference to the efforts that resulted from the Jerusalem meeting. Unfortunately, there is no evidence of a worldwide famine outside of Acts 11:28. However, we know of several local food shortages in the mid–first century. Josephus (*Ant.* 20.51) refers to a famine during the middle of the 40s (i.e., likely only a few years earlier than the Jerusalem meeting). There may have also been another famine a few years later (*Ant.* 3.320).

86. The makeup of the assembly in Antioch is unknown. However, there must have been both Jews and non-Jews. We do not know, however, if most in the assembly were Jewish, non-Jewish, or if the group was evenly mixed.

87. Since Jews were not prohibited from eating with gentiles, the reason for the separation of Jews and non-Jews is uncertain.

88. It is unclear exactly what happened. Paul says that Peter "drew back and separated himself." Did Peter eat the meal at a table with Jews, leaving non-Jews to their own table? Did Peter, the other Jews in the assembly, and the people from James celebrate their own meal to which non-Jews were not invited?

Paul was furious. He interpreted Peter's action as a betrayal of the previous agreement. And so, as he himself narrated the events, he "opposed [Peter] to his face, because he stood self-condemned" (Gal 2:11). Paul went further and asked Peter, "If you, though a Jew, live like a Gentile and not like a Jew, how can you compel the Gentiles to live like Jews?" (Gal 2:14). Unfortunately, we cannot be sure of the result of the confrontation. Paul ended his account of the incident here. But we can hazard a guess that Paul came out the loser; the community probably sided with Peter. We can hypothesize this because—given the situation faced by the addressees of the letter in which Paul reported the events—it would have been in Paul's best interest to proclaim his victory. But, there is no such proclamation. Paul's silence strongly suggests the opposite; Paul, having tried to shame Peter and the others, was himself humiliated.

But, regardless of the outcome, Paul soon left Antioch and headed west. From this point on, he began founding communities composed primarily, if not exclusively, of non-Jews.[89] From his letters, we know that he set up assemblies in Galatia (in central Asia Minor), in the cities of Philippi and Thessalonica (in the Roman province of Macedonia), and in Corinth (the capital of the Roman province of Achaia). It is possible that he also set up other communities but there is no solid evidence to support such a claim.[90]

Summary and Conclusions

In the first few decades of its existence, the Jesus movement saw rapid and dramatic change. The movement began with Jesus of Nazareth who, while wandering through the rural agricultural and fishing villages of Galilee, exorcised, healed, and proclaimed the imminent arrival of the kingdom of God. Jesus and his followers proclaimed the love of God for the outcasts of Judean (i.e., Jewish) society, "sinners and tax collectors." To the best of our knowledge, Jesus preached only to "the lost sheep of the house of Israel" (Matt 15:24).

Following Jesus's death, his followers did not disband but rather gathered together in Jerusalem. They believed, based on their personal experience, that the deity had vindicated Jesus by raising him from the dead. Although they

89. Paul himself tells us that his communities were composed of non-Jews in 1 Cor 12:2, Gal 4:8, and 1 Thess 1:9.

90. Although from his letters, we know that Paul taught elsewhere—at Ephesus, for example, or Troas (both in Asia Minor)—there is no evidence to suggest that he established communities in those places. Although there was an assembly at Ephesus, it was almost certainly created before Paul arrived there.

continued to emphasize the imminent arrival of the kingdom, they also began to shift their focus somewhat. More emphasis was placed on the original proclaimer of the kingdom than on the kingdom itself. Jesus was acknowledged by his followers as the risen Messiah (Christ) and the Son of Man who would return in the near future to usher in the kingdom.

Within a few years of Jesus's death, as the movement expanded from Jerusalem into the Syrian city of Antioch, Jesus followers began to preach to non-Jews. The latter expressed an interest and were, it seems, welcomed into some Jewish assemblies of Jesus followers. Not surprisingly, the acceptance of non-Jews into the assemblies provoked controversy. Some Jesus followers insisted that non-Jews in the assemblies convert to Judaism while other Jesus followers, including Paul—who claimed he had been commissioned by the deity to preach to non-Jews—insisted that non-Jews remain in the assemblies as non-Jews. Paul eventually met with the Jerusalem leaders, who acknowledged the legitimacy of his position.

Meanwhile, as the movement spread into non-Jewish territory, the emphasis on Jesus, the movement's founder, also began to shift. While his original disciples, following their leader's death, had proclaimed Jesus the Messiah of Israel, others (like Paul) proclaimed him as the Son of God whose death had made possible reconciliation for sinners. Paul and others like him insisted that Jesus's death provided non-Jews with the opportunity to abandon their idolatrous past and become reconciled to the one true deity.

CHAPTER 3

From Idols to a Living and True God

W hy would pagans have been interested in the Jesus movement's radically monotheistic message to worship one God and one God only? The polytheism that characterized Greco-Roman religion pervaded virtually all of society. To commit oneself to only one deity (and a foreign one at that!) to the exclusion of the traditional gods was a bold step that could carry very real social consequences. Although in the middle of the first century there was no official, empire-wide suppression of the Jesus movement, nevertheless, adopting the absolute monotheism required by the movement could alienate others, including friends and family.

In order to better understand the ramifications of such a move, in this chapter we will first explore the religious beliefs and practices that dominated Greco-Roman society, that which we normally call "paganism." We will then turn our attention to the message of the Jesus movement as exemplified by one of its most important missionaries, Paul of Tarsus. Although Paul was not the only Jewish Jesus follower to take the message of the Jesus movement to non-Jews, he is the only one whose message has survived.

Paganism in the Eastern Empire

An intriguing narrative from the Acts of the Apostles provides a good point of entry into our investigation of paganism in the eastern Roman Empire. The Acts story recounts a journey of the apostle Paul and his companion Barnabas through Lycaonia, an area in south central Asia Minor (currently, the Turkish province of Konya). Whether or not we accept the historicity of this passage (Paul himself never mentions anything about either Lycaonia or the episode narrated by Acts), this particular text nevertheless gives us access to the religious landscape of the time.

As Acts tells the story, while in Lycaonia, Paul and Barnabas visited the city of Lystra. Compared to some of the great Asian cities mentioned in the New Testament—Ephesus, Pergamum, or Sardis, for example—Lystra was a relatively small town; it probably held no more than a few thousand residents. Regardless, as the story goes, Paul and Barnabas entered the city and there encountered a man with disabilities; he "could not use his feet and had never walked, for he had been crippled from birth." While he was preaching, Paul noted that this man was listening to him. "And Paul, looking at him intently and seeing that he had faith to be healed, said in a loud voice, 'Stand upright on your feet.' And the man sprang up and began to walk" (14:10). For our purposes, what is particularly interesting about this episode is not the healing miracle itself but what followed.

The people of Lystra were greatly impressed. They shouted out, "'The gods have come down to us in human form!' Barnabas they called Zeus, and Paul they called Hermes, because [Paul] was the chief speaker. The priest of Zeus, whose temple was just outside the city, brought oxen and garlands to the gates; he and the crowds wanted to offer sacrifice" (14:11–13). Paul and Barnabas were horrified by the actions of the multitude; they attempted to stop the sacrifice:

> [Paul and Barnabas] tore their clothes and rushed out into the crowd, shouting, "Friends, why are you doing this? We are mortals just like you, and we bring you good news, that you should turn from these worthless things to the living God, who made the heaven and the earth and the sea and all that is in them. In past generations he allowed all the nations to follow their own ways; yet he has not left himself without a witness in doing good—giving you rains from heaven and fruitful seasons, and filling you with food and your hearts with joy" (14:14–17).

With such words, Paul and Barnabas were able to prevent the Lycaonians from offering the sacrifice to them.

As mentioned earlier, our interest in this account focuses less on the actions of Paul than on the reaction of the crowd. Its response to the miraculous healing communicates four basic but essential characteristics of Greco-Roman religion. First and most obvious is its polytheism. The Lycaonian people claimed that *gods* (plural) had appeared and they mentioned two deities in particular, Zeus and Hermes. Second, the crowd's reaction suggests the belief that the gods were like humans, at least to some extent, and interacted with them. Third, the episode indicates that the gods could and sometimes would *help* humans, in this case by healing. Fourth, as the end part of the passage suggests, humans believed that they could also provide something for the gods; the gods could be honored with animal sacrifice. We will examine each of these points in turn.

There Were Many Gods

To say that the hellenized people of Paul's time worshipped many gods is a bit of an understatement. The deities worshipped numbered in the hundreds. While there was some regional variation, the same major deities were, for the most part, venerated throughout the whole of the eastern Roman Empire.[1] We can divide these deities into two categories, the gods of the Greeks and foreign gods. The former comprised the pantheon of the ancient Greek city-states, a pantheon that eventually spread throughout the hellenized eastern Mediterranean. The latter included those deities that had originated elsewhere, primarily from the East.

The Greek pantheon consisted of twelve immortals. Zeus, of course, was the high god, the most important deity of all; he ruled over all the other Olympian deities. Zeus's wife (and sister) was Hera. The others gods included Poseidon, Athena, Apollo, Artemis, Aphrodite, Hermes, Demeter, Dionysus, Hephaestus, and Ares.[2] Alexander and those who succeeded him had taken some of these deities to the East. But many had previously migrated, before Alexander's time, often as a result of colonies created by the Greek city-states.

It is important to note, however, that there were often significant differences among gods with the same name. For example, there was a temple of Zeus in virtually every city in the Hellenistic world. But, the deity in many

1. Regional variation would have been pronounced in an area like Egypt where Egyptian gods continued to be worshipped. Of course, in Judea, deities other than the God of the Jews were rare (other than in parts of Judea with a significant pagan population). In the western empire, Roman deities predominated.

2. Although the Greeks and Romans each had their own pantheon, there was a remarkable correspondence between the major deities of each group. This is hardly surprising since we know that Greek influence on Roman culture goes back to at least the sixth century BCE. Indeed, Greek settlers colonized Sicily and parts of the southern Italian peninsula as early as the eighth century BCE. Below is a list of Greek gods followed by their Roman counterparts: Zeus = Jupiter; Hera = Juno; Poseidon = Neptune; Athena = Minerva; Apollo = Apollo; Artemis = Diana; Aphrodite = Venus; Hermes = Mercury; Demeter = Ceres; Dionysus = Bacchus; Hephaestus = Vulcan; and Ares = Mars.

of the eastern temples was frequently an indigenous deity, thinly disguised as Zeus. We can see another good example in the goddess Artemis. In Greece, Artemis was thought to be a beautiful and graceful huntress; she was portrayed as such by the Athenian playwright Euripides (*Hippolytus* 73–87). But this incarnation of the goddess differs markedly from the stiffly posed Asian Artemis of Ephesus, from whose torso hung rows of pendants (variously interpreted as breasts, bull testicles, or bees' abdomens). Apparently, when Greek colonists originally arrived in Ephesus, they had identified a local Asian goddess with their own Artemis. Although the Artemis of Ephesus ultimately acquired many of the Greek goddess's characteristics, sculptural representations of her form did not change much. As these examples show us, although there existed a commonly recognized group of "Greek" deities, there was nevertheless some (often significant) local variation.

Besides the Greek gods that were worshipped throughout the Hellenistic world, there were also foreign deities, gods and goddesses from places other than Greece. But unlike the examples discussed above, these gods were *not* identified with the deities of the Greeks. Rather, for some reason, they were able to maintain their original (foreign) identities. Such gods and goddesses included Atargatis from Syria, Isis and Serapis from Egypt, Cybele and Attis from Asia Minor, Bendis and Sabazios from Thrace, and Mithras from Persia. Although foreign in origin, these deities were worshipped throughout the eastern Roman Empire *alongside* the traditional Greek gods. Indeed, in some cases, the popularity of some foreign gods outstripped that of many traditional Greek gods. But how did these gods keep their foreign identities? Why were they not simply assimilated to the existing Greek deities? Why were they accepted at all?

An inscription from the Greek island of Delos (ca. 200 BCE) can help us answer these questions. The inscription, composed by an Egyptian priest of the god Serapis, gives a detailed account of the arrival, resistance to, and eventual acceptance of that deity by the inhabitants of the island. According to the inscription, the priest's grandfather traveled from Egypt to the Greek island approximately a century before the inscription was carved. "Our grandfather Apollonius, an Egyptian from the priestly class, having brought his god with him from Egypt, continued serving his god, according to ancestral custom and, it seems, lived for ninety-seven years."[3] As the text tells us, upon his ar-

---

3. *IG* XI.4 1299. This inscription is sometimes known as the Serapis Aretology. The translation here and following is from Richard S. Ascough, Philip A. Harland, and John S. Kloppenborg, *Associations in the Ancient World: A Sourcebook* (Waco: Baylor University Press, 2012), 133–34.

rival in Delos, Apollonius set up the statue of Serapis, presumably in his own home, and served it as he had previously, "according to ancestral custom." In other words, he established a household cult of Serapis in his new homeland. Apollonius himself acted as the cult's priest, presumably leading those in his household (and possibly other local Egyptian immigrants) in the worship of Serapis.

The inscription then tells us how the responsibility for the household cult passed to Apollonius's son and then eventually to his grandson, the author of the inscription (also named Apollonius). But after the youngest Apollonius took over the cult, the god ordered him to construct a more proper temple for his worship: "The god instructed me through a dream that I should dedicate his own temple of Serapis and that he was not to be in rented rooms anymore. Furthermore, he would find the place where the temple should be located, indicating this by a sign. And this is what happened." Having been shown by the god where the temple was to be established, Apollonius bought the land and began to set the temple up.

Meanwhile, a group of locals, who opposed the establishment of the temple to the foreign god, took Apollonius to court. Toward the end of the inscription, in a hymn of praise to the deity, we learn the ultimate outcome of the court case: Serapis himself miraculously stymied the opposition in court. Unfortunately, the details of what actually happened are not narrated. The inscription only provides the result: "all the community marveled at [Serapis's] divine power." Whatever happened, the cult of Serapis was accepted as a legitimate religious enterprise on Delos. What began as an attempt of one immigrant family to maintain ties to its native culture ended with the recognition of the foreign deity by the Greek inhabitants of the island.

Over the course of several centuries, other foreign gods were introduced into various Hellenistic cities. They too were probably brought by immigrants, although some were introduced otherwise. Lucian of Samosata, a satirist from the second century CE, relates how the snake-figured deity, Glycon, was brought to Paphlagonia (north central Turkey) by a certain Alexander of Abonouteichos. As Lucian tells the story, Alexander discovered a tiny live snake in an egg at the site of a temple that was being constructed for Asclepius, a god of healing. Lucian, who considered Alexander a charlatan, claimed that the latter had previously planted the egg. However the egg made it to the construction site, the little snake's appearance caused an uproar. The people of Paphlagonia hailed the arrival of the god. Alexander then set up an oracle at the site, complete with a large talking snake (*Alexander the False Prophet* 12, 26). As Lucian tells the story, Alexander procured a large, tame snake that he held on his lap. Over the snake's head, Alexander placed "a serpent's head of linen, which had something of a human look, [which] was all painted up, and . . . would open and close its mouth by means of horsehairs, and a forked black tongue like a snake's, also controlled by horsehairs, would dart out" (*Alexander the False Prophet* 12). Furthermore, "[by fastening] crane's windpipes together and [passing] them through the [snake's false] head," Alexander also gave the snake the ability to speak. From outside the sanctuary, an assistant "spoke into the tube . . . so that the voice issued from his canvas [god]" (*Alexander the False Prophet* 26). The oracle apparently drew enormous crowds and made Alexander rich, much to Lucian's chagrin.

But alongside of transplanted foreign deities and the twelve traditional gods of the Greek pantheon, a multitude of lesser gods were revered. These included, among many others, the twin gods Castor and Pollux, favored by sailors; Hecate, a goddess associated with crossroads and magic;[4] Eros, the god of love and desire; Pan, the god of the countryside; the Graces, the Muses, and the Furies. Some deities were associated with particular locations; certain nymphs, for example, were linked to rivers, forests, meadows, or springs. Other gods or goddesses were tied to natural phenomena like the sun (the god Helios), the moon (Selene), the sea (Thetis or Leucothea), or the winds.[5]

Heroes, typically human beings who had achieved immortality, were also widely worshipped. The healing deity Asclepius, mentioned in the story of Glycon's arrival at Paphlagonia, was one of these hero-deities. During his lifetime, he was alleged to have been a great healer; following his death, he was granted immortality by Zeus. The cult of Asclepius was widespread; peo-

---

4. In one of his satires, Lucian has one of his characters recount a vision of Hecate: "I . . . went off by myself into the wood. . . . When I was under cover, there came first the barking of dogs, and I supposed that my son Mnason was at his usual sport of following the hounds, and had entered the thicket with his companions. This was not the case, however; but after a short time there came an earthquake and with it a noise as of thunder, and then I saw a terrible woman coming toward me, quite half a furlong in height. She had a torch in her left hand and a sword in her right, ten yards long; below, she had snake feet, and above she resembled the Gorgon, in her stare, I mean, and the frightfulness of her appearance; moreover, instead of hair, she had the snakes falling down in ringlets, twining about her neck, and some of them coiled upon her shoulders. . . . Well, at the sight of her I stopped, at the same time turning the gem that [an] Arab gave me to the inside of my finger, and Hecate, stamping on the ground with her serpent foot, made a tremendous chasm, as deep as Tartarus; then after a little she leaped into it and was gone. . . . Then I saw everything in Hades, the River of Blazing Fire, and the Lake, and Cerberus, and the dead, well enough to recognize some of them" (*Lies* 22–24 [Harmon]).

5. The ancient historian Herodotus, for example, tells us that the Athenians honored the north wind, Boreas, because he had destroyed the ships of the invading Persians (*Hist.* 7.189).

ple traveled great distances to his temples—particularly those at Epidauros (Greece) and Pergamum (western Turkey)—seeking cures for their ailments. Besides Asclepius, there were other hero-deities, such as Heracles (Hercules to the Romans), Orpheus, and Prometheus. Of these three, Heracles was the most popular. He was venerated throughout the ancient world as an omnipresent helper of human beings; he was thought to have the ability to avert evil and so his image often appeared on amulets.[6]

Various personifications of human qualities, emotions, or desires were also considered worthy of divine honors, including figures like Arete ("virtue"), Eirene ("peace"), Eudaimonia ("prosperity"), Nike ("victory"), Ploutos ("wealth"), or Tyche ("fate" or "fortune"). *Agatha Tyche* ("good fortune") had temples in cities throughout the empire; a libation to *Agatha Tyche* was also customary at formal meals. While *Tyche* could be capricious, *Agatha Tyche* was beneficent.

Rome (as the goddess Roma), Rome's emperors, and their families were also revered as being in some way divine. The acknowledgment of the divinity of a ruler was hardly new. The divinity of emperors had been recognized in the East for centuries. Alexander, as we have already seen, was hailed as the son of Zeus-Ammon in Egypt. Several Hellenistic rulers that followed him identified themselves with Dionysus (e.g., Ptolemy XII and Antiochus VI) or claimed divinity without identifying themselves with any particular god (e.g., Antiochus II and Antiochus IV).[7] In the West, however, the notion of an emperor's divinity was a later development. Among the Romans, it first appeared in connection to Julius Caesar who was hailed as *divus Iulius* ("Julius, the god") after his assassination in 44 BCE. His adopted son Octavian—who would later be known as Caesar Augustus—claimed the title *divi filius*, "son of god."

The emperors who followed Augustus likewise claimed divinity. Temples built to honor them were everywhere, remarkably, even in Caesarea, in Judea. The divine emperor's portraits were also ubiquitous; as many as fifty thousand pictures of Augustus appeared in the towns and cities of the empire during his reign.[8] We may wonder if people really believed that the Roman emperors were

---

6. The phrase "O Heracles!" was common on the lips of ordinary people as evidenced by the comment by the orator Aelius Aristides, who sarcastically called it "the daily praise [of Heracles] by all men" (*Or.* 40.1).

7. Ptolemy XII was called Neos Dionysus ("the new Dionysus") and Antiochus VI, Epiphanes Dionysus ("the manifestation of Dionysus"). Antiochus II was simply called Theos ("the god") and Antiochus IV was called Epiphanes ("the manifestation" of the divine).

8. Michael Peppard, *The Son of God in the Roman World: Divine Sonship in Its Social and Political Context* (Oxford: Oxford University Press, 2011), 91.

truly gods. In answer to that, one noted scholar has suggested the following: "Sophisticated [people] may not have believed that the emperor was a god, nor did the courtiers who saw him, but they sacrificed to him, as though he was a god, and perhaps they covered the conflict of evidence with a metaphysical metaphor—god made manifest, son of god, the least of gods but the highest of mortals, son of Apollo, Hercules on earth. Most people probably did not bother with the demarcation; the emperor was clearly both man and god."[9] In other words, what the people actually *thought* about the emperor's divinity was less important than how they *acted*; they behaved toward him as they behaved toward the gods: they built temples, offered sacrifice, poured out libations, and held festivals, all in his honor.

As the discussion of the divinized emperors suggests, there was not a clear demarcation between gods and human beings in the Greco-Roman world. There was rather an in-between state in which existed those who were more than human but not gods, at least not gods in the same sense as the Olympian deities. This was the territory not only of the Roman emperors; other people also resided there, people considered to be more than human. In one way or another, these individuals were thought to have access to the divine realm; consequently, they had knowledge and or capabilities beyond those of ordinary mortals. Some scholars have referred to these people as "divine men," others as simply "holy men." However, a better label, more recently introduced is "freelance religious experts."[10]

Such religious experts cannot be easily categorized. Some were philosophers;[11] some were healers and exorcists; others were prophets who could predict the future; still others were wonder-workers who were reputed to have the ability to still storms, prevent plagues, and talk to animals. Alexander of Abonouteichos, mentioned earlier, was one of these specialists. So was the philosopher Apollonius of Tyana. He was an important teacher, exorcist, and healer who could also allegedly predict the future.[12] It is important to note that

---

9. Keith Hopkins, *Conquerors and Slaves,* SSRH 1 (Cambridge: Cambridge University Press, 1981), 242.

10. I have taken the label from Heidi Wendt, who describes such experts as "any self-authorized purveyor of specialized religious skills, teachings, and related services . . . [who] operated outside existing institutions and had to earn their recognition and legitimacy, often through demonstrations of skill and learning." See Heidi Wendt, "*Ea Superstitione:* Christian Martyrdom and the Religion of Freelance Experts," *JRS* 105 (2015): 185.

11. Most prominently, the ancient philosophers Pythagoras and Empedocles could be considered such.

12. The historian Dio Cassius tells us a particularly intriguing story of one such un-

we find such religious experts not only in the pagan milieu but also within Judaism; one such Jewish expert was Honi the circle-drawer, so named because, during a drought, he drew a circle around himself and informed God that he would not leave the circle until it rained. Rain did come.[13] Hanina ben Dosa was another such Jewish religious expert. Among other things, it was alleged that he could heal from afar (b. Ber. 34b). Furthermore, Jewish writers, including Philo and Josephus, portrayed Moses in such a manner.[14] He was "the greatest and most perfect" of all men and his ascent of Mount Sinai was seen as a kind of apotheosis.[15]

Besides freelance religious experts and Roman emperors, demons also fell between the divine and the human realm. Originally, it was thought that they could bring either good or evil to people. Hesiod, one of the oldest known Greek poets, called them "invisible wardens for the whole human race . . . tending to justice . . . and dispensing wealth" (*Works and Days* 144–47).[16]

---

named freelance religious expert from the third century CE. This person, labeled a *daimon* ("spirit") by Dio, acted as follows: "Claiming to be the famous Alexander of Macedon, and resembling him in looks and general appearance, he set out from the regions along the Ister, after first appearing there in some manner or other, and proceeded through Moesia and Thrace, revelling in company with four hundred male attendants, who were equipped with thyrsi and fawn skins and did no harm. It was admitted by all those who were in Thrace at the time that lodgings and all provisions for the spirit were donated at public expense, and none—whether magistrate, soldier, procurator, or the governors of the provinces—dared to oppose the spirit either by word or by deed, but it proceeded in broad daylight, as if in a solemn procession, as far as Byzantium, as it had foretold. Then taking ship, it landed in the territory of Chalcedon, and there, after performing some sacred rites by night and burying a wooden horse, it vanished" (*Rom. Hist.* 80.18.1–3 [Cary]). It is difficult to know what to make of the activity of this "spirit" (i. e., religious expert). Dio gives us no more information because he relates the story as an explanation for another event (the emperor Elagabalus's adoption of his cousin whom he renamed Alexander). Consequently, we can only speculate. This individual claimed to be Alexander the Great but in his actions (his performance of Bacchic rites and leading a Bacchic retinue) he resembled Dionysus. Why did he bury a wooden horse? Was it some allusion to the Trojan war? Was that in some way connected to Alexander or Dionysus? Unfortunately, we will never know. Perhaps those who encountered him understood their significance; perhaps they did not. Regardless, they honored him, likely because they feared him. They fed and lodged him while he was on his journey.

13. References to Honi are found in m. Ta'an. 3.8; b. Ta'an. 19a; and Josephus, *Ant.* 14.22.

14. See Wayne A. Meeks, "Moses as God and King," in Jacob Neusner, ed., *Religions in Antiquity: Essays in Memory of Erwin Ramsdell Goodenough* (Leiden: Brill, 1968), 354–71.

15. The description of Moses as "the greatest and most perfect" comes from Philo, *Moses* 1.1.

16. Translation from Stanley Lombardo, *Hesiod: Works and Days and Theogony* (Indianapolis: Hackett, 1993).

But as time went on, demons came to be seen almost exclusively as malicious entities. Illnesses were blamed on them. People who acted irrationally were considered under their power or "possessed" by one or more of them.

Curiously, demons had no cult. They were feared, not venerated. Magicians used charms, chants, and spells in order to control them. Once control was gained, a magician—for a fee, of course—could force demons to do his or her bidding: to foretell the future, to curse a rival, or to bring about a romance. But it was not only magicians who could control demons. Some freelance religious experts also had power over them. They could drive demons out of individuals possessed by them. As we have seen, Jesus of Nazareth was one such person; Apollonius of Tyana was another.

From our perspective, the people in the hellenized portion of the Roman Empire recognized a staggering number of supernatural beings. They acknowledged the gods of the Greek pantheon, a number of foreign deities, gods tied to specific locations, nature deities, divinized heroes, personified human qualities, Rome herself, the emperor, demons, and even some religious experts. The gods existed not only in the peoples' hearts and minds, they were literally everywhere in the ancient world.

Statues of deities appeared in and around the various temples that filled the towns and cities, in the streets, in market places, and in town halls. Household deities occupied virtually every home. One ancient author estimated that, at his time, there were thirty thousand statues of deities scattered across the empire.[17] Besides statues, there were also friezes and mosaics of the gods. They decorated the homes of the elite and appeared both inside and outside public buildings. Furthermore, temples were crowded with testimonials—painted on wood or inscribed in stone—that described the benefits obtained from one god or another. Votive offerings of hands, feet, eyes, and ears, molded in terra-cotta or precious metal, filled the precincts of temples, attesting to cures effected by a particular god or goddess.

Finally, anyone interested in the arts or any kind of public entertainment would have encountered the gods over and over again. Virtually every artistic performance would have featured them in one way or another. Choirs sang their praises. Stories of the gods were acted out on stage in theaters across the empire. Literature, both poetry and prose, was chock full of their exploits. Sporting events were not exempt. They were usually connected to festivals in

---

17. The author, who lived in the second century CE, was Oenomaus. He is cited in the fourth-century Christian writer Eusebius, *Prep. Gos.* 5.36.2 (cited in Ramsay MacMullen, *Paganism in the Roman Empire* [New Haven: Yale University Press, 1981], 31).

honor of one deity or another. Clearly, the Greco-Roman world was not only polytheistic; it was exuberantly so. As one scholar has put it, for the ancients, the "gods overflowed like clothes from an over-filled drawer which no one felt obliged to tidy."[18]

The Gods Were like Humans and Interacted with Them

Some philosophically minded groups, like the Epicureans, thought that the gods—although they existed—had nothing to do with the activities of humans. But most people, like the Lycaonians represented in the Acts story, believed that the gods regularly interacted with people. It was commonly assumed that one deity or another would occasionally appear on earth, unexpectedly, and in human form.

Physiologically, the gods were thought to resemble humans. Although they were considered immortal, they were not unchanging (or immutable as monotheistic theologians would describe their deity). The gods ate and drank; they also experienced pleasure and pain. Immortality did not protect them from injury. Homer's *Iliad*, for example, recounts that Aphrodite was wounded with a spear. According to the Latin novel *The Golden Ass*, Cupid (Eros to the Greeks) was burned by hot oil from a lamp.

The gods were not only thought to resemble humans physiologically, their psychological makeup was quite similar as well. They experienced joy, sadness, anger, and sexual desire. They married and they had children. They even cheated on their spouses. Indeed, Zeus was famous for his sexual adventures. He had affairs with both goddesses *and* human women. Among the former was Leto who, as a result of her liaison with Zeus, gave birth to the deities Artemis and Apollo. The human women that Zeus seduced included Europa, Io, Semele (the mother of Dionysus), and Danaë (the mother of Perseus).

Zeus's sexual appetite was only matched by the profound jealousy of his wife, Hera, who typically sought vengeance on her husband's human sexual partners. For example, when she found out that Zeus had previously promised Semele, one of his mortal conquests, anything that she might desire, Hera suggested that Semele ask Zeus to show himself to her in all of his divine glory.

---

18. R. T. C. Parker, *Polytheism and Society at Athens* (Oxford: Oxford University Press, 2005), 387. Although Parker's comment had to do with the city of Athens during the classical period, it easily applies to the Greco-Roman world.

Although Zeus tried to dissuade Semele, it was to no avail. Zeus reluctantly granted her request and Semele perished, consumed by fire.

As with Hera's retaliation against her husband's mistresses, the gods sometimes punished humans because they were angry. In Hera's eyes, Semele had overstepped her bounds by submitting to Zeus's advances. But sometimes the humans who were punished were blameless. For example, in *The Golden Ass*, mentioned above, Venus (Aphrodite to the Greeks) was infuriated because a beautiful human named Psyche was getting more attention than Venus herself; furthermore, people sometimes mistook the human woman for the goddess.[19] The goddess was indignant: "So! Here I am, the progenitor of creation, the very origin of nature—Venus, the nurturer of the whole planet—and I'm placed in the position of divvying up my exalted privilege with a human wench and seeing my name, cherished in heaven, desecrated by terrestrial trash! I suppose that I'll be invoked jointly with her and endure precarious worship by proxy. An adolescent who's going to die someday will be hauling her face around as if it were my image . . .[but] she's not going to chortle over stealing my prerogatives. I'll make sure that she pays in plenty for that imposter beauty" (*The Golden Ass* 4.30).[20] Venus tried to follow through on her threat by commanding her son Cupid to cause Psyche to fall in love with the vilest mortal imaginable. Fortunately for Psyche, Venus's plot was thwarted; Cupid himself fell in love with Psyche.

Others who accidentally crossed a deity, however, were not as fortunate as Psyche. For instance, the Roman poet Ovid tells the story of the man Actaeon who, while hunting, accidentally stumbled across the goddess Diana (Artemis to the Greeks) as she was bathing. Shamed and dishonored by being seen naked by a mortal, the angry goddess transformed Actaeon into a stag. His hunting dogs immediately turned on him and tore him to pieces (*Metamorphoses* 3.138–252).

While sometimes the gods interfered in human affairs because they were angry, at other times they sought to put people to the test. When the hero of Homer's *Odyssey* finally returned to his home country, he headed to his house, disguised as a beggar. There he encountered many would-be suitors vying for his wife's hand. When he begged for food, one of the suitors,

19. We see something like this in several Greek novels. In a novel by Chariton entitled *Chaereas and Callirhoe*, Callirhoe, because of her extraordinary beauty, was often mistaken for Aphrodite. Similarly, in *The Ephesian Tale* by Xenophon of Ephesus, the heroine Anthia was mistaken for Artemis.

20. The translation of this and other passages of this work in the pages that follow are from Sarah Ruden, *The Golden Ass: Apuleius* (New Haven: Yale University Press, 2011).

Antinoös, hurled a footstool at him, intending to drive him away. The rest quickly chastised him:

> A poor show, that—hitting this famished tramp—
> Bad business, if he happened to be a god.
> You know that they go in foreign guise, the gods do,
> Looking like strangers, turning up
> In towns and settlements to keep an eye
> On manners, good and bad. (*Odyssey* 17.483–87)[21]

The suitors of Odysseus's wife, although hardly positive characters in the story, nevertheless were wise enough to be appalled by Antinoös's actions; the beggar, they insisted, might be a god in disguise.

We hear a similar kind of story from Ovid. As he tells it, the gods Jupiter and Mercury (the Roman counterparts to the Greek gods Zeus and Hermes) disguised themselves as weary travelers and, while wandering in Asia Minor, sought out hospitality from the locals.[22] But everyone they approached sent them away. Finally, an elderly couple, Philemon and Baucis, welcomed the gods-in-disguise. They provided them with food and drink. The gods therefore rewarded the old couple while destroying their stingy neighbors (*Metamorphoses* 8.611–724).

The gods, however, did not interact with human beings only to punish or test them. Sometimes, they intervened to help them. This brings us to our third characteristic of Greco-Roman paganism.

The Gods Would Sometimes Help Humans

Although the ancients credited the gods with much of their good fortune (e.g., bountiful harvests, good health, and the like), in this section we will focus on divine aid that was provided more directly to individual human beings. Ancient literature provides us with numerous examples. According to Homer's *Iliad*, for instance, Apollo decided to assist the Trojans in their struggle against the Achaeans, despite his claim elsewhere that mortals were not worth fighting

21. Translation by Robert Fitzgerald, *Odyssey: Homer* (New York: Farrar, Straus, and Giroux, 1989). This particular passage suggests that the gods were interested in justice among humans. Although this is not necessarily a prominent idea in ancient Greek religion, it does appear at times. See, for example, Hesiod, *Works and Days* 280–83.

22. The readers of the Acts story about Paul and Barnabas being mistaken for these gods most likely would have recognized its similarity to the other tale.

over. When the Trojans were imperiled, Apollo, in the likeness of a warrior, held the Achaeans at bay so the Trojans could flee to safety (*Illiad* 21.461–67, 590–611). In various places in the *Odyssey*, Athena likewise appeared among humans, primarily to help Odysseus and his family. In one instance, disguised as an older man, she advised Odysseus's son, Telemachus (*Odyssey* 2.267–305). Elsewhere, she took the form of Telemachus himself. In that guise, she gathered a crew and prepared a ship for a journey that the real Telemachus was about to make (2.382–92).

The gods were also sometimes credited with saving individuals in peril. A second-century-CE soldier named Apion wrote in a letter to his father: "I give thanks to the lord Serapis because, when I was in danger at sea, he saved me straightaway" (BGU 423).[23] In the Greek novel *An Ephesian Tale*, two separated lovers, Anthia and Habrocomes, endure many dangers trying to find one another. They wander over land and sea, suffering "robbers' threats and pirates' plots and pimps' insults, chains, trenches, fetters, poisons, and tombs." When finally reunited, they credit Isis for both protecting them and restoring them to one another. At the temple of Isis, they pray: "To you, greatest goddess, we owe thanks for our safety; it is you, the goddess we honor most of all, who have restored us" (5.13).[24]

The gods were also believed to be able to treat diseases and physical disorders. In the role of healer, the goddess Isis is again conspicuous. The ancient historian Diodorus of Sicily claims: "[Isis] finds her greatest delight in the healing of mankind and gives aid in their sleep to those who call upon her, plainly manifesting both her very presence and her beneficence toward men who ask her help" (*Library of History* 1.25.3). Other gods besides Isis were also credited with healing. But the most famous was surely Asclepius, the deified human healer, mentioned above.

Healings accomplished by Asclepius typically happened at one of his temples, known as an Asclepium. In the ancient world, an Asclepium functioned much as a hospital does in ours.[25] Although many of these sanctuaries were scattered throughout the hellenized world, the most famous was at Epidaurus in Greece. Sometimes, after a successful healing, the subject would place a votive offering—such as a model of a body part, made of terracotta or precious

---

23. The letter in its entirety along with an English translation can be found in Adolf Deissmann, *Light from the Ancient East* (Grand Rapids: Baker, 1978), 179–80.

24. Translated by Graham Anderson in *Collected Ancient Greek Novels*, ed. B. P. Reardon (Berkeley: University of California Press, 1989).

25. The noted second-century-CE physician, Galen, began his study of medicine at the Asclepium in Pergamum in western Asia Minor in order to learn about treatment.

metal (mentioned earlier)—in the Asclepium. At other times, an inscription would be dedicated to the god. One such inscription, found at Epidaurus, describes a remarkable cure of a blind woman: "Ambrosia from Athens [was] blind in one eye. She came as a supplicant to the god. Walking about the sanctuary, she ridiculed some of the cures as being unlikely and impossible, the lame and blind becoming well from only seeing a dream. Sleeping there, she saw a vision. It seemed to her the god came to her and said he would make her well, but she would have to pay a fee by dedicating a silver pig in the sanctuary as a memorial of her ignorance. When he had said these things, he cut her sick eye and poured medicine over it. When day came she left healthy" (A4).[26]

As many of the examples presented above demonstrate, the gods were typically understood to be compassionate. Consequently, humans frequently called upon them for aid. Illness was one of the most popular reasons for seeking the aid of the gods; it was, however, not the only one.

Humans Could Provide Something for the Gods

While the gods were believed to be compassionate and sometimes willing to help mortals in trouble, it was also thought that humans could benefit the gods. Indeed, people were expected to honor them regularly and especially following an act of divine beneficence. This could be done in many ways. Votive gifts could be provided following a healing, as we have already seen. Small daily cultic acts could also be performed: one could honor a god by saluting his or her image as one passed (sometimes by blowing a kiss); one could offer the household gods a bit of food; one could pour out a few drops of wine in a deity's honor at the end of a meal; or one could recite a prayer of thanksgiving

---

26. The translation is from Lynn R. LiDonicci, *The Epidaurian Miracle Inscriptions: Text, Translation and Commentary*, SBLTT 36 (Atlanta: Scholars Press, 1995), 88–89. It should be noted that Asclepius not only cured human beings. One inscription from Epidaurus tells of the miraculous "healing" of a drinking-cup: "A baggage-carrier was traveling to the sanctuary, and when he was just over a mile away, he fell over. He got up, opened his bag and looked at the things inside which were all shattered. When he saw that his master's usual drinking-cup was broken, he was upset and sat down and tried to put the pieces together. A traveler saw him and said, 'You idiot, why are you mending that cup? It's quite pointless! Even Asclepius in Epidauros could not make that whole again.' When he heard this the slave put all the pieces in the bag and went on to the sanctuary. On arriving he opened the bag and took out the cup which had become whole. He told his master what had happened and what had been said, and when his master heard this he dedicated the cup to the god." This anecdote is cited in Emily Kearns, *Ancient Greek Religion: A Sourcebook* (Chichester: Wiley-Blackwell, 2010), 305–6.

for one's good fortune. But, among the many different ways of honoring the gods, the most important was animal sacrifice.

The importance of animal sacrifice was demonstrated in the story of the healing of the lame man by Paul quoted at the beginning of this chapter: "the priest of Zeus ... brought oxen and garlands to the gates [of the city]" because "he and the crowds wanted to offer sacrifice" to Paul and Barnabas, those the crowds had mistaken for gods. Obviously, the priest thought it essential to offer sacrifice because Zeus and Hermes had honored the town by visiting in person. Furthermore, they had also performed a miracle in the people's presence. The sacrifice of oxen in this account is significant; the bigger and more expensive the animal, the more the god was honored. The very expensive sacrificial gift of two or more oxen (the noun is plural in the Acts account but the number is not specified) was not typical. A more common sacrifice would have involved the slaughter of one, smaller, and much less expensive animal: a pig, goat, sheep, or some kind of domestic bird. In this case, however, the priest deemed this generous sacrifice suitable for such an extraordinary occasion.

Regular sacrifice (at civic festivals honoring one god or another, for example) was thought to assure good fortune. As one ancient philosopher put it, "we honor the gods [with sacrifice] in the wish that they will turn away evil from us and bring us good" (Theophrastus, *Peri Eusebeias*, frag. 12).[27] A human would offer a deity something that the latter desired—the smoke from the roasted meat of the sacrificial victim—and in turn the god would provide something of benefit to the human, health or good fortune, for example.

We see this in the story from Acts, although in that case the process was reversed. Hermes and Zeus had done something for the Lycaonians (or so it was believed). The gods had both honored the Lycaonians with their appearance and they had healed one of their number. In turn, it was thought only proper that the Lycaonians return the favor by offering a significant sacrifice to the gods.

What did a sacrifice look like? First of all, it was not usually performed within a temple building itself. Rather, it took place in the open air, usually on an altar in front of the temple. The animal was led to the altar; drops of water or sometimes kernels of grain were dropped on its head, causing the animal to nod its head. This was taken as a sign that the victim was agreeable. The throat of the animal was then slit (a large animal, like an ox, would be first stunned with a blow to the head); some of the victim's blood was poured on the altar and, following that, the god's portion—the tail, the bones, and the

---

27. Translation by Kearns, *Ancient Greek Religion*, 214 (slightly modified).

fat—was burned on the altar. Meanwhile, the *splanchna*, the internal organs, were roasted on spits and eaten, usually by the priest(s) and a select circle of worshipers. The rest of the meat was then boiled and eaten by the sacrificer(s) and companions. Typically, some of it was given to the temple. Any leftovers would be taken home for later consumption or sold at the meat market.[28]

Was Paganism in Decline?

Although the Jesus movement clearly had significant success attracting pagans into its ranks, the reason for its success is not immediately clear. It has often been claimed that the movement's success can be credited, in large part, to the decline of paganism in Hellenistic and Roman times. One noted scholar, writing in the 1920s, described paganism during that period as follows: "Twilight was indeed falling on the Olympians, in spite of external show. . . . What was happening can be seen in the one great temple a Greek city planned to a Greek god; Apollo's temple at Didyma was still unfinished four centuries later, not for lack of money at Miletus, but for the lack of that living faith which had formerly enabled cities to complete their temples in a generation."[29] With the loss of "that living faith," it was often claimed, all that remained was magic and superstition, both of which were easily swept away by the vitality of the Christian message.

More recent scholarship has challenged this idea, clearly demonstrating that paganism was alive and well during Roman times, even into the mid–third century CE.[30] Nevertheless, although paganism continued to thrive, the

28. It is important to note that animal sacrifice was not a phenomenon restricted to Greco-Roman paganism. Jews also sacrificed to their deity. However, there was one, very significant difference between pagan and Jewish sacrifices. It had to do, not with the way that the sacrifice was performed (indeed the manner in which the sacrifice was done was similar in both cases), but rather *where* the sacrifice was performed. For Jews, there was only one place where sacrifice could be offered to their deity, the temple in Jerusalem. To the contrary, there were hundreds of temples dedicated to the pagan gods throughout the empire and so sacrifice could be offered in many locations. It is unlikely that Jesus followers were taught to reject sacrifice. Rather, for them, sacrifice to their deity would have been impractical because it would have involved a trip to Jerusalem. Furthermore, following the destruction of the temple in 70 CE, it would have been altogether impossible.

29. W. W. Tarn, *Hellenistic Civilisation*, 3rd ed. (New York: New American Library, 1974), 336–37.

30. On the vitality of paganism, see in particular, Robin Lane Fox, *Pagans and Christians* (New York: Knopf, 1987) and MacMullen, *Paganism.*

Hellenistic and Roman periods brought change. Different religious practices were introduced, new religious ideas were explored, and temples to previously foreign deities were constructed. All of this could be said to add up to some kind of dissatisfaction with the traditional religion, at least in some quarters. Indeed, one noted sociologist of religion has asserted, "people do not embrace a new faith if they are content with the older one."[31] But do we see specific evidence of such dissatisfaction within paganism?

It could be argued that a growing interest in monotheism or at least a kind of quasi-monotheism in the Roman period demonstrates such dissatisfaction. The notion that there was only one God was not unknown in the ancient Greek world. However, it was found almost exclusively among the philosophers. The pre-Socratic philosopher Xenophanes (ca. 570–ca. 478 BCE) criticized the deities that appeared in the writings of Homer, arguing that their deeds were "matters of reproach and censure among men; theft, adultery, and mutual deceit" (Fragment 11). Such gods, he argued, were created by humans; humans gave the gods "their own dress and voice and form." But Xenophanes was not content to criticize the deeds of the human-created-gods. He went even further, insisting that there was "one god . . . greatest among gods and men, [who is] not at all like mortals in body or in thought" (Fragment 23).[32] Xenophanes was not promoting monotheism per se, as evidenced by his assertion that the one deity is the "greatest among gods." But he was moving in that direction. The philosophy of the later Stoics (in Hellenistic and Roman times) also tended toward monotheism; the Stoics believed that the divine was a kind of cosmic force that pervaded all of reality.

In Roman times, the notion of monotheism (or at least something like it) began to appear outside of philosophical circles; it started to infiltrate popular culture. Some of the eastern deities that had become popular, notably Serapis, Isis, and Mithras, were sometimes described in at least a quasi-monotheistic way. For example, the goddess Isis, when she appeared to the man-turned-ass Lucius in Apuleius's *Golden Ass*, described herself as: "the mother of the universe, queen of all the elements, the original offspring of eternity, loftiest of the gods, queen of the shades, foremost of heavenly beings, single form of gods and goddesses alike. I control by my will the dazzling summits of the sky, the wholesome breezes of the sea, the despairing silences of the dead below"

---

31. Rodney Stark, *The Rise of Christianity* (New York: HarperCollins, 1997), 37.

32. Translation by J. H. Lesher, *Xenophanes of Colophon: Fragments; Translation, Text, and Commentary*, Phoenix Supplement 30 (Toronto: University of Toronto Press, 1992). The translation of frag. 23 has been slightly altered.

(11.5). Isis's claim that she is the "single form of gods and goddesses alike" is worth noting for, by itself, it sounds like a monotheistic claim. On the other hand, Isis also claims that she is the "loftiest of the gods" which implies that she is not the only deity; she does describe herself, however, as the one in charge.

Another example of a move toward monotheism can be seen in the growth of the cult of the deity *Theos Hypsistos* (meaning "the most high god"). Although sometimes the designation *hypsistos* was tied to Zeus (i.e., Zeus, *theos hypsistos*, "Zeus, the most high god") or another deity, at other times *Theos Hypsistos* stood alone. This "most high god" was widely worshipped, particularly throughout Asia Minor, and the worship of this deity can be traced back as far as the second century BCE.[33] Interestingly enough, *Theos Hypsistos* was not linked to specific festivals. Nor do we have evidence that animals were sacrificed to "the most high god." It seems that this deity was conceived, unlike the other gods in Greco-Roman paganism, as a kind of abstract high god.[34] The growth of the worship of *Theos Hypsistos* suggests, if not a disillusionment with polytheism per se, at least a kind of monotheistic impulse.

The increased interest in fate during Roman times has also been touted as evidence of the erosion of the power of paganism. It seemed to many at the time that fate's control was all-encompassing. Even the gods were considered subject to it. In one of Lucian's satiric dialogues, *Zeus Catechized,* Zeus was brazenly asked why people should continue sacrificing to him since fate controls everything. Furthermore, the protagonist wondered why people should be blamed for their evil deeds since fate controls their actions. Not surprisingly, Zeus could provide no answer to these questions. He merely became annoyed by the questioner and refused to discuss such matters with him any more.[35]

33. We see a reference to this deity in Acts 16:16–18.

34. On *Theos Hypsistos*, see Stephen Mitchell, "The Cult of Theos Hypsistos," in *Pagan Montheism in Late Antiquity*, ed. Polymnia Athanassiadi and Michael Frede (Oxford: Clarendon Press, 1999), 81–148.

35. We can also see the attention to fate reflected in Apuleius's novel, *The Golden Ass.* In that work, following Lucius's accidental self-transformation into an ass, he is continually knocked about by the forces of capricious fate. As an ass, he encountered brutal criminals of every stripe; he was sold or traded from one cruel master to the next; he was overworked, starved, beaten, and frequently threatened with death. Every time he seemed about to escape his situation, fate intervened to block him. The frustration felt by Lucius at the hands of fate must have felt familiar to many of Apuleius's readers. Regardless, toward the end of the novel, Lucius was provided with a solution to his asinine predicament. Isis promised him salvation from fate in return for his lifelong service to her (11.16). Following the protagonist's transformation on the day following Isis's appearance, the priest of Isis addressed the ass-turned-human Lucius: "You have scraped the bottom of many and various hardships. You were driven off course by great

Alongside the growth of fate's status, the worship of its personification—the goddess *Tyche* ("Fate") in the East and her Latin counterpart, *Fortuna* ("Fortune" or "Fate"), in the West—became widespread. Nearly every major city in the East had a temple dedicated to *Tyche*. If she controlled everything, it was reasoned, then perhaps she could be appeased by prayer and sacrifice, in the way that the other gods had been.

An increased interest in magic, it has been argued, provided yet another sign that traditional religion was losing influence during Roman times. If one believed that fate could not be controlled by the gods, perhaps an incantation could do the trick.[36] Evidence of magic's amplified relevance appeared throughout the empire; leaden curse tablets were common and manuals focused on magic's use circulated. One scholar has noted that in Roman times, "People who should have known better [came] to credit [magical] invocations with an efficacy that, in some previous century, would never have been believed."[37]

The escalation of magic's importance is reflected throughout the book of Acts, a work that is filled with magicians, astrologers, and wonder-workers of various kinds. The author is careful to distinguish his hero, Paul, from people like Bar-Jesus (13:4-12) or the sons of Sceva (19:11-17) who competed with the apostle for the attention of the crowds. Acts demonstrates repeatedly that such individuals were nothing more than charlatans; Paul alone wielded true power, the power of God. Indeed, Acts tells us that Paul's power was demonstrated so effectively in the city of Ephesus that those who had previously practiced magic burned their costly manuals (Acts 19:19).

---

storms, gigantic cyclones of Fortune, but you have reached at last this haven of rest and altar of mercy. . . . [Fortune] can now run wild somewhere else and find some other victim for her cruelty; for incursions of chance, there is no opening in the lives of those our majestic goddess has claimed as her own" (11.15-16). Here we can see a marked difference between Apuleius's novel and Lucian's satiric dialogue with Zeus vis-à-vis fate. According to Lucian's satire, the gods themselves were subject to fate but, to the contrary, Apuleius's novel claimed that the great deity Isis had power over fate; those who pledged themselves to her would be protected from it.

36. Interestingly enough, the growth in the importance of fate and magic was not necessarily unrelated. In fact, in a spell from a later Greek papyrus, we see magic as a way to free oneself from one's predetermined evil fate. The papyrus instructs one to tell an angel that has been summoned, "'Greetings, lord. Both initiate me by these rites I am performing and present me [to the god] and let the fate determined by my birth be revealed to me.' And if he says anything bad, say, 'Wash off from me the evils of fate. Do not hold back, but reveal to me everything, by night and day and in every hour of the month, to me, [insert name], son of [insert father's name]'" (PGM 13.608-17; translation from *The Greek Magical Papyri in Translation, Including Demotic Spells*, ed. Hans Dieter Betz, 2nd ed. [Chicago: University of Chicago Press, 1992], brackets original).

37. MacMullen, *Paganism*, 70.

All in all, one might conclude that the increased interest in monotheism, fate, and magic suggests some dissatisfaction with traditional religion. Nevertheless, it is also worth noting that the three phenomena mentioned above were not new. Notions of monotheism (of a sort), ideas about fate, and magical practices had been around for centuries. But in the Hellenistic and Roman periods, they began receiving greater emphasis than they had previously. Consequently, it would seem to be more accurate to describe paganism at this time as undergoing change rather than deterioration.

Regardless, such change could, at least in part, explain the missionary success of the Jesus movement among pagans but it could not account for it completely. What other factors were in play? Before we attempt to answer that question, we need to look at what the Jesus movement offered to its potential converts. What was the message that was disseminated by the movement's missionaries? It is to this that we will now turn.

The Jesus Movement's Message to Pagans

What do we know about the spread of the Jesus movement into the hellenized cities of the Roman Empire? First, from Paul's letters, we know that a number of Jewish Jesus followers preached to non-Jews in the movement's early years. For example, we know that Barnabas, Paul's one-time companion, preached to gentiles (1 Cor 9:6; Gal 2:1, 9, 13). Apollos, another Jewish Jesus follower, also reached out to non-Jews; he appeared in Corinth after Paul had left that city (1 Cor 1:12; 3:4–6, 22; 4:6; 16:12). Furthermore, Paul tells us of two Jewish missionary couples, Prisca and Aquila (1 Cor 16:19, Rom 16:3–4); and Andronicus and Junia (Rom 16:7) in connection with non-Jewish communities.[38]

Unfortunately, we do not have anything like a complete picture of the message that these earliest Jesus followers preached. We can safely assume that Barnabas, Apollos, and the two couples mentioned above preached a message similar to Paul's.[39] But we also know that other Jewish missionaries in the movement preached a somewhat different message to non-Jews. Paul,

---

38. Prisca and Aquila are also mentioned in Acts 18:2 (although in Acts, Prisca is named Priscilla). It is from that source that we learn that they are Jewish. In Rom 16:7, Paul refers to Andronicus and Junia as *syngeneis*, a Greek term that can mean "kin" or "countrymen." By this, he probably means that, like him, they were Jews.

39. We can assume this with all but Apollos because of Paul's personal association with them. We can make a similar assumption about Apollos because, in 1 Corinthians (where Apollos is mentioned), the apostle does not offer any corrective to his preaching.

for example, tells us of missionaries to Galatia who insisted that Jesus followers be circumcised; not surprisingly, he insisted that their message was illegitimate (cf. Gal 1:6–9). Paul also condemned a group of preachers who visited Corinth sometime after Apollos had left that community. Paul labeled them "super-apostles" (2 Cor 11:5; 12:11). Although we cannot be sure what they preached, Paul's antipathy toward them may suggest that their message was not compatible with his.[40]

In a catalogue of hardships found in 2 Corinthians, Paul lists "danger from false brothers and sisters" as one of the difficulties that he had to endure while preaching his message (11:26). Regardless of what he meant by "danger," the label "false brothers and sisters" indicates that Paul faced some in the Jesus movement who taught a message that he considered illegitimate. Unfortunately, no other information about the content of their teaching and belief appears. Indeed, our only reliable source for reconstructing the earliest message of Jesus followers to non-Jews comes from Paul. Consequently, we must rely on his message. At the same time, however, we must constantly remind ourselves that we do not have a complete picture; there were other messages—some compatible with Paul's teaching and others not—that circulated about which we know little or nothing.

What did Paul preach when he first entered a new city? In the book of Acts, we see a number of missionary speeches made by Paul. Unfortunately, those speeches do not reflect the words of the historical Paul.[41] Instead, the author himself, like other historians of his day, composed the speeches attributed to Paul; he also created the discourses credited to other noteworthy figures in the work. This is easily confirmed by two facts: first, Paul's speeches in Acts sound very much like the speeches of Peter and Stephen in that same work, meaning that all these speeches reflect the author's own thinking, rather than that of the characters delivering the speeches. Second,

40. There have been many attempts to reconstruct the message of the "super apostles." In my opinion, Paul does not give us enough information to draw any sound conclusions.

41. As mentioned earlier, Acts was written decades after the apostle's death, most likely by someone who had not known the apostle personally. According to Christian tradition, Luke (who was also the author of Acts; cf. Luke 1:1–4 and Acts 1:1–2) was a traveling companion of Paul. But the origins of that tradition seem relatively late; it first appears in Irenaeus in the late second century (*Ag. Her.* 3.1.2). Although some contemporary scholars affirm that Luke was a companion of Paul (based in part on the so-called "we" passages: 16:10–17; 20:5–15; 21:1–8; 27:1–28:6), other evidence from the text of Acts makes such a possibility highly unlikely. Most notably, there are significant inconsistencies between Paul's letters and Acts, particularly with respect to chronology and theology.

Paul's speeches in Acts do not sound much like what we find in his own letters.

Consequently, we are left only with Paul's letters to determine what Paul said when he first began preaching to non-Jews. Unfortunately, in those letters, nowhere does the apostle give us the *original* message that he had preached in a particular community. This is because, when he wrote his letters, he no longer had any need to *convert* his readers. They had already been converted, baptized, and become members of the assemblies of Jesus followers. Paul's letters instead focused on specific problems that the various assemblies were struggling with.[42] But despite this, the letters are not totally devoid of the kind of information that we seek. We can garner enough information from them to reconstruct something close to Paul's original message.

One passage from Paul's letters that seems to represent a fair summary of his early teaching appears at the beginning of 1 Thessalonians, the earliest of the letters that we possess (ca. 50 CE). The teaching appears in the context of Paul's praise for the community. He recounts that Jesus followers elsewhere had spoken about the Thessalonians with admiration, specifically: "How you turned to God from idols, to serve a living and true God, and to wait for his son from heaven, whom he raised from the dead—Jesus, who rescues us from the wrath that is coming" (1 Thess 1:9–10).

In this passage, the beliefs of the Thessalonians—the beliefs that Paul had originally taught them—are summed up in four essential points. The first is the belief in the one "living and true" deity. Paul principally taught all of his potential converts that they would have to turn their backs on their traditional gods, here called "idols."[43] Second, Paul informed them that the "living and true" God had a son, Jesus, who had died and was raised from the dead. Third, Paul referred to impending doom, the "wrath that is coming." Finally, the apostle emphasized the possibility of rescue from that wrath by Jesus, God's son. In the pages that follow, we will examine each of these points individually, fleshing out each with information gathered from elsewhere in Paul's letters. Following that, we should be able to reconstruct with some confidence Paul's original preaching to his non-Jewish audiences. For the sake of clarity, we will address the four points in a somewhat different order than Paul articulated them in 1 Thess 1:9–10.

42. The exception is Paul's letter to the Romans. He did not found the community at Rome but he wrote in preparation for a visit to that city. Nevertheless, he presumed that the members of his audience were all Jesus followers.

43. "Idol" (*eidōlon*), literally meaning a shadowy thing without substance, is the Greek term that was typically used by Jews to describe false gods. It appears frequently in the Septuagint, the Greek translation of the Jewish Scriptures.

One "Living and True" Deity

To his non-Jewish audience, Paul would have first proclaimed the God of the Jews as the only "living and true God." This God, Paul would have continued, had set the Jews apart as his chosen because, although all the other nations rejected this deity, the Jews did not. To the Jews, God sent prophets, the most notable of them being Moses, through whom God delivered the Torah (which Paul usually calls simply "the Scriptures").[44] But, at the same time, Paul would have insisted, this deity was not the God of the Jews only. Rather, he was the true deity of both Jews and non-Jews alike.

Paul may have referred to the important Jewish prayer, the Shema, to support such an assertion.[45] This prayer, found in Deuteronomy 6:4, declares the oneness of God; that is to say, it affirms that this deity is the *one* God of all creation: "Hear (*shema*), O Israel, the Lord is our God, the Lord is one." For Paul, this prayer's proclamation of God's oneness meant that he was the God of both Jews and non-Jews. For example, in his letter to the Romans, Paul asks, " . . . is God the God of Jews only? Is he not the God of Gentiles also? Yes, of Gentiles also, since God is one . . ." (Rom 3:29–30).

But Paul would not have relied on the Shema alone to affirm the notion that the "living and true" God of the Jews was also the God of the non-Jews. He would have also pointed to the figure of Abraham, the patriarch of the Jews; for Paul, God's words to Abraham (as recounted in the Scriptures) proved that he was concerned with all humanity, not simply the Jews. In his letter to the Galatians, for example, Paul asserted the following: "The Scripture, foreseeing that God would justify the nations (NRSV: gentiles) by faith, declared the gospel beforehand to Abraham, saying, 'All the nations shall be blessed in you'" (Gal 3:8).[46] Here Paul loosely quoted Gen. 12:3 to argue that the blessings of God had been promised—through Abraham—not just to the Jews but to all the nations. Paul likewise quoted Gen. 17:5 to make a similar point in his letter to the Romans: " . . . [God's] promise [is]

---

44. Paul also referred to the Scriptures in his letter to the Romans as "the oracles of God" (Rom 3:2).

45. Since we find allusions to this prayer in several of Paul's letters (e.g., 1 Cor 8:4–6; Gal 3:20), this suggests that he taught it to all of his potential converts.

46. The Greek term *ethnē* can be translated either "gentiles" or "nations." The NRSV prefers "gentiles" in the early part of the verse (which is a fair translation), but I have substituted "nations" in order to clarify the connection that Paul makes between his claim that God would justify the nations in the early part of the verse and the quotation of Gen. 12:3 at the end.

... guaranteed to all [Abraham's] descendants, not only to the adherents of the law but also to those who share the faith of Abraham—for he is the father of all of us, as it is written, 'I have made you the father of many nations'" (4:16–17).[47]

Paul would then likely have moved on to point out that the non-Jews, although they should have recognized the "living and true God," refused to do so. Paul spoke of this in Romans: "For what can be known about God is plain to [non-Jews], because God has shown it to them. Ever since the creation of the world his eternal power and divine nature, invisible though they are, have been understood and seen through the things he has made. So [the non-Jews] are without excuse; for though they knew God, they did not honor him as God or give thanks to him, but they became futile in their thinking, and their senseless minds were darkened. Claiming to be wise, they became fools; and they exchanged the glory of the immortal God for images resembling a mortal human being or birds or four-footed animals or reptiles" (Rom 1:19–23). Here Paul made the argument that the non-Jews— those who did not have the advantage of God's direct revelation—should nonetheless have been able to infer the existence of the true deity by contemplating creation. But rather than acknowledging the creator, they turned their attention to images created in the form of animals or humans (i.e., pagan statues of gods).[48]

Although God could have destroyed all of the idolatrous people at this time, he did not. To the contrary, he allowed them to continue in their idolatry. Paul made this point later in the same letter where he asserted that the deity "in his divine forbearance . . . had passed over the sins previously committed" (Rom 3:25). But God's tolerance was not without limit. As the passage from 1 Thessalonians has already shown us, Paul taught that there would be a final reckoning and it would be a terrible event.

---

47. Caroline Johnson Hodge has recently made the provocative argument that this phrase should be translated more along the following lines: " . . . [God's] promise [is] . . . guaranteed to all [Abraham's] descendants, not only to the adherents of the law but also to those who share the faithfulness [vs. the NRSV's 'faith'] of Abraham—for he is the father of all of us, as it is written, 'I have made you the father of many nations.'" See her work, *If Sons, Then Heirs: A Study of Kinship and Ethnicity in the Letters of Paul* (Oxford: Oxford University Press, 2007), 79–91.

48. This argument is similar to one put forward by another Hellenistic Jew, possibly from around the same time. See *Wisdom of Solomon* 13–14.

"The Wrath That Is Coming"

As Paul's reference to coming wrath in the 1 Thessalonians passage indicates, the apostle, like most others in the early Jesus movement (and Jesus himself), thought apocalyptically. That is to say, Paul believed that he was living at the end of an age that was dominated by evil powers. Paul envisioned the world as being under the control of Satan (cf. 2 Cor 4:4). But Paul also believed that such a situation was not destined to last much longer. The time was coming soon when the world would be wrested away from Satan and his minions. At that time, "the day of the Lord," would appear like "a thief in the night." Devastation would overtake the idolaters. Paul briefly describes such a scenario toward the end of 1 Thessalonians: "When [people] say, 'There is peace and security,' then sudden destruction will come upon them, as labor pains come upon a pregnant woman, and there will be no escape!" (1 Thess 5:2–3). The idolaters could then expect to experience God's wrath: "[God] will repay according to each one's deeds" (Rom 2:6). All humans, Paul would have asserted, "must appear before the judgment seat of Christ, so that each may receive recompense for what has been done in the body, whether good or evil" (2 Cor 5:10). But Paul also taught that there was hope for idolatrous gentiles; God's wrath could be avoided, in part, through the past action of Jesus, God's son.

"God's Son . . . Whom He Raised from the Dead"

As we have seen above in Paul's message to the Thessalonians, the coming wrath of God could somehow be avoided. How? Paul would have insisted that God offered reconciliation to the idolatrous gentiles by sending his son, Jesus. As he says in his letter to the Romans, "God sent his own Son in the very likeness of sinful flesh" (Rom 8:3). But, although God's son was righteous, he was crucified by the "rulers of this age" (1 Cor 2:8). It is unclear exactly what Paul meant by the "rulers of this age." Did he mean the Romans? Or did he mean demonic powers?[49] In some respects, it does not really matter because, for someone thinking apocalyptically (as did Paul), the worldly powers functioned as mere puppets for the demonic forces that opposed God.[50]

49. Since Paul called Satan "the god of this age" (2 Cor 4:4), by analogy he could have been speaking of demonic powers when he referred to the "rulers of this age" in 1 Cor 2:8.

50. A good example of this way of thinking appears in Revelation 12 and 13. Rev 12:3 described Satan as "a great red dragon, with seven heads and ten horns, and seven diadems on his heads." In the chapter that follows, Rome was described in similar bestial terms, as a

Regardless, the "rulers of this age" executed God's son. Paul would likely have emphasized the irony of Jesus's seemingly shameful death by pointing out that his death served as expiation for sins and would ultimately destroy the power of the demonic forces that dominated the age. Paul would then have explained that God vindicated Jesus by raising him from the dead; he now resided in heaven with his father, the deity (Rom 8:34). Indeed, because of his faithfulness, God had made him "Lord," "[giving] him the name that is above every name" (Phil 2:9). As Lord, Jesus would soon return to judge the world (2 Cor 5:10).

"Rescue from the Coming Wrath"

Because of Jesus's expiatory sacrifice, idolatrous non-Jews could now avoid the coming wrath. All they had to do, Paul would have pointed out to them, was to reject their past idolatrous ways and to pledge themselves to the one true God, the God of the Jews, who had raised his son from the dead. As Paul says in his letter to the Romans: "if you confess with your lips that Jesus is Lord and believe in your heart that God raised him from the dead, you will be saved" (Rom 10:9).

Those who accepted Paul's message would then have been baptized, at which point they would have received the Spirit (cf. Rom 8:15; Gal 4:6). Their baptism, Paul would have told them, had brought them into a new community in which their everyday roles in society no longer mattered. In his letter to the Galatians, Paul quotes the words from a baptismal liturgy, likely used by himself and others both before and after him: "[You] have clothed yourselves with Christ. There is no longer Jew or Greek, there is no longer slave or free, there is no longer male and female; for all of you are one in Christ Jesus" (Gal 3:27–28).[51] Participation in this utopian community, Paul would have insisted, gave its members a foretaste of the new age, the age that would be inaugurated by the return of God's son, Jesus. When Jesus returned, the idolaters would experience God's wrath, but those who

---

great beast, "having ten horns and seven heads; and on its horns were ten diadems, and on its heads were blasphemous names" (Rev 13:1). The text then goes on to say that "the dragon gave [the beast] his power and his throne and great authority" (Rev 13:2). In short, Rome's power came from Satan.

51. There are a number of reasons that scholars believe that Paul was quoting a baptismal formula here, including the fact that we also see it (or something very like it) in 1 Cor 12:13 and Col 3:9–11.

joined the assembly of Jesus followers would escape it and dwell together with Jesus.

Based upon all that we have pulled together, an abbreviated version of Paul's message would have sounded something like the following:

> Friends, I am here to tell you that there is only one God. This God is not like the deities that you worship. He is the master of the whole world. You may know him as the God that the Jews worship. I assure you, however, that he is the God of all humanity. Although all people should have been able to infer his existence, most (all but the Jews) turned their backs on him; they worshipped so-called gods in the form of human beings or even animals. But despite the idolatrous actions of the majority of humanity, up to now God has been patient with those who rejected him. But his patience will not last forever.
>
> Indeed, very soon, there will be a reckoning; idolaters will pay for their sins, not just their sin of idolatry but all of the other sins that their idolatry led them into. The "day of the Lord," when God's wrath will be unleashed, is coming soon; it will appear suddenly and without warning, like a "thief in the night." When people are most complacent, when they say, "There is peace and security," then, beware! Sudden destruction is on the way. It will come as quickly and irreversibly as labor pains come upon a pregnant woman. Once the process begins, there will be no stopping it. But do not despair! For you there is a way out. But only if you take action now. Let me explain.
>
> In his mercy, the true God sent his righteous son, Jesus, into this corrupted world. But the powers-that-be did not realize who he was. In fact, they saw him as a threat to their power and they killed him in a most abhorrent way: they crucified him. But, the story did not end there. God vindicated his son by raising him from the dead; indeed, he raised him up to heaven where he now dwells with his father. There God made him "Lord" of all things. He will soon come back to destroy the evil powers that have enslaved humankind and he will judge everyone. Idolaters will experience the wrath that they deserve. But it is not too late for you. Even though you now worship so-called gods instead of the one, true God, you still have time to renounce those counterfeit deities. The true God, long ago, promised to Abraham—the patriarch of the Jews—that all people could share in God's blessing. Jesus's death has now made that possible. His death broke the power of sin and evil and it made amends for human sin. Because of his salvific death, you now have the opportunity to repent of your idolatry

and turn to God. While there is still time, join Christ and his community by being baptized. You will be baptized into a community in which the old distinctions no longer matter; "there is no longer Jew or Greek, there is no longer slave or free, there is no longer male and female; but all are one in Christ Jesus."[52]

Summary and Conclusion

In this chapter, we focused on two different belief systems. We began by briefly surveying Greco-Roman paganism. We identified four important characteristics of Greco-Roman paganism from Acts' narrative of a healing by Paul and the crowd's reaction to it (14:8–18): 1) it was polytheistic; 2) gods were similar to humans, and they interacted with them; 3) gods sometimes helped humans; and 4) humans honored the gods, above all with animal sacrifice. Following our survey, we considered some of the changes taking place in paganism during the Hellenistic and Roman periods.

Next, we turned to the message that Jewish Jesus followers offered to their pagan audiences. Using Paul's letters, particularly a passage from 1 Thess 1 (supplemented by material from elsewhere in his letters), we isolated four important components of his initial message to non-Jews: 1) there was only one "living and true" deity; 2) that deity had a son, Jesus, who had died and had been raised from the dead; 3) the end of the current age, along with God's wrath, was coming soon; and 4) those who turned to the one, true God would be rescued from the coming wrath as a result of Jesus's salvific death.

It is now important to ask why this teaching attracted believers. What about it was compelling? Answering this question will comprise our task in the next three chapters. They are organized according to the three antithetical statements in the traditional baptismal formulation cited above: "there is no longer Jew or Greek, there is no longer slave or free, there is no longer male and female" (Gal 3:28). For the sake of clarity, however, the chapters will not appear in precisely that order.

---

52. I am indebted to Calvin J. Roetzel for the idea of creating a facsimile of Paul's preaching. For Roetzel's attempted reproduction see his work, *The Letters of Paul: Conversations in Context*, fifth edition (Louisville, KY: Westminster John Knox, 2009), 87–88.

Inside the Movement

CHAPTER 4

No Longer Jew or Greek

The cities in which the Jesus movement found its first pagan adherents were ethnically diverse. During the so-called *Pax Romana* ("Roman peace")— usually reckoned from the time of the accession of Emperor Augustus (27 BCE) to the death of Marcus Aurelius (180 CE)—travel was safe; the roads were well-maintained and the sea was (relatively) free of pirates. Consequently, there was a significant amount of movement by travelers, merchants, and immigrants. People in large cities would have been used to encountering people from a variety of places.[1]

Furthermore, despite the Hellenistic cultural patina that covered the eastern Roman Empire (resulting from Alexander's conquest centuries earlier),

---

1. A quick glance at a few of the writers who lived during the *Pax Romana* can give us an idea of the ease of mobility at that time. The novelist Apuleius, whom we have encountered several times already, was born in north Africa at Madaura, in what is now Algeria; he studied in both Athens and Rome, and then traveled extensively throughout Asia Minor and Egypt. The satirist Lucian, also mentioned in the previous chapter, was born in Syria (at Samosata, which is now in eastern Turkey, on the banks of the Euphrates River) and during his lifetime, he traveled throughout Asia Minor, Greece, Italy, and Gaul (now France). The philosopher Epictetus was born at Hieropolis (now Pamukkale, Turkey) and spent his youth as a slave in Rome. After he gained his freedom, he began to teach philosophy in the capital. When the emperor Domitian (who reigned 81–96) expelled all philosophers from Rome, Epictetus settled at Nicopolis in western Greece. Paul himself was born at Tarsus (in what is now south central Turkey). Although we do not know much about his childhood, he likely spent some time in Jerusalem, underwent a conversion experience in or near Damascus, preached for a number of years in the area of what is now Jordan and southern Syria, moved to Antioch (on the Syrian coast), and from there traveled throughout Asia Minor and Greece. Following a journey to Jerusalem, he traveled to Rome. It is possible that he died in that city (as tradition has it) but it is also possible that he left Rome and journeyed to Spain, an intended destination that he mentions in his letter to the Romans (15:28).

many people still held tightly to their particular ethnicities. We know, for example, that many ethnic clubs or associations (of Alexandrians, Cilicians, Cretans, Italians, Lycians, Pergaians, Phrygians, Pisidians, Samothracians, Sidonians, and Tyrians—not to mention Judeans [i.e., Jews]) popped up in the various cities of the empire. Although the people in most of these clubs were thoroughly hellenized—that is to say, they spoke Greek, lived in cities organized on the Hellenistic model, and worshipped Greek gods—they were clearly unwilling to abandon their particular ethnic identity entirely.[2]

In this chapter, we consider the Jesus movement from the perspective of ethnicity, both Jewish and "Greek" (i.e., Hellenistic). Ethnicity represents one of the most curious aspects of the movement. Jesus and his original followers were all Jews. As far as we know, Jesus did not concern himself with non-Jews but viewed his mission as focused on "the lost sheep of Israel" (Matt 15:24). But for some unknown reason, early on, when the movement spread beyond the borders of Judea, non-Jews were welcomed into it.[3] By the end of the first century, there were probably more non-Jews than Jews in the movement. In the early second century, the Jesus movement, now labeled "Christianity," even began to define itself *against* Judaism.

In the following pages, we will look at the Jesus movement through two different lenses. The first lens is that of Judaism. Although the Jesus movement eventually transformed itself from a Jewish to a non-Jewish undertaking, it nevertheless continued to hold on to a number of beliefs and practices that had heretofore applied only to the Jews. These included the worship of the God of the Jews to the exclusion of all other deities and reverence for the Jewish Scriptures. As such, even as it transformed itself into a non-Jewish movement, it still retained its Judean roots.[4] Even though most of the members of the assemblies in the large cities of the empire were non-Jews (as far as we know), the early Jesus movement would have likely been viewed as a Jewish, or at least a quasi-Jewish, phenomenon.

---

2. Obviously, the Judeans did not worship the Greek gods. However, they would have been the lone exception.

3. Paul himself, who likely had his change of heart regarding Jesus followers (from being a persecutor to a participant) only a few years after Jesus's death, began preaching to non-Jews. Indeed, as we saw in chapter 2, Paul viewed his visionary experience as a commission to preach to non-Jews (Gal 1:15–16). Nevertheless, Paul was probably not the first to bring non-Jews into the movement.

4. In the middle of the first century, the movement had an even stronger connection to Judaism, in that its most influential people—including the leaders of the Jerusalem assembly (James, Peter, and John), Paul, Barnabas, and others—were all Jews.

This brings us to the second lens though which we will view the Jesus movement, that of pagan culture. Throughout the chapter we will ask why a Jewish movement would attract non-Jews. We will begin our discussion by considering the attraction that some cults connected with eastern ethnic groups (such as the Egyptians) had during Hellenistic and Roman times. We will then turn to examine the appeal that one of these groups, the Jews, held for many in pagan society.

Next we will turn to Paul's message. While at first glance it would seem that what Paul preached would have sounded quite alien to a pagan audience, there were in fact some interesting connections between the core of Paul's teaching (as laid out in the previous chapter) and certain pagan beliefs. So although Paul's message would have presented a significantly different way of looking at the world than those in his audience were accustomed to, enough connections likely existed to have made his preaching palatable to an interested pagan. Finally, we will turn to the figure of Paul himself and look at him against the backdrop of other freelance religious experts of his time. Ultimately, we will see that it was not just Paul's message but the person of Paul himself (and other missionaries like him) that helped grow the membership of the Jesus movement in its early years.

Non-Jewish Assemblies and Judaism

What were the assemblies of the early Jesus movement in the large hellenized cities like ethnically? It is sometimes claimed that the Jesus movement transcended ethnicity. As such, it would have differed significantly from the various ethnic clubs mentioned above. Indeed, on the surface, the phrase of the baptismal rite, "there is no longer Jew or Greek"—the title of this chapter—does suggest a multiethnic movement. Nevertheless, if we look a bit more closely at that phrase, we will see that it is not as culturally neutral as it first appears. This is because the juxtaposition of "Jew" and "Greek" is somewhat peculiar.

The meaning of the first group mentioned in the baptismal phrase, "Jew" (*Ioudaios* in Greek), would seem to be obvious. We normally think of a Jew (like a Christian or a Muslim) as someone who practices a certain *religion*. But, in the ancient world, things would have looked somewhat different. From the standpoint of the larger Hellenistic society, the Greek term *Ioudaios* would have pointed not just to a religion but to a particular ethnic identity, an identity not unlike those tied to the clubs noted above. Although throughout the New

Testament the word *Ioudaios* is almost always translated "Jew," it can also be rendered "Judean," as noted earlier. That is to say, the label *Ioudaios* indicated a person whose ethnic roots could be traced to the territory of Judea. Consequently, "Judean" may be closer than "Jew" to the meaning that the term *Ioudaios* would have carried in the empire's cities.

What would it mean if a (pagan) resident of a large port city like Ephesus had a neighbor who was a *Ioudaios*? The resident would certainly have perceived that his or her neighbor had different religious practices but, from the (pagan) resident's point of view, the *Ioudaios* would have also been perceived as someone who had come from a different part of the world (or perhaps his or her ancestors did). Consequently, the Ephesian neighbor of the *Ioudaios* would not have been surprised that some of the customs from the Judean homeland were still practiced in Ephesus: for example, male "Judean" infants were circumcised, certain foods were avoided, labor was eschewed for one day during the week (the Sabbath), and the "Judean" deity was worshipped. Although from our standpoint these practices are all religiously oriented (i.e., mandated by the God of the Jews), to the Ephesian neighbor they would likely have been perceived as ethnically determined customs as much as strictly religious practices.

The word in the baptismal formula that stands opposite "Jew" (or "Judean"), is "Greek." That this term is used in conjunction with the term *Ioudaios* is somewhat surprising for, while *Ioudaios* pointed to a *specific* ethnicity at that time, the label "Greek" did not. It simply meant a hellenized person; virtually any Greek speaker living in the eastern part of the Roman Empire could have been considered a "Greek." This would have included a Greek-speaking Syrian, a Greek-speaking Egyptian, or even a Greek-speaking Italian. This juxtaposition between *Ioudaios* and Greek raises an important question: why is one term in this contrast very specific (*Ioudaios*) but the other term very general (Greek)? This is certainly not the case with the other pairs of antitheses: male-female and slave-free.

The answer can probably be traced back to the time of the origin of the baptismal formula. The odd juxtaposition of *Ioudaios* and Greek suggests that this phrase arose in a particular ethnic context, specifically a Jewish (or, if one prefers, a Judean) one. The words of the baptismal ritual doubtless point back to the earliest days of the movement, likely around the time that non-Jews were first brought into the assemblies. The point of view of the baptismal formula is obviously Jewish. As far as the formula is concerned, there are only two kinds of people: Jews and non-Jews (i.e., Greeks).

This is significant because what, on the surface, sounds like one thing to us—a statement indicating that ethnicity does not matter—would have sounded quite different to pagans at the time. To them the juxtaposition of *Ioudaios* and Greek would have sounded much more particularistic; pagans would not have heard, "your ethnicity does not matter," but instead something like, "it does not matter if you are a Jew or not." A pagan hearing such a statement would likely have assumed that the assembly of Jesus followers was a Jewish-oriented group that allowed non-Jews to join. A rough analogy would be my Irish family members telling their friends, "Come celebrate St. Patrick's Day with us. It doesn't matter whether you are Irish or not." In both cases one ethnicity (whether Judean or Irish) has been set over against all others. Granted, there is a certain ethnic tolerance in each statement, but neither could really be labeled "multi-cultural" in the full sense of the word; rather, each has a specific ethnic focus.

But, despite the particularistic, Jewish, character of the phrase, the statement does indeed claim that, in the assembly, one's Jewish or non-Jewish background was unimportant. It specifically claims: "There is *no longer* Jew or Greek." That is to say, once one joined the assembly of Jesus followers, it did not matter whether one was Jewish or whether one came from a non-Jewish background. As the end of the baptismal formula claims, all were now "one in Christ Jesus." That is to say, all those in the assembly, Jewish or not, were considered legitimate members.

Nevertheless, a pagan who thought about joining the local assembly of Jesus followers could hardly ignore the somewhat Jewish (or Judean) character of the assembly. Those trying to recruit new members, people like Paul, Barnabas, or Apollos, were all Jews/Judeans. The God worshipped in the assembly—to the exclusion of all other deities—was the God of the Judeans. The Scriptures that were read were Jewish and all the stories told were about Judeans: Abraham, Sarah, Moses, David, and even Jesus. In other words, a pagan joining an assembly of Jesus followers may have been perceived by his or her neighbors as betraying his or her ethnicity by worshiping the Judean God.[5] As one scholar has put it, "what we call 'conversion,' ancients saw as de-

---

5. The reverence that people had for their own indigenous deities can be illustrated by the example of Artemis of Ephesus. Artemis was reputed to have been born just outside the city of Ephesus and she was a source of great pride to the local citizens of that city (as was her temple). The Ephesians believed that Artemis privileged the city by showering blessings on it; they also believed that she protected it. Any slight to Artemis or her temple could have had severe repercussions for the city itself. According to the book of Acts, a riot broke out in Ephesus because the locals were afraid that Paul's preaching would somehow denigrate the status of the goddess. One of the Ephesian locals, a certain Demetrius, argued that, as a result

serting ancestral customs for foreign laws."[6] This is not to say that conversions to Judaism did not happen. Some people did convert. But many who greatly admired the Jews did not.

The relationship between the Jesus movement and Judaism was something that various assemblies struggled with. Paul, most notably, argued that the assemblies that he founded should *not* embrace a Judean/Jewish lifestyle (other than by worshipping the Judean God and revering Jewish Scriptures of course). However, the communities that Paul had founded in Galatia decided—after the apostle had left their region—that males should be circumcised. That is to say, the Galatians decided to change their lifestyles in order to live fully in the manner of ethnic Judeans. They probably believed that if they worshipped the Judean God and his son, they should also live in accordance with the customs of others (i.e., the Jews) who did so.

The community that produced the Gospel of Matthew felt similarly. The Gospel itself claimed that the law (i.e., the Jewish Torah) was in force for the members of that community; Jesus is quoted as saying that the law would be in force until the end of time: "For truly I tell you, until heaven and earth pass away, not one letter, not one stroke of a letter, will pass from the law" (Matt 5:18). Elsewhere in the Gospel, Jesus tells those around him, "If you wish to enter into life, keep the commandments," presumably meaning the commandments of the Torah (Matt 19:17).

The community that produced the Gospel of Mark seems to have moved in the opposite direction; it rejected at least some Jewish ritual practices. The Gospel's author, for example, interpreted one of Jesus's sayings to mean that the distinction between kosher and non-kosher foods had been abolished (Mark 7:19). The communities responsible for the Gospels of Luke and John reflected a similar move away from Jewish practices. In fact, these latter communities went so far as to draw bright lines between their assemblies and Judaism.[7] But,

---

of Paul's ability to attract people to his movement, there was a danger "that the temple of the great goddess Artemis will be scorned, and she will be deprived of her majesty that brought all Asia and the world to worship her" (Acts 19:27). What is not said here by Demetrius, but would certainly have been in the back of his mind, was the worrisome possibility that Artemis would withdraw her protection from the city were she "deprived of her majesty." Were the goddess to turn her back on Ephesus, the city would have been susceptible to natural disasters, disease, famine, or even attack.

6. Paula Fredriksen, "Why Should a 'Law-Free' Mission Mean a 'Law-Free' Apostle?" *JBL* 134 (2015): 642. In this quotation, Fredriksen is speaking about conversion to Judaism, but the same would apply to a pagan joining the Jesus movement.

7. The Gospel of John, in particular, characterized "the Jews" (as a whole) as the enemies

even if many assemblies of Jesus followers in the large cities of the empire did not uphold the entirety of the Torah (e.g., they did not circumcise the males in the community, keep the Sabbath, or avoid forbidden foods), from the point of view of their pagan neighbors, they still acted a lot like Jews.

The Judeocentric focus of the early Jesus movement raises an important question about the missionary accomplishments of Paul and others: specifically, *why* was the movement successful? Why would a pagan want to join what appeared to be a Jewish group? Before we try to answer this question, we will first turn our attention to the worship of other foreign (i.e., ethnic) deities in the Hellenistic world. A brief investigation of that phenomenon may help us understand how someone like Paul was able to bring converts into what looked like an ethnic movement.

Eastern Religions in the Cities of the Empire

As noted in a previous chapter, there were a number of ethnic deities that were successful at gathering adherents in the cities of the empire. Perhaps the most notable of these were the Egyptian deities Isis and Serapis. These gods were able to gain popularity without sacrificing their ethnic identities. They had, in effect, been accepted into the Hellenistic pantheon. By the Roman period, a native-born Corinthian or Ephesian would have had no qualms about venerating Isis, Serapis, or any number of other "foreign" gods. Indeed, the protagonist of Apuleius's novel, *The Golden Ass*, although born and raised in Greece, eventually dedicated his life to Isis.

How can we explain the attraction of these foreign deities? Unfortunately, there is no single answer to this question. One factor undoubtedly had to do with the flow of various peoples though the large Mediterranean cities following the hellenization of the eastern Mediterranean area. Catherine Bell, a noted scholar of religion, suggested that intense and sustained exposure to plurality could eventually weaken the established order and values of a society and allow people to experiment: "[The] exposure to plurality—that is, to other value systems and alternative forms of social organization . . . can begin to undermine the coherent sense of a unifying order that underlies a traditional society. Some people opt for new or foreign ways of doing things. . . . People have choices that they never had before, whether they want them or not. The mere existence of choices among

---

of Jesus. This is in contrast to the other Gospels that characterize Jesus's enemies as a particular group of Jews (e.g., the chief priests, the Pharisees, or the Sadducees).

ways of thinking and acting relativizes what was once deemed absolute, raises questions, necessitates decisions, and promotes experimentation."[8] Although Bell here is speaking about secularization in a more contemporary setting, her words can easily be applied to the situation of those in the hellenized cities of the eastern Mediterranean. The continual flow of various kinds of people through the Hellenistic cities following Alexander's conquest inevitably brought change, some of which was religious change. Eastern merchants and immigrants brought their gods with them as they migrated into the great Mediterranean cities. Furthermore, as a result of the continual warfare from the time of Alexander's death (323 BCE) until the establishment of the *Pax Romana* (27 BCE), hundreds of thousands of enslaved ethnic peoples came from the East, bringing their deities with them. Eventually, many of these eastern gods found a following among the native inhabitants of the Hellenistic cities.

But ethnic diversity does not explain everything. Another important factor was the Greek (and Roman) reverence for antiquity.[9] Eastern civilizations were believed to be much more ancient than those of the Greeks and Romans. As such, eastern civilizations were accorded great respect. The fifth-century-BCE historian Herodotus, for example, noted that from the first Egyptian king until the most recent: "There had passed 341 generations of men, and that in each generation there had been one priest and one king. Now 300 generations of men is equivalent to 10,000 years, since there are 3 generations of men in 100 years, and the 41 remaining generations in addition to the 300 add up to 11,340 years" (*Histories* 2.142.1–2).[10] From Herodotus's perspective, 11,340 years was a much older lineage than that of the Greeks. Because of the reputed age of

8. Catherine Bell, *Ritual: Perspectives and Dimensions* (Oxford: Oxford University Press, 1997), 200.

9. In the words of one scholar: "During the Hellenistic and Roman periods, the general principle seems to have been that the older and more eastern things were, the more divine and the more credible they were, inasmuch as human beings were closest to the gods in the earliest times and in the East" (Louis H. Feldman, *Jew and Gentile in the Ancient World* [Princeton: Princeton University Press, 1993], 177).

10. Translation by Andrea L. Purvis in *The Landmark Herodotus*, ed. Robert B. Strassler (New York: Pantheon, 2007). A history of Egypt that likewise claimed a longer history for the Egyptian civilization than that of the Greeks was written by Manetho, an Egyptian priest in the early third century BCE. However, it should be noted that it was not just Egyptian civilization that was considered more ancient than the civilizations of the Greeks. A history of Babylon, written in the third century BCE by Berosus, a Babylonian priest, made a similar claim for that civilization. In the second century CE, a writer named Philo from the city of Byblus pointed to Phoenician writings that claimed that the gods and heroes of Phoenicia had brought civilization to humanity.

Egyptian civilization, Herodotus and others like him insisted that the Greeks had originally learned about their gods from the Egyptians.[11] However, it was not only knowledge of the gods that the Greeks acquired from the Egyptians. Practices that characterized Greek religion also came from Egypt: "the Egyptians were . . . the first to assign altars, statues, and temples to the gods and to carve their figures in relief on stone" (*Histories* 2.4).[12]

Given the belief in the antiquity of Egyptian civilization and the religious practices that derived from that civilization, the worship of Egyptian deities by non-Egyptians becomes a bit more understandable. Rather than being seen as betraying one's own ethnicity, it could instead be justified as the performance of a more original (and hence more authentic) form of worship. Indeed, in *The Golden Ass*, Isis appeared to the novel's protagonist and made a claim that would support this understanding. "The whole world," the goddess noted, "worships my power under an abundance of images, a variety of rituals, and an array of names." Some peoples, she continued, have called her Venus, others Minerva, others Diana, still others Proserpina, Ceres, Juno, Bellona, Hecate, or Rhamnusia. But, ultimately the goddess insisted that her real name was Isis, the one that originated with the Egyptians (*The Golden Ass* 11.5).

In sum, we have seen two reasons why Greeks may have been attracted to non-Greek deities. The first had to do with the sustained exposure that hellenized people had to religious plurality; this, in turn, led to experimentation. Of course, with the coming of Rome and the pacification of the empire following Augustus's ascent to power (the *Pax Romana*), such diversity only intensified. Travel became much easier than it had been in the past and more and more people moved about. But Greco-Roman reverence for antiquity provided another reason for the rise in popularity of non-Greek deities. Since the eastern civilizations were believed to be much more ancient that that of the Greeks, their religious practices were revered for their antiquity. For some, their antiquity also affirmed their authenticity.

Pagan Interest in Judaism

The antiquity of another eastern civilization, that of the Jews or Judeans, also attracted interest in the Greek world. A number of Jewish writers trumpeted the antiquity of their nation and the accomplishments of their lawgiver, Moses.

11. E.g., Herodotus, *Hist.* 2.50; cf. Lucian, *Goddess* 2–3.
12. Trans. Purvis, slightly modified. See also Herodotus, *Hist.* 2.50–51 and 2.58–59.

The most famous of these was Josephus. In the early volumes of his *Jewish Antiquities* (whose very title emphasizes his nation's ancient pedigree), Josephus drew almost exclusively from the first five books of the Scriptures—believed by him (and all Jews of his time) to have been authored by Moses. Moses, Josephus claims, "was born two thousand years ago, to which ancient date the [Greek] poets never ventured to refer even to the birth of their gods, much less the actions or laws of mortals" (*Jewish Antiquities* 1.16).

Other Jewish writers likewise made claims for the antiquity of their nation. Two writers of the second century BCE, Eupolemus and Artapanus, presented rather fanciful accounts of such. The first, Eupolemus, dismissed claims by the Egyptians, Phoenicians, and the Greeks that they had first created the alphabet. Instead Eupolemus insisted, Moses was its inventor: "He first taught the alphabet to the Jews, and the Phoenicians received it from the Jews, and the Greeks received it from the Phoenicians."[13] Eupolemus's claim for the Jewish creation of the alphabet, in effect, credited Moses as the originator of civilization (or at least, the creator of its most important tool).

The Jewish writer Artapanus likewise made exaggerated claims for Moses's early influence on humankind: "As a grown man he bestowed many useful benefits on mankind, for he invented boats and devices for stone construction and the Egyptian arms and the implements for drawing water and for warfare, and philosophy. Further he divided the state [of Egypt] into 36 nomes. . . . On account of all these things then Moses was loved by the masses, and was deemed worthy of godlike honor by the priests and called Hermes, on account of the interpretation of the sacred letters."[14] Here Artapanus cleverly dismissed Egyptian claims that theirs was the most ancient civilization by insisting that they learned everything from Moses.

But it was not only Jewish authors who asserted the antiquity of the Jews. Pagan authors made similar claims. Alexander Polyhistor, an early-first-century-BCE writer, traced the name "Judea" to the descendants of the Syrian goddess Atargatis. A Phoenician historian named Claudius Iolaus connected the Jews to Cadmus, the purported founder of the ancient Greek city of Thebes. The Roman scholar, Pliny the Elder, claimed that the Essenes (the

---

13. Eupolemus is only preserved in fragments that appear in Eusebius, *Prep. Gos.* and Clement of Alexandria, *Miscellanies.* The material above comes from Eusebius, *Prep. Gos.* 9.26.1. The fragments can be easily accessed in James H. Charlesworth, *The Old Testament Pseudepigrapha*, ABRL (Garden City, NY: Doubleday, 1985), 2.865–72.

14. Like Eupolemus, Artapanus is preserved in fragments that appear in Eusebius, *Prep. Gos.* The above text is from 9.27.4–6. It and other fragments are also found in Charlesworth, *Old Testament Pseudepigrapha*, 2.889–96.

Jewish group responsible for the Dead Sea Scrolls) had been in existence for "thousands of ages" (*Natural History* 5.73).[15]

Although the antiquity of the Jewish people interested non-Jews, there were other attractions as well. Jewish authors promoted their nation as a philosophically minded people. In his *Against Apion*, Josephus asserted that the Jewish understanding of the deity was in line with that of the philosophers: "In fact, Pythagoras, Anaxagoras, Plato, the Stoics who succeeded [Moses], and nearly all the philosophers appear to have held similar views concerning the nature of God. These, however, addressed their philosophy to the few, and did not venture to divulge their true beliefs to the masses who had their own preconceived opinions; whereas our lawgiver [Moses], by making practice square with precept, not only convinced his own contemporaries, but so firmly implanted this belief concerning God in their descendants to all future generations that it cannot be moved" (*Against Apion* 2.168–69).

Because of its importance in Greco-Roman philosophy, a number of Jewish writers also promoted Judaism as providing an efficient path to self-control or self-mastery, something believed to be very important, not only to philosophers but to just about everyone at that time. Philo, for example, pointed to the Jewish way of life—notably, law observance—as promoting self-control: "The [Jewish] law holds that all who conform to the sacred constitution laid down by Moses must be exempt from every unreasoning passion and every vice in a higher degree than those who are governed by other laws" (*Special Laws* 4.55). Moses, Philo insisted, understood the destructive character of the passions: "[Moses] observed and therefore discarded passion in general and detesting it, as most vile in itself and in its effects, denounced especially desire as a battery of destruction to the soul, which must be done away with or brought into obedience to the governance of reason, and then all things will be permeated through and through with peace and good order" (*Special Laws* 4.95).

Consequently, Philo argued that the law was given by God as the remedy for a fruitless life lived devoid of reason: "He who gave abundance of the means of life also bestowed the wherewithal of a good life . . . for the good life [people] needed laws and ordinances which would bring improvement to their souls" (*On the Decalogue* 17). The improvement to the people's souls would come about because the law would train them to domesticate their passions and tame their desires. For example, the Jewish dietary restrictions were explained by Philo in this way: "All the animals of land, sea, or air whose flesh is the finest and fattest, thus titillating and exciting the malignant foe pleasure, [Moses]

15. Feldman, *Jew and Gentile*, 177–200.

sternly forbade them to eat, knowing that they are a trap for the most slavish of the senses, the taste, and produce gluttony, an evil very dangerous to both soul and body" (*Special Laws* 4.100).[16]

But, again, it was not just Jewish writers who made the link between Judaism and philosophy. The Greek historian Megasthenes and the philosophers Theophrastus and Clearchus (all writing around the end of the fourth century and the beginning of the third century BCE) saw a connection between the laws of Plato and the Jewish law. As a result, they understood the Jews to be philosophers. Other pagan authors perceived an even more direct connection between Judaism and philosophy, making the claim that some of the greatest (pagan) philosophers, including Aristotle, had derived their wisdom from the Jews.[17]

The Godfearers

Some pagans who were interested in either the God of the Jews or Jewish religious practices are sometimes referred to as Godfearers, a label that comes from the book of Acts.[18] These Godfearers sometimes even participated in some way with Jewish communities and adopted some Jewish ritual practices.[19] Josephus provides us with information about these Godfearers (although he does not use that label). He claims that "[the pagan] masses have long . . . shown a keen desire to adopt our religious observances; and there has not been one city, Greek or barbarian, nor a single nation, to which our custom of abstaining from work on the seventh day has not spread, and where the fasts and the lighting of lamps and many of our prohibitions in the manner of food are not observed" (*Against Apion* 2.282). Philo also remarks on pagan interest in the Jewish law: "not only the Jews but almost every other people, particularly those which take more account of virtue, have grown so far in

16. Stanley K. Stowers, *A Rereading of Romans: Justice, Jews, and Gentiles* (New Haven: Yale University Press, 1994), 42–52.

17. Feldman, *Jew and Gentile*, 203–4, 209–14.

18. Such pagans are labeled "those fearing God" in Acts 13:16 and 13:26. Alternatively, pagan sympathizers are called "those worshipping God" elsewhere in the work (Acts 13:50, 17:4, and 17:17).

19. According to Acts, Paul spoke to both Jews and Godfearers when preaching his message in a synagogue in Asia Minor (Acts 13:16–41). The fact that Paul mentioned "Israelites" (i.e., Jews) *and* Godfearers in his address to a synagogue suggests that Godfearers sometimes attended the synagogue service.

holiness as to value and honor our laws." For Philo, this is a truly remarkable phenomenon: "Throughout the world of Greeks and barbarians, there is practically no state which honors the institutions of any other. . . . We may fairly say that mankind from east to west, every country and nation and state [show] aversion to foreign institutions. . . . It is not so with ours. They attract and win the attention of all, of barbarians, of Greeks, of dwellers on the mainland and islands, of nations of the east and the west, of Europe and Asia, of the whole inhabited world from end to end" (*On the Life of Moses* 2.18–20). Obviously both Philo and Josephus were exaggerating when they made the claims that "there has not been one city, Greek or barbarian, nor a single nation" that has not adopted some Jewish practices or that the law has won the attention of the "whole inhabited world from end to end." However, hyperbole aside, there must have been some truth to their statements.[20]

Further evidence for pagan interest in Jewish practices and beliefs appears in the New Testament Gospels. The introduction to the story of Jesus healing the slave of a centurion (a Roman military officer) in Luke's Gospel is particularly instructive. The healing miracle is set up as follows: "A centurion [at Capernaum] had a slave whom he valued highly, and who was ill and close to death. When he heard about Jesus, he sent some Jewish elders to him, asking him to come and heal his slave. When they came to Jesus, they appealed to him earnestly, saying, 'He is worthy of having you do this for him, for he loves our people, and it is he who built our synagogue for us'" (Luke 7:2–5).

Although in Matthew's version of the same story, the centurion himself approached Jesus, the Lukan version, cited above, had Jewish elders approach Jesus. Note their efforts to persuade Jesus. They told him, "he loves our people" and, more significantly, "[he] built our synagogue for us." Although this Roman officer presumably continued his pagan religious practices—for example, as a soldier, he would have been expected to participate in the pagan military cult of his unit—he nevertheless felt a strong enough attraction to Judaism to finance the building of a synagogue, a synagogue that he likely attended whenever possible.[21]

---

20. Cf. Philo's report on pagans keeping the Sabbath: "For who has not shown his respect for that sacred seventh day, by giving rest and relaxation from labor to himself and his neighbors, freemen and slaves alike, and beyond these to the beasts? . . . Again, who does not every year show awe and reverence for the fast, as it [i.e., the Day of Atonement] is called, which is best kept more strictly and solemnly than the holy month of the Greeks?" (*Moses* 2.19–23). The "holy month" that Philo mentioned pointed to certain months agreed upon by the Greeks in which military action was forbidden.

21. Although it is likely that the plea by the Jewish elders was not historical, the fact that

As the above evidence suggests, some pagans showed more than a superficial interest in Judaism. They actually had some religious interaction with the Jewish community. While some of these pagans eventually converted to Judaism, most did not. Perhaps such Godfearers did not want to abandon their own gods. Godfearers may have instead merely added the Jewish God to the pantheon of their traditional gods, like the Greeks who worshipped Isis or Serapis alongside of their own Greek gods,[22]

Nevertheless, the very existence of pagan Godfearers raises the possibility that some of these Godfearers joined the earliest urban assemblies of Jesus followers. Indeed, many scholars have argued for such a possibility. But while such a scenario is possible, we cannot be sure of it. The shift from synagogue to Jesus assembly could certainly have been an easy transition for some Godfearers. But for others—those unwilling to give up their own gods, for example—the path from synagogue to assembly of Jesus followers would have been blocked. For pagans unwilling to give up their own deities, the Jesus movement's unwavering commitment to absolute monotheism would have precluded their acceptance into an assembly.[23]

---

the author wrote the story in this way provides proof that such an argument by Jewish leaders was believable to the audience. There is also inscriptional evidence of another pagan, in this case an aristocratic woman, whose actions were comparable to those attributed to the centurion in Luke's story. In the late nineteenth century, an inscription was discovered at the site of the ancient Phrygian city of Acmonia (currently Ahat Köyü in western Turkey) that told of a certain Julia Severa who had funded the building of a synagogue. We know from other evidence that this woman could not herself have been a Jew; elsewhere she was labeled a "high priestess," presumably a priestess of a pagan cult.

22. In this case the worship of the God of the Jews would correspond more closely with the growth of other foreign cults, like that of Isis, for example. For most, the worship of Isis did not replace the worship of the traditional gods. Rather, it supplemented it.

23. On the other hand, perhaps for some pagans, the Jesus movement's connection to Judaism was not strong enough (or was not strong enough in the right way). The various comments by both Josephus and Philo regarding Godfearers indicates that one of the primary attractions that Judaism held for pagans was the possibility of law observance to one extent or another. Philo, in one of the passages cited above, indicated that many non-Jews had come "to value and honor our laws" (*Moses* 2.17). Josephus, in a number of places, likewise focuses on Jewish law observance. He noted in one place, "many have agreed to adopt our laws" (*Ag. Ap.* 2.123). Elsewhere, he claims that "our laws . . . have to an ever increasing extent excited the world at large" (*Ag. Ap.* 2.280). In other places, both Philo and Josephus noted that non-Jews had been attracted to Sabbath observance (Philo, *Moses* 2.19-23; Josephus, *Ag. Ap.* 2.282), to the observance of Jewish festivals, or to Jewish dietary laws (Josephus, *Ag. Ap.* 2.282). Such observances would have been discouraged in the Jesus movement, at least in Paul's communities.

Judaism and the Jesus Movement:
An Appealing Connection or an Ethnic Liability?

Earlier in this chapter we had asked if the perceived Judeocentric focus of the early Jesus movement represented a liability among the pagans to whom preachers like Paul appealed. Why, we inquired, would a pagan want to join what appeared to be a Jewish group? We are now in a better position to answer that question.

Although a fair amount of anti-Jewish sentiment existed in the ancient world, nevertheless, as we have seen, some pagans were drawn to Judaism for one reason or another. It seems that for some, the antiquity of the Judean people attracted them; for others, it was Judaism's monotheism; for still others, the promise of law observance struck them as an attractive means to self-mastery. For one reason or another, these people believed that Judaism represented an ancient and authentic mode of life and worship. In short, while the Jewish nature of the Jesus movement may have alienated some people, it likely induced others to pay at least some attention to the preaching of Jesus followers.

However, attracting the attention of an audience could be a far cry from winning it over. How would a preacher like Paul—a Judean Jesus follower intent on convincing non-Jews to join their movement—have kept his audience engaged for more than a few moments? How would he have convinced anyone to join an assembly of Jesus followers? Although we looked briefly at Paul's preaching in the last chapter, in the next section we will attempt to contextualize the message that he delivered to prospective pagan converts. As we will see, there were some connections that would likely have made a message like Paul's at least somewhat compatible to beliefs already held by members of his audience.

Paul's Message: The Judean God and His Son in the Pagan World

In the last chapter, we examined a passage from 1 Thessalonians that presented a concise summary of what was likely Paul's initial preaching to prospective pagan converts (1 Thess 1:9–10). From it we extracted four important components of Paul's initial message. The first was Paul's insistence that there was only one living and true deity. Paul's second point was that, although the true God had thus far allowed the idolatrous gentiles to survive and even prosper, a reckoning would take place in the very near future. At that time, God's righteous wrath would be unleashed on the idolaters. Paul's third point was that God's son, Jesus, played and would continue to play an important role in the drama that was unfolding. God had recently sent his son, Jesus, into the world but the latter had been crucified by the "rulers of this age." Nevertheless, following his death, Jesus was raised from the dead by the deity. Although now dwelling with God in heaven, he would return in the near future to usher in a new age. The fourth component of Paul's initial preaching was related to the third: because of Jesus's salvific death, it would now be possible for the idolatrous gentiles to be reconciled to God and, consequently, be rescued from the coming wrath. Of course, for Paul's pagan audience, the sin that was most significant was their idolatry.

One would hardly think that these ideas would sound compelling to a non-Jewish audience. Indeed, all of them seem dependent on the Jewish idea of absolute monotheism and the notion that there was only one, true God. This seems, at least on the surface, to run counter to the polytheistic culture of Greco-Roman society. How did preachers like Paul gain any traction with their prospective pagan audiences? In order to answer this question, we now turn our attention to each of the four components of Paul's message that we extracted from 1 Thess 1:9–10. Viewed separately we will discover some interesting connections to ideas already held by those in the larger pagan culture.

One, True God

The first of the Pauline components mentioned above was, of course, the acknowledgment of one, true God, to the exclusion of all others. But, as we have already seen, monotheism was compatible with some of the Greek and Roman philosophical ideas of the time. Even outside philosophical circles, there was some movement in popular culture toward monotheism. Indeed, Judaism's absolute monotheism may have contributed to pagan attraction to that religion. So although absolute monotheism may have been a difficult hurdle for some pagans, it was certainly not a completely new idea to many of them.

Judgment, the End of the Present Age, and the Establishment of a New Era

The second idea that we distilled from 1 Thess 1:9–10 was the notion that there would soon be a divine reckoning, when all humans—including the idolatrous pagans—would be judged. At that time, God would "repay according to each one's deeds," to borrow a phrase from Paul's letter to the Romans (2:6). This idea, of course, came from Jewish apocalypticism, a worldview that envisioned the present age as corrupt and run by the demonic forces of Satan. But, as we have already noted, according to apocalyptic thinking, this corrupt age would not endure forever. At some point in the very near future, the deity would step in to right things. At that time, he would establish a new age.

Although there are no close Greco-Roman parallels to the apocalyptic idea of a soon-to-come divine judgment, there are elements of Paul's apocalyptic thinking that would not have sounded completely alien to a pagan audience. Most notable would be the notion of the present as an age of corruption. Like other Jewish apocalyptic thinkers, Paul understood the present age as an era overrun by evil powers. Indeed, in one place in his writings, he even referred to Satan as the "god of this age" (2 Cor 4:4). Presumably, he also understood the human rulers of the age as acting in concert with Satan and his minions (cf. 1 Cor 2:6–8).

However, when Paul spoke to pagan audiences, his apocalyptic message was probably somewhat different from what we see in other apocalyptic writings. In his preaching to non-Jews, he likely focused on idolatry as one of the principal reasons for the current state of affairs. We can be fairly certain of this because of what Paul writes to the Romans, an assembly that the apostle clearly identifies as a non-Jewish community (Rom 1:5–6, 13; 11:11–14; 15:14–33). In that work, Paul adds an interesting twist to the typical Jewish apocalyptic belief in the corruption of the present age. As we saw in the previous chapter, Paul insisted that society had been overrun by evil because humanity, particularly gentile humanity, had turned its back on the true deity in order to worship idols. Since all but the Jews disregarded the true deity, God handed the idolatrous humans (i.e., pagans) over to their passions (Rom 1:24, 26, 28). Their minds, which were supposed to control their desires, instead became debased (Rom 1:28). No longer able to control themselves, they committed all kinds of "wickedness, evil, covetousness, [and] malice." They were "full of envy, murder, strife, [and] deceit" (Rom 1:29). In short, as Paul tells the story in Romans, the corruption of the present age came about because of the sin of idolatry.[24] Although Paul said nothing about what preceded humankind's turning away from the true deity in his letter to the Romans, his narrative certainly presupposed a better time, a time prior to humanity's corruption.[25]

---

24. Although Paul also indicted Jews later in Romans, his focus in this letter, as in all of his others, was on non-Jews.

25. Although many scholars point to the Adam and Eve story of Gen 2–3 as providing

Although Paul's narrative in Romans 1 has its closest parallels in another Jewish text, the Wisdom of Solomon (14:12–31), the idea that civilization had devolved was common in the ancient world.[26] In Greek literature, the idea goes back as far as Hesiod (late eighth century BCE) who spoke of four separate ages in his "Works and Days." The original age, Hesiod contended, was a golden era when people "lived like gods, not a care in their hearts, Nothing to do with hard work or grief, And miserable old age didn't exist for them" (132–34).[27] Over time, Hesiod insisted, things degenerated. The golden age was followed by two less ideal ages, those of silver and bronze. Finally, humanity found itself in its present circumstances: "This is the Iron Age. Not a day goes by a man doesn't have some kind of trouble. Nights too, just wearing him down. I mean the gods send us terrible pain and vexation" (204–8).[28] However, Hesiod, unlike Paul, did not envision an end to the decline. The future, he believed, would bring an even worse age.

Roman writers also spoke of the corruption of the present era. They wrote of an initial golden age when the deity Saturn ruled directly over humans. As in Hesiod's golden age, there was no strife or labor. Neither was there warfare (e.g., Ovid, *Metamorphoses* 1.89–112). Since that time, however, humans had become greedy, licentious, and belligerent. Roman authors of the late republic and early empire, when Rome was plagued with civil wars and political instability, longed for a return to the golden age.

During a brief period of peace and political stability in the mid–first century BCE, the Roman poet Virgil predicted its return with the birth of a child. With this child's appearance, there would come an end to the "brood" of the age of iron and a beginning of the "reign of Saturn," the golden age:

> Now is come the last age of Cumaean song; the great line of the centuries begins anew. Now the Virgin returns, the reign of Saturn returns; now a new generation descends from heaven on high. Only do you, pure Lucina,

---

the background to Paul's narrative (and in that story, there is a description of humanity prior to Adam and Eve's disobedience), the fact that Paul's story focuses on gentiles in Romans 1 (note especially Rom 1:23) indicates that Paul is *not* alluding to the Adam and Eve story here.

26. Stowers, *A Rereading of Romans*, 85–100.

27. Translation by Stanley Lombardo, *Hesiod: Works and Days and Theogony* (Indianapolis: Hackett, 1993).

28. We see a similar understanding of the decline of ages in Dan 2.31–43 although for Daniel, the four ages all precede a time when "the God of heaven will set up a kingdom that shall never be destroyed" (2:44).

smile on the birth of the child, under whom the iron brood shall at last cease and a golden race spring up throughout the world! Your own Apollo now is king! . . . Unbidden, the goats will bring home their udders swollen with milk, and the cattle will not fear huge lions. The serpent, too, will perish, and perish will the plant that hides its poison; Assyrian spice will spring up on every soil. But as soon as you can read of the glories of heroes and your father's deeds, and can know what valour is, slowly will the plains yellow with the waving corn, on wild brambles the purple grape will hang, and the stubborn oak distil dewy honey (*Eclogue* 4.5–30 [Fairclough & Goold]).

Although the true identity of the particular child named here by Virgil remains unknown, the poet would—in his later epic poem, the *Aeneid*—acknowledge Augustus as the savior who would reestablish the golden age. In that later poem, Virgil's protagonist Aeneas—while visiting his dead father in the underworld—encountered innumerable souls not yet born. Aeneas's father identified many of them for him, including the soul of the man who was to become Augustus: "And this . . . is he whom you so often hear promised you, Augustus Caesar, son of a god, who will again establish a golden age in Latium amid fields once ruled by Saturn" (*Aeneid* 6.791–94 [Fairclough & Goold]).

The poet Horace also envisioned Augustus as the savior, come to restore the golden age. Horace wrote that, since the beginning of Augustus's reign: ". . . the ox ambles over the pastures in safety; Ceres and kindly Prosperity give increase to their crops . . . the home is pure, unstained by any lewdness, custom and law have gained control over the plague of vice. . . . Each man spends all day until sunset in his own hills, wedding the vine to the unmarried trees; then he returns happily to his wine and requests your divine presence at the second course" (*Odes* 4.5 [Rudd]).

Like these Greek and Roman authors, Paul also anticipated the inauguration of a new age following the conclusion of the current age. But unlike the Roman poets, the apostle did not expect Augustus, the *divi filius* ("son of a god") to inaugurate that era. Rather, it would be brought about by Jesus, the son of the *true* God. Therefore, although Paul inherited the notion of a coming age—in which the evil of the current, corrupt age would be overcome—from apocalyptic Judaism, his proclamation of it may have resonated with his pagan audience; similar ideas had been circulating throughout the pagan world, promoted by supporters of Augustus, Rome's first emperor.

The Death and Resurrection of Jesus, the Son of God

The notion that a remarkable individual had died (or been killed) and then raised from the dead sounds to us as if it could only have originated within the Jesus movement. Consequently, we are inclined to presume that such a story would have been difficult for a pagan audience to accept. Surprisingly, however, it would not necessarily have sounded so strange to pagan ears. Several pagan counterparts can be found, particularly in the stories of the heroes Asclepius and Heracles, both of whom were divinized after their deaths.[29] While there are some similarities between the stories of both Asclepius and Heracles and Paul's account of Jesus, the most impressive comparisons are with Heracles.[30]

Heracles was part mortal and part divine, the son of Zeus and the mortal Alcmene. Because of the dreadful torments that he suffered toward the conclusion of his life, he ended his life by immolating himself on a pyre.[31] But unlike most mortals, he did not just die. As the second-century-CE author Apollodorus told the story, "While the pyre was burning a cloud is said to have enveloped Heracles and to have raised him up to heaven with a crash of thunder" (2.7.7).[32]

Heracles's apotheosis corresponded somewhat to Paul's narrative about Jesus who, after his death, was raised from the dead and taken to heaven where he resided "at the right hand of God" (Rom 8:34; cf. 1 Thess 1:10; Phil 2:9). Other points of comparison between Heracles and Jesus focused on their suffering and obedience. Cynic philosophers in particular viewed Heracles's suffering and his obedience to the will of Zeus as things to be imitated in their own lives.[33]

29. The parallels between Jesus and Heracles were recognized by the second-century Christian, Justin Martyr (e.g., *1 Apol.* 21.1; *Dial.* 69.3). They were also acknowledged by Celsus, the second-century opponent of Christianity (Origen, *Cels.* 3.22ff.). Besides these two divinized heroes, there were also several pagan deities that were reputed to have been raised from the dead, including Dionysus, Adonis, and the Egyptian deities Osiris and Horus.

30. David E. Aune, "Heracles and Christ: Heracles Imagery in the Christology of Early Christianity," in David L. Balch, Everett Ferguson, and Wayne A. Meeks, eds., *Greeks, Romans, and Christians: Essays in Honor of Abraham J. Malherbe* (Minneapolis: Fortress, 1990), 3–19.

31. Unlike in our culture, suicide was not necessarily considered a deplorable act in ancient times. It was sometimes viewed as an honorable death. Heracles's death was considered such by many.

32. Translation by Michael Simpson in Leonard Baskin, ed., *Gods and Heroes of the Greeks: The Library of Apollodorus. Translated with Introduction and Notes* (Amherst: University of Massachusetts Press, 1976).

33. Regarding the latter, see the comments of Epictetus: "Nay, [Heracles] had no dearer

Paul likewise emphasized the suffering and obedience of Jesus and encouraged the imitation of both. Indeed, he tied his own suffering as an apostle to Jesus's suffering and death (2 Cor 4:7–12), and he also insisted that Jesus's suffering provided a model for all members of the Jesus movement.[34] For example, he claimed that Jesus followers were "joint heirs with Christ" because "we suffer with him so that we may also be glorified with him" (Rom 8:17; cf. 1 Thess 1:6).

For Paul, Jesus was also an exemplar of obedience. When contrasting Jesus to Adam, Paul claims, "just as by the one man's disobedience the many were made sinners, so by the one man's obedience the many will be made righteous" (Rom 5:19). Likewise, in Philippians, Paul emphasizes Christ's death as an act of obedience: "Being found in human form, he humbled himself and became obedient to the point of death—even death on a cross" (Phil 2:7–8). Those in Paul's audience were encouraged to act as selflessly as had Jesus (Phil 2:2–4).

Admittedly, the Heracles myth differs from the story of Jesus in a number of ways. For one, Heracles killed himself while Jesus was killed by others (the "rulers of this age," as we saw earlier). Furthermore the stories about Heracles do not really focus on his death but rather on his apotheosis. Paul's narratives about Jesus's demise, to the contrary, focus heavily on his death rather than his resurrection. Indeed, it was Christ's death on the cross that was particularly significant for Paul's theology. Regardless, despite these differences between the story of Heracles and the narrative of Jesus as Paul would have proclaimed it, there were some analogies, particularly when the Heracles myth was filtered through the lens of the Cynic philosophers.

The Beneficial Nature of Jesus's Death

One idea that appears frequently in Paul's letters, as it must have likewise materialized in his oral presentations, was the idea that Jesus's death was ultimately a positive thing: Jesus died, Paul insisted, so that human beings could be reconciled to God (e.g., Rom 3:21–26). But the idea that Jesus's death was in some

---

friend than God. That is why he believed himself to be a son of Zeus, and was. It was therefore in obedience to his will that he went about clearing away wickedness and lawlessness" (*Disc.* 2.16.44 [Oldfather, slightly revised]).

34. Although Paul rarely mentioned the suffering of Jesus, he frequently referred to his crucifixion, an obviously painful death. In 2 Cor 4:10, the word that Paul used for the "dying" of Jesus was *nekrōsis*, a term that emphasized the *process* of his death, that is Jesus's suffering prior to his death.

way beneficial to others would, like some of his other ideas, have sounded somewhat familiar to pagan ears. Indeed, the notion that someone would die for others or even die for an idea, was a very old one in the Greek world.

In Homer's *Iliad*, for example, the warrior Achilles refused to fight because he was feuding with the Achaean leader, Agamemnon. But Achilles learned through a prophecy that he had two choices. If he took part in the war, his participation would ensure the Achaean victory over the Trojans, but it would also result in his death. Alternatively, if he refused to fight the Trojans, he would live a long life but his people would be defeated (*Iliad* 9.410–16). Achilles, of course, eventually chose the former; the Achaeans won the war but at the cost of Achilles's life.

Another example having to do with the Trojan War concerned Iphigenia, the daughter of the Achaean leader, Agamemnon. As the story was told, the Achaeans were stranded in the port of Aulis, unable to sail against Troy because of contrary winds. Earlier, Agamemnon had affronted the goddess Artemis and she had responded with the unfavorable winds. To make things right, Agamemnon learned that he would have to offer a sacrifice to the goddess, but not just any sacrifice; he was required to sacrifice his daughter, Iphigenia. Agamemnon summoned Iphigenia to the port on the pretext of marrying her to Achilles. But when she arrived at Aulis, she learned the awful truth. Nonetheless, she ultimately accepted her fate; she told her mother: "Listen, mother, to what I have been thinking. I have decided to die. . . . It is through me that the ships will be able to sail. . . . I offer my body for Hellas. Sacrifice me and destroy Troy" (Euripides, *Iphigenia at Aulis* 1374–99 [Kovacs]). In both of these cases, both Achilles and Iphigenia consciously chose death in order to benefit others. Achilles decided to fight, knowing that it would mean his own death and Iphigenia allowed herself to be slaughtered so that the Achaeans could sail against the Trojans, to a war that they were honor-bound to fight.

But the Greeks did not just tell stories of people dying for others. They also celebrated those who died for their ideas or principles. Probably the best example of such a person was the philosopher Socrates whom the Athenian assembly unjustly condemned to death. Although his friends hatched a plan for his escape, Socrates refused to take advantage of it. Instead, he believed that he was obliged to carry out the sentence. Consequently, he drank the hemlock given to him and died. Socrates's willingness to die rather than compromise his principles was lauded by many for centuries following his death (e.g., Epictetus, *Disc.* 4.1.164–66).

In sum, there was much in Paul's message that would have sounded familiar to members of his pagan audience. First, the idea of monotheism would not have been totally foreign to them. Second, while the notion of a divine judgment at the end of the age would have probably been new to them, the idea that the present age was both corrupt and coming to an end would not have been. Nor would the notion that a new, idyllic age would arrive in its place. Third, the story of the death and resurrection of Jesus resembled stories of the divinized heroes, especially Heracles. Finally, the idea of someone dying for something, whether for principles or for others, had been around for centuries; consequently, Paul's claim that Jesus's death was for the benefit of others would have been intelligible.

Of course, this is not to dispute the originality of Paul's proclamation (or that of other Jewish, Jesus-following missionaries). It is simply to point out that elements of Paul's message would have been comprehensible to some pagans. Nor is it to say that becoming a Jesus follower would have been easy. There was much in the movement that was antithetical to the culture of the time. We will consider this issue more fully in a later chapter. For now, however, we turn our focus from Paul's message and concentrate instead on the figure of the apostle himself.

Paul: A Judean Religious Expert

In the last chapter, we introduced the idea of freelance religious experts. We described these freelance experts as individuals who operated outside of normal institutional channels. As such, they had to earn their own recognition and establish their own legitimacy. They typically achieved such with public demonstrations of their learning, power, or contact with the divine realm. Successful figures like Alexander of Abonoteichos easily illustrate the appeal that such freelance experts could have.[35]

Given the Greco-Roman fascination with the civilizations of the East, it is hardly surprising to see that a number of popular freelance religious experts originated in that part of the world.[36] Indeed, we can even see this fascination with the East exhibited by the author of Matthew's Gospel who told of the

35. This and the following pages are indebted to the writings of Heidi Wendt, including chapters from her book that had not yet been published while I was writing this but which she generously shared with me. The book has since been published: *At the Temple Gates: The Religion of Freelance Experts in the Roman Empire* (New York: Oxford University Press, 2016).

36. Probably the most famous example was the first-century-CE miracle-working philosopher, Apollonius, who hailed from the eastern city of Tyana (in the area of what is now Cappadocia in Turkey).

arrival of a group of traveling *magoi* (translated by the NRSV as "wise men") "from the east," come to pay homage to the newly born king of the Jews (Matt 2:1–12). By calling these men *magoi* and claiming that they came from the East, the author probably meant to indicate that they were astrologers who, having read the news of the birth of Jesus in the heavens from their eastern homeland, traveled west to honor the new king.[37]

Among eastern religious experts, Jewish (or Judean) experts were, it seems, popular. We know from several historians that both Jewish and Egyptian cults were abolished in the city of Rome during the reign of the emperor Tiberius (14–37 CE).[38] Although Josephus blamed the trouble on a few rogue priests of Isis and a couple of corrupt Jews, it seems more likely that the fault lay with freelance religious experts, some of them Jewish, who were perceived by the rulers to be troublemakers.[39]

Another example of a Jewish religious expert comes from the book of Acts. There, we encounter the story of a Jewish *magos* (translated by the NRSV as "magician") and prophet named Bar-Jesus that Paul and Barnabas encountered on the island of Cyprus (Acts 13:6–12).[40] Bar-Jesus (also named Elymas in the account), it seems, functioned as a religious advisor to the proconsul, Sergius Paulus.[41] Of course, from the standpoint of the author of Acts, the advisor was merely a charlatan because he "opposed [Paul and Barnabas] and tried to turn the proconsul away from the faith" (13:8).

A third example comes from the pen of the Roman satirist, Juvenal, who mocked a certain Jewish woman whom he described as "an interpreter of the laws of Jerusalem . . . [and] a trusty go-between of highest heaven." She, so claimed Juvenal, would interpret dreams "for the minutest of coins" (*Satires* 6.544–47). This woman appeared in a passage that satirized a whole range of freelance religious experts—eunuchs in service to the goddess Bellona, an Egyptian priest of Anubis, Armenian *haruspices* (people who read the

---

37. The people of the East, and particularly Babylon, were noted for their astrological expertise.

38. Suetonius, *Tib.* 36.1, Tacitus, *Ann.* 2.85.11–17, and Josephus, *Ant.* 18.65–84.

39. Heidi Wendt, "Iudaica Romana: A Rereading of Judean Expulsions from Rome," *JAJ* 6 (2015): 97–126.

40. The term *magos* is the same term that we saw in the story of Jesus's birth in the Gospel of Matthew (*magos* is singular and *magoi* is plural). The term could be used either positively or negatively. In Matthew's Gospel, it was intended positively to indicate eastern religious specialists. In the Acts passage, it is intended negatively and so a "magician" or even a "charlatan" would be indicated.

41. Josephus also seems to have known about this Bar-Jesus (*Ant.* 20.142).

future in the entrails of sacrificed animals), and Chaldean astrologers—all swindlers in Juvenal's eyes (*Satires* 6.314–610), but well-received by the general populace.

These various examples demonstrate the prevalence and, with most people, popularity of eastern, and particularly Jewish (Judean), religious experts in the culture of the time. In light of this, wandering Jewish preachers like Paul, Barnabas, and Apollos may have found pagan audiences predisposed to pay some attention to them. To put it another way, it is possible that the early missionary success of the Jesus movement had as much to do with the messengers as the message itself.

Paul's ability to demonstrate his religious expertise would have been essential for, by his own admission, he was not a powerful speaker, a talent one might expect in a wandering preacher. As he himself acknowledged: "When I came to you [in Corinth], brothers and sisters, I did not come proclaiming the mystery of God to you in lofty words or wisdom" (1 Cor 2:1).[42] Elsewhere, one of his detractors even noted that "his speech [was] contemptible" (2 Cor 10:10). Given his less-than-impressive speaking ability, it would be difficult to credit his success unless he possessed other strengths. Clearly those other strengths had to do with his religious expertise. But what talents did Paul have?

For one thing, he had an extensive knowledge of the ancient Jewish scriptural tradition. Based on that alone, he may have been able to stir up a bit of interest when he arrived in a new city. But besides his scriptural knowledge, Paul could have also claimed the ability to communicate directly with the divine realm. In two of his letters, he referred to his vision of God's heavenly son (Gal 1:15–17; 1 Cor 15:8). In another letter, he mentioned that he had been "caught up to the third heaven—whether in the body or out of the body I do not know" and that there he had "heard things that are not to be told, that no mortal is permitted to repeat" (2 Cor 12:2–4).

But, perhaps most importantly, Paul also claimed the ability to provide "a demonstration of the Spirit and of power" (1 Cor 2:4). He made a similar claim in a letter to the Thessalonians, where he also mentioned "power" and "the Spirit" (1 Thess 1:5). The Greek term that is translated "power" in both of these texts could sometimes mean a work of wonder or a miracle. Given the context of the two passages in question, this appears to be the term's meaning.[43]

---

42. This is in contrast to the character of Paul described in Acts. There he was portrayed as an eloquent speaker who, for example, made a famous speech in Athens at the Areopagus (Acts 17:19–34). But, as mentioned earlier, this speech, like Paul's other speeches in Acts, owed more to the author of Acts than to Paul.

43. The reference to the "Spirit" in these passages refers to the "Spirit of God" that pos-

Another passage from yet a different letter confirms this. There he reminded his audience that the "signs of a true apostle were performed among you with utmost patience, signs and wonders and mighty works" (2 Cor 12:12; cf. Rom 15:18–19). In short, Paul not only *preached* in the cities where he was trying to convince people to join his movement; he also *worked wonders* of some kind.

Based upon all of this information, we can conclude that Paul was perceived by his pagan audiences as a kind of itinerant Judean religious expert, an expert who could quote the sacred Scriptures of the Jews, tell of his mystical encounters, and work wonders. Elsewhere, Paul informs us that he was proficient in speaking in tongues and that he could also prophesy.[44] Unfortunately, he gives us few other specifics regarding his abilities. Regardless, physical demonstrations of his religious expertise would have allowed Paul to attract an audience so that he could deliver his message about the crucified and resurrected Son of God. Just as importantly, Paul's impressive demonstrations would have provided credibility for that message.

Paul was undoubtedly careful to credit his extraordinary abilities to the Spirit of God that possessed him. Furthermore, Paul would have promised that those who joined his assembly (i.e., those who submitted to baptism) would themselves receive the Spirit (1 Cor 12:13; cf. 1 Cor 3:16; Rom 8:9). This would mean that *they* would also possess the ability to do the kinds of things that they saw Paul doing. Indeed, in one of his letters, Paul unequivocally connects the presence of the Spirit with miracle working in the community (Gal 3:5). But, perhaps more importantly, Paul also told his audiences that their possession of the Spirit (or more accurately, the Spirit's possession of them) promised that they, like Jesus, would ultimately overcome death: "If the Spirit of him who raised Jesus from the dead dwells in you, he who raised Christ from the dead will give life to your mortal bodies also through his Spirit that dwells in you" (Rom 8:11).[45] Such a promise would surely have caught the interest of some in the crowd.

---

sessed Paul and enabled him to perform such "signs and wonders and mighty works." It is not clear that he intended a real distinction to be drawn between a "demonstration of power" and a "demonstration of the Spirit" in 1 Cor 2:4. It is possible that, by using the phrase "a demonstration of the Spirit and power," he employed a rhetorical technique called *hendiadys*, which is the use of two words to express one idea. In other words, a better way to express Paul's phrase would probably be "a demonstration of power that comes from the Spirit."

44. In 1 Cor 14:18, Paul claimed the ability to speak in tongues. The context of the whole chapter (1 Cor 14) suggests that he could also prophesy.

45. This promise should be understood as an elaboration of the point made in 1 Thess 1:9–10 about their escape from the coming wrath.

Summary and Conclusion

As we have seen, the Jesus movement began as an exclusively Jewish under-taking. To the best of our knowledge, during Jesus's lifetime, non-Jews were neither encouraged to join nor welcomed into the movement. Following Je-sus's death, his followers in Judea continued to consider the movement an exclusively Jewish one. But when the movement spread beyond the confines of Jewish territory, things began to change. At first, a few non-Jews were wel-comed into the movement and some mixed assemblies (i.e., assemblies of Jews and non-Jews) were created. The assembly at Antioch, mentioned by Paul in Gal 2:11–14 represented one such mixed community. At some point, however, missionaries from the movement (people like Paul, Barnabas, and Apollos) began founding non-Jewish communities in the large cities of the eastern empire. Indeed, by the middle of the first century, the assemblies about which we know the most—those founded by Paul in Galatia, Philippi, Thessalonika, and Corinth—were made up almost exclusively of non-Jews. It is hardly likely that Jews were excluded from these assemblies; it is much more probable that they saw little reason to join. Nevertheless, even though these assemblies were made up almost entirely of non-Jews, they retained a decidedly Jewish charac-ter: the Jewish God was worshipped (as was his son, Jesus), Jewish Scriptures were read, and Jewish apocalyptic expectations predominated.

Furthermore, in this chapter, we have seen that a number of things would have attracted non-Jews to Paul and his message. For one thing, among some people, there may have been some dissatisfaction with their traditional religion or at least the desire to explore other options. Second, the Jewish presupposi-tions behind Paul's message (such as absolute monotheism or the apocalyptic view of history) may not have been as foreign to non-Jews as we may have first anticipated. The phenomenon of Godfearers indicates that at least some pagans found various aspects of Judaism appealing. Third, some parts of Paul's message would have resonated with his audience. Some pagan parallels to the story of Jesus's death and resurrection, although not precise, nevertheless existed. Fourth, the perception of Paul as a Jewish freelance religious expert, who could interpret sacred texts, communicate directly with the divine realm, and work wonders both attracted people to his message and legitimated that message. Finally, his promise of the Spirit to members of his community, which would grant them special powers and guarantee them life beyond the grave, would also have been particularly attractive.

CHAPTER 5

No Longer Male and Female

Greco-Roman culture was patriarchal. This reality was reflected in both the family and society at large. In the family, the *paterfamilias* ("family father") was in charge; his wife was considered drastically inferior to her husband, "like a grown-up child."[1] The husband was to some extent responsible for her actions, good or bad. Several ancient writers used the metaphor of horse and rider to describe a marriage. One argued that if the horse (the wife) was vicious, it was usually the fault of the rider (Xenophon, *Oeconomicus* 3:13; cf. Plutarch, *Advice to Bride and Groom* 8). In other words, the husband was obligated to control his wife, train her as he would tame his horse.[2] Most believed that the wife's faults ultimately traced back to her husband; even if she cheated on him, the husband was considered at fault, "much as [today] we might criticize parents for overindulging or spoiling their children."[3]

The extent that a husband dominated the matrimonial relationship can be illustrated by comments by Plutarch in his *Advice to Bride and Groom*. In that work, he made a number of recommendations concerning the proper behavior of both a husband and wife. Regarding the latter, Plutarch advised her to be modest, to eschew expensive clothing and makeup, to stay indoors, to keep quiet, and communicate only through her husband. Furthermore, she should have no feelings of her own but take on those of her husband and she should worship only her husband's gods (10–31). Perhaps most notably, she

---

1. Paul Veyne, "The Roman Empire," in *From Pagan Rome to Byzantium*, vol. 1 of *A History of Private Life*, ed. Paul Veyne (Cambridge, MA: Belknap, 1987), 39.

2. We see this attitude toward woman as unable to control their own emotions among a number of ancient philosophers, Aristotle (*Eth. Nic.* 7.7.6 and *Pol.* 1.5.6; 3.2.10).

3. Veyne, "Roman Empire," 39.

should not be displeased by her husband's dalliances with slaves or prostitutes; it was, Plutarch insisted, out of respect for her that he "[shared] his debauchery, licentiousness, and wantonness with another woman" (16).

But it was not only the wife who was expected to honor and obey the *paterfamilias* in the patriarchal family. Children, and especially sons, were dominated by their fathers. In the city of Rome itself, a son was under the authority of his father as long as the latter lived. "Psychologically, an adult [Roman] male whose father was alive found himself in an intolerable situation. He could do nothing without his father's consent: he could not sign a contract, free a slave, or draw up his will. He possessed only his [allowance] . . . and even that could be revoked."[4]

The importance of family in the ancient world can hardly be overestimated. The family into which one was born, to a great extent, determined his or her future. An individual born of slaves would, as an adult, probably labor as a slave. The son of a tradesman or a craftsman—a baker or a shoemaker, for instance—would most likely live out his life engaged in that same trade, learning the appropriate skills from his father at an early age. If, however, a child was fortunate enough to be born into an aristocratic family, that child would either be groomed to rule (if a male) or raised to marry well (if a female).

But, as mentioned above, patriarchy existed not only in the family, it extended to society at large. Indeed, societal gender roles were grounded in the family. Older males dominated not only the home but public life as well.[5] Sons were raised to lead, daughters to follow. A male child would have opportunities that a female child would not. A female would forever be (at least theoretically) under the control of a male, whether that male be her father, husband, or next of kin. Even the terrain of the city was imagined according to gender. Public space, where men dealt with other men, was considered masculine. On the other hand, domestic space, where women conducted their business, was imagined as feminine.[6]

Did the Jesus movement challenge the patriarchal assumptions of the larger society? The claim of the baptismal formula alluded to in the title for this chap-

---

4. Veyne, "Roman Empire," 28.

5. The emperor himself was considered the *paterfamilias* of the empire.

6. This is not to say that there was no crossing of the borders that separated these gendered spaces. Women were frequently found in public spaces, particularly women of the lower socioeconomic strata. Their families could not afford the luxury of them remaining at home; their labor was necessary to make ends meet. Upper status women, however, were expected to remain out of the public's gaze, unless accompanied by a husband, as Plutarch's comment (quoted above) indicates.

ter, "there is no longer male and female," suggests that it did. In the following pages, we will explore the impact of the Jesus movement on notions of family, particularly the patriarchal family; we will also explore the movement's attitudes about gender and particularly the roles that women could or (should) play.

The early years of the Jesus movement were generally characterized by a disregard for the patriarchal family in favor of the "family" constituted by those in the movement; at the same time, there existed some flexibility in the roles played by women. But as time went on, the patriarchal family became more important and the role of women more constrained, at least for the most part. This is not to say that the dominant mores of the larger culture totally extinguished the radical ideas promoted by the historical Jesus. While in some cases this was true, in other cases Jesus's ideas took root and endured.[7]

We will divide each of the following sections into three. In each section, we will consider first, the topic of one's family of origin, next, the issues of marriage and divorce, and finally, gender roles, and particularly, the roles that women could play. When considering the second topic, marriage and divorce, we will examine the matter of celibacy since, as we will see—particularly in the writings of Paul—the option of celibacy was tied to questions regarding the benefit (or lack thereof) of marriage. We will address these three issues chronologically, first at the time of the movement's origin, during Jesus's lifetime, and then following his death. In the latter segment, we will consider especially how opinions in the movement changed (or in some case, remained the same) as time progressed.

Family, Gender, and the Historical Jesus

What was Jesus's response to the hierarchical structure of the patriarchal family? How were his disciples supposed to deal with their own families of origin? What about marriage? Were Jesus's followers to marry or not? If one were already married, should he or she stay married? What if one partner followed Jesus and the other did not? What about gender roles? How much did women matter to the historical Jesus? Did he specifically reach out to them? Were their roles in the movement less restrictive than in the dominant society? In this section we will attempt to answer all of these questions, beginning with the subject of one's patriarchal family of origin.

7. Ultimately, some of those ideas, such as Jesus's prohibition of divorce, even changed the standards of Greco-Roman culture (although this process took centuries).

Family of Origin

Curiously, the "family values" that many contemporary Christians connect to their tradition did not originate with the historical Jesus. Jesus's teaching about family was both radical and shocking; it challenged the strict hierarchy of the patriarchal family in Greco-Roman society as well as the Jewish scriptural command to honor one's parents. For example, according to a saying recorded in Matthew's Gospel, Jesus tells his followers to "call no one your father on earth, for you have one Father—the one in heaven" (Matt 23:9). By this, did Jesus mean that the honor that one was to accord one's biological father should be given *only* to the deity (and *not* to one's father)? Or did he mean simply that one should honor God *more than* one's biological father? In this case, the answer is not obvious.

However, a different saying, preserved in Q (Matt 10:37; Luke 14:26) and the Gospel of Thomas, suggests that the more radical interpretation of the previous command is more likely. In the Gospel of Thomas version of the second saying, Jesus announced, "Whoever does not hate father and mother cannot be my disciple, and whoever does not hate brothers and sisters . . . will not be worthy of me" (Gos. Thom. 55; cf. 101). The Q version of the same saying states: "If anyone does not hate his own father and mother, he cannot be my disciple and if anyone does not hate son and daughter, he cannot be my disciple" (Q 14:26). Here it is not a matter of more or less. The command is straightforward. One should *hate* one's father (and mother and siblings). Most scholars are convinced that the historical Jesus must have said something very much like this. The norms of Greco-Roman society, Judaism, and the later Christian tradition all insist that one respect and honor one's family members—particularly one's parents—and, as a result, it seems highly unlikely that this saying would have been attributed to Jesus by the later tradition. It must have come from Jesus himself.[8]

The author of Matthew's Gospel was clearly troubled by the radical nature of the saying that he inherited from Q and so he modified it to say: "Whoever loves father or mother *more than me* is not worthy of me; and whoever loves son or daughter *more than me* is not worthy of me" (Matt 10:37, emphasis added). This version of the saying has Jesus emphasize the love for him *over*

---

8. This method of determining the authenticity of a saying or action is usually called the criterion of dissimilarity. That is to say, if a saying (or action) is dissimilar to the norms of Greco-Roman society, to those of Judaism at the time, and to those of the later movement, it probably came from Jesus. To put it differently, there is no obvious reason why a later writer would make something like this up.

that of one's family. It does not imply that one was to no longer love his or her family members.

Luke also did his best to soften the impact of the saying; his version reads: "Whoever comes to me and does not hate father and mother, wife and children, brothers and sisters, yes, and even life itself, cannot be my disciple" (Luke 14:26). By adding the phrase "yes, even life itself," Luke's version shifts the emphasis away from the command to hate one's parents and siblings. As a result, it emphasizes the importance of discipleship over everything. It thereby sounds at least somewhat less radical than the original, which commanded those who followed him *to reject* their kinfolk.[9]

The saying that commands hatred of parents and siblings lines up to some degree with yet another saying of Jesus recorded in Q: "Do not think that I have come to bring peace on earth; I have not come to bring peace, but a sword. For I have come to separate son from father, and daughter from her mother, and daughter-in-law from her mother-in-law" (Q 12:51–53; cf. Matt 10:34–36; Luke 12:51–53). Note that this saying differs a bit from the earlier sayings in Matthew (10:37), Luke (14:26), and the Gospel of Thomas (55) in that in the Q saying there is nothing about separation from one's siblings. Rather the alienation brought by Jesus appears between generations (children and their spouses over against parents and in-laws). One author has suggested the following: "[This] attack is on the Mediterranean family's axis of power. . . . The family is society in miniature. . . . It is not just a center of domestic serenity; since it involves power, it invites the abuse of power, and it is at that precise point that Jesus attacks it."[10] The suggestion that Jesus in this saying attacks the power of the patriarchal family—although it does not account for Jesus's rejection of siblings in some of the previous sayings (and in one of the sayings that will follow)—does seem to line up, at least somewhat, with Jesus's command discussed earlier, to "call no man father."

Another radical passage about family that also appears in Q seems to focus more on family loyalty (and particularly respect for one's father) than power. When asked by Jesus to follow him, a potential disciple answered, "'Lord, let me first go and bury my father.' But [Jesus] said to him, 'Follow me, [and] let the dead bury their own dead'" (Q 9:59–60; cf. Matt 8:21–22; Luke 9:59–60). Jesus's command to "let the dead bury their own dead" is particularly

9. There is a similar passage in the Gospel of Mark that is close in meaning to the above sayings in the Gospels of Thomas and Luke although it is not as radical. It mentions Jesus's followers leaving (rather than hating) "brothers or sisters or mother or father or children" for Jesus's sake (10:29; cf. Matt 19:29 and Luke 18:29).

10. John Dominic Crossan, *Jesus: A Revolutionary Biography* (New York: HarperCollins, 1989), 60.

alarming in light of the way the patriarchal family was conceived at the time. According to the norms of both Judaism and the larger Greco-Roman society, one's parents were to be honored both in life and in death. Jesus's command to let the dead bury their own dead overturned those norms; to follow that command would ultimately result in the young man's father remaining unburied and dishonored, easy prey for scavenging animals.[11]

The Gospel of Mark presents us with yet another shocking narrative about Jesus and his family. As the Gospel reports the story, Jesus's family attempted to disrupt his activities when he was in the town of Capernaum: "Then [Jesus] went home; and the crowd came together again, so that [Jesus and his disciples] could not even eat. When [Jesus'] family heard it, they went out to restrain him, for they said, 'He has gone out of his mind.'" (3:19–21).[12] As these few sentences indicate, Jesus's family was not only unsympathetic to his activities, it was embarrassed by them.[13] Believing him to be mentally ill, the family came to take him away, presumably back to Nazareth where he could be controlled. As the story continues, Jesus's family arrived at the house in Capernaum where he was and "standing outside, they sent to him and called him" (3:31). Jesus, however, ignored them. Turning to those around him, he asked: "'Who are my mother and my brothers?' And looking at those who sat around him, he said, 'Here are my mother and my brothers! Whoever does the will of God is my brother and sister and mother'" (3:34–35; cf. Luke 8:21 and Gos. Thom. 99:2). According to this narrative, Jesus redefined the meaning of family for his followers. He turned his back on his biological family in favor of "those who do the will of God."

A saying that appears in the Gospel of Luke, also likely authentic, seems analogous to the above Markan episode: "A woman in the crowd raised her

11. Although it was mentioned in chapter 2 that Jesus's teachings were not in opposition to the Jewish law, this is a possible exception. However, this does not mean that Jesus rejected Judaism. Indeed, the Therapeutae, mentioned by Philo in his work *On the Contemplative Life* 18, who demonstrated a similar attitude to family, would not have been considered to be outside of Judaism.

12. The NRSV translates this as follows: "When his family heard it, they went out to restrain him, for people were saying, 'He has gone out of his mind.'" The addition of "people" (suggesting people other than Jesus's family) is unwarranted. The original text simply says, "they were saying," and this points back to the original subject, Jesus's family. I have therefore adjusted the translation above accordingly.

13. Although this episode is recorded in a Gospel written a generation after Jesus's death, there is no reason to believe that the Gospel writer invented it. The rejection of Jesus by those in his hometown of Nazareth was similar (Mark 6:2–6). Furthermore, the Gospel of John also tells us that "[Jesus'] brothers did not believe in him" (John 7:5).

voice and said to [Jesus], 'Blessed is the womb that bore you and the breasts that nursed you!' But he said, 'Blessed rather are those who hear the word of God and obey it!'" (Luke 11:27–28). Here a woman shouting from the crowd extolled Jesus's mother for giving birth to and for nursing such a remarkable son. Although the unknown woman praised his mother, Jesus corrected her, countering that "those who hear the word of God and obey it" should *instead* be commended.[14] As in the earlier Markan story, familial ties are toppled here in favor of "those who hear the word of God and obey it."

Marriage and Divorce

Although the historical Jesus seems to have challenged traditional family structures, there is one dimension of family relationships that he upheld. He believed that marriages should not be broken up and so he prohibited divorce. On the surface, this seems odd. If Jesus opposed the traditional family of those related by blood, why did he not likewise condone the dissolution of marriages? Unfortunately, we cannot be sure. The Gospels give us two different reasons.

According to the Gospel of Mark, the reason that Jesus gave for prohibiting divorce is that it ran contrary to the will of the creator: "From the beginning of creation, 'God made them male and female.' 'For this reason a man shall leave his father and mother and be joined to his wife, and the two shall become one flesh.' So they are no longer two, but one flesh. Therefore what God has joined together, let no one separate" (Mark 10:6–9). According to Jesus's reasoning in this passage, God created two genders, intending that a man and a woman unite with one another. Once that had happened, they should remain together.

But we see something different in a saying from the Q document. Matthew's version of the Q saying states: "Anyone who divorces his wife . . . causes *her* to commit adultery; and whoever marries a divorced woman commits adultery" (Matt 5:32, emphasis added).[15] The first line in this command is

14. The fact that Jesus is correcting the woman can be seen by Jesus's use of the phrase, "Blessed *rather . . .*"

15. The Matthean text actually says, "anyone who divorces his wife, *except on the ground of unchastity*, causes her to commit adultery; and whoever marries a divorced woman commits adultery." I have removed the italicized phrase above because it is likely a later attempt (probably by the author of Matthew) to make Jesus's stern command a bit more palatable. We will return to the italicized phrase later in the chapter.

a bit puzzling. Why would a divorced woman be accused of adultery? The assumption must be that a divorced woman would need to either remarry or resort to prostitution in order to survive. Obviously, either option would force her to engage in sexual relations with someone besides her original husband. Consequently, a man divorcing his wife would, in one way or another, make her an adulteress. The second line of the saying is clear enough on its own; it prohibits any man from marrying a divorced woman because such a man would engage in sex with someone who was someone else's (original) wife. Consequently, both partners—the man along with the woman—would be committing adultery.

Luke's version is a bit easier to understand. It states: "Anyone who divorces his wife and marries another woman commits adultery; and anyone who marries a woman divorced from her husband commits adultery" (Luke 16:18). While Matthew's version of the saying makes both parties of a divorce guilty of adultery, curiously, Luke's version only accuses offending males of adultery. Nothing is said about women; apparently, divorced women would be blameless (perhaps even if they remarried?). Regardless, according to both Matthew's and Luke's versions of this saying, the proscription seems to be less a condemnation of the couple's separation (as in the Markan prohibition) than it is a denunciation of remarriage. For Q, separation is not the real problem; remarriage is.

Did Jesus prohibit divorce (in the sense of separation) because it was contrary to the created order or was he really against remarriage for those who had separated from their original spouses? Since these options are not mutually exclusive, it is possible that he condemned both acts: separation (on the basis of the created order) as well as remarriage (since it is that act that ultimately causes the adultery). Unfortunately, we cannot know his reasoning for certain. We can, however, be confident of the prohibition.[16]

Jesus's prohibition of divorce raises again the question about his views on family. As we saw above, the historical Jesus seems to have encouraged his followers to abandon their families of origin in favor of "those who did the will of God," presumably meaning Jesus's followers. But, did he go even farther than that, perhaps urging them to create their own families (of those who would do the will of God) by marrying while at the same time rejecting their blood kin? Or did he simply urge those of his followers who had already been married to remain so? These are difficult questions to answer, quite simply because

16. Since, at the time, divorce was relatively easy in both Judaism and pagan society at large, the prohibition of it almost certainly came from the historical Jesus.

we lack sufficient evidence to come to a definitive conclusion. But there are some hints from which we may be able to derive a tentative conclusion. First of all, to the best of our knowledge, the historical Jesus was unmarried.[17] In this regard, his status was somewhat unusual; marriage and procreation were generally encouraged within Jewish culture.[18] Jesus's unmarried status could by itself suggest that Jesus encouraged unmarried people to remain unmarried, as he was.

There is also one saying—likely an authentic saying of the historical Jesus—that points in that direction: "There are eunuchs who have been so from birth, and there are eunuchs who have been made eunuchs by others, and there are eunuchs who have made themselves eunuchs for the sake of the kingdom of heaven" (Matt 19:12).[19] Curiously, this saying mixes the literal with the metaphorical. In the three different phrases that mention eunuchs, the first two references are obviously meant literally: 1) some men are eunuchs because they were born without testes and, 2) some men are eunuchs because they were castrated for one reason or another. The third mention of eunuchs, however, those who are "eunuchs for the sake of the kingdom of heaven," could hardly have meant that men were literally expected to castrate themselves for the sake of the kingdom.[20] Instead, it metaphorically points to those who have acted like eunuchs: they have renounced sex (and presumably marriage) "for the sake of the kingdom." In short, the saying seems to indicate that Jesus approved of those who acted like eunuchs—i.e., lived a celibate life—for the sake of the kingdom.

In sum, our evidence suggests that the historical Jesus commanded his followers to reject their families of origin, that is, their parents and siblings. His reasons for doing so, however, are not clear. Perhaps he meant to undermine the power of the patriarchal family. Perhaps he felt that *any* attachment (family likely being the strongest) was detrimental to the proclamation of the

---

17. That Jesus was married has been suggested many times. However, such suggestions lack evidence. A Coptic papyrus that mentioned Jesus's wife surfaced in 2012, but it has since been established that the papyrus is a modern forgery.

18. Of course, there were exceptions. The Essenes and the Therapeutae, two Jewish "monastic" type groups were celibate.

19. The saying's radical nature suggests that Jesus said it or something close to it. It is likely that the final phrase of the verse, "Let anyone accept this who can," was added later, in a somewhat desperate attempt to domesticate its radical nature.

20. The fourth-century-CE historian Eusebius tells us that the Christian theologian Origen castrated himself because of this saying (*Hist. eccl.* 6.8). Eusebius's story, however, is probably fictional.

kingdom. Regardless, he also commanded those among his followers who had already established families by marriage to preserve those marriages. Wives and husbands were, as Jesus saw things, indissolubly linked. Finally, based on rather meager evidence, we can tentatively conclude that Jesus encouraged those of his followers who were unmarried to remain celibate, as he was.

The Role of Women in the Movement at the Time of Jesus

Although the historical Jesus was unmarried and seems to have recommended celibacy to those around him, he did not avoid the company of women. The Gospels narrate stories of Jesus healing women on a number of occasions (Mark 5:25-34; Luke 8:2; 13:10-17). On one of these occasions, the healing of the woman with a hemorrhage, Jesus even credited the woman for effecting her own healing: "Daughter, your faith has made you well" (Mark 5:34).[21] The Gospels also contain several stories in which Jesus interacted closely with women, sometimes despite the objections of those around him (e.g., Mark 7:24-29; 14:3-9; Luke 7:36-50; John 4:7-29).

The historical Jesus also directed his teaching toward women as well as men. While not all teachers at the time would have believed teaching women to be a worthwhile undertaking, Jesus apparently did.[22] Indeed, some of his parables featured women in the leading role. Among his parables, we encounter a number of "gender-symmetrical pairs."[23] That is to say, while some parables feature men as their primary character, there are, at times, comparable parables that highlight the role of a woman. Examples include: the parable of the mustard seed featuring a male as protagonist (Luke 13:18-

---

21. Although it is difficult to authenticate individual miracles (i.e., whether they actually happened as narrated), there are enough healings of women in the Gospel accounts to assume that Jesus did treat women as well as men. There are also enough examples of Jesus crediting the people healed by their own belief that it is reasonable to assume the historicity of Jesus's belief that the faith of those being healed actually worked the healing (e.g., Mark 7:29; 10:52; Luke 7:9, 50). Consequently, it is likely that at least the statement, "Daughter, your faith has made you well" is authentic (Geza Vermes, *The Authentic Gospel of Jesus* [London: Penguin, 2003], 9-10, 420). Compare this statement to Jesus's words to the sinful woman in Luke 7:50: "Your faith has saved you."

22. Many philosophers of the time, for example, did not believe that women could benefit from moral instruction. See below, n. 45.

23. Gerd Theissen and Annette Merz, *The Historical Jesus: A Comprehensive Guide* (Minneapolis: Fortress, 1998), 220.

19), and the parable of the leaven, featuring a female (Luke 13:20–21); the parable of the lost sheep, featuring a male protagonist (Luke 15:3–7) and the parable of the lost coin, featuring a female (Luke 15:8–10); the parable of the persistent (male) friend (Luke 11:5–8) and the parable of the persistent widow (Luke 18:1–8).

But Jesus did not just minister to women. He also had female followers. While some women traveled with Jesus, there were others who, it seems, owned homes into which he and his itinerant followers were welcomed (Mark 1:29–31; Luke 10:38–42; cf. John 11:1–27). Of the female itinerants who traveled with Jesus, we know the names of a few, including Mary of Magdala (more commonly known as Mary Magdalene), Joanna (the wife of Herod's steward), Susanna, another woman named Mary (identified only as the mother of James and Joses), and Salome (Luke 8:2–3; Mark 15:40). In his letter to the Romans (16:7), Paul sends greetings to a certain Andronicus (a male) and Junia (a female). These two were probably husband and wife. Paul identifies them as "fellow countrymen" (i.e., Jews), "prominent among the apostles," who "were in Christ before I was." Since Paul likely became a Jesus follower within a few years of Jesus's death, the fact that Andronicus and Junia were part of the movement before Paul opens up the possibility that Junia would have also been a female follower of the historical Jesus.

Although we do not know how most of these women became Jesus's followers, we can infer something about one of his female followers, Mary of Magdala. But it is important to first recognize that the well-known identification of Mary of Magdala as a reformed prostitute has no basis in the New Testament. Rather, the idea comes from the later conflation of two narratives, the mention of Mary of Magdala in Luke 8:2 and a story about a sinful woman—probably a prostitute—whom Jesus encountered at a meal in the house of a Pharisee in the chapter immediately before Mary's name is mentioned (Luke 7:36–50).[24]

The credible knowledge that we have about Mary comes from an aside by the author of Luke's Gospel. From that aside, we learn that Mary had previously been the victim of demon possession; seven demons possessed her. She was exorcised, presumably by Jesus and, as a result, became one of his followers (Luke 8:2).[25] We learn elsewhere that Mary, along with several other women,

24. This idea arose in the Latin Church somewhere around the sixth century. Curiously, in the Greek Church, the idea does not occur; Mary of Magdala is not considered a reformed prostitute in that tradition.

25. Although the text does not explicitly say that it was Jesus who exorcised her, it seems a reasonable supposition.

observed the crucifixion (Mark 15:40–41; Matt 27:55–56; John 19:25–27). Jesus's male followers, to the contrary, had all fled by then.[26] Furthermore, according to one strand of tradition, Mary was the first witness of Jesus's resurrection (Mark 16:9 and John 20:11–18; cf. Matt 28:1, 9 where she, along with "the other Mary," were the first witnesses).[27]

Despite the fact that the story of Mary of Magdala as a reformed prostitute arose as an imaginative product of the later church, nevertheless, a connection between the historical Jesus and prostitutes has some historical basis. There is a story of Jesus speaking with such a woman in Luke 7:36–50 (mentioned above).[28] Although in that passage, the woman is simply labeled a "sinner," her sin was likely prostitution.[29] There is also a saying from Matthew's Gospel, likely authentic, in which Jesus told the temple priests and elders who had questioned his authority that "the tax collectors and the prostitutes are going into the kingdom of God ahead of you" (Matt 21:31). The fact that we have a story of Jesus interacting with a prostitute as well as an authentic saying that specifically mentions prostitutes entering the kingdom of God suggests that he, at times, associated with them.

In sum, from the evidence that we have, it seems reasonable to assume that Jesus both ministered to women and viewed them as potential partners in the movement. Some women, like his male disciples, followed him on his travels; others, although they did not travel with him, accepted him into their homes. Furthermore, women were as much the focus of his teachings as men and some were credited with an active role in their own transformation (whether from illness to health or from a sinful to a non-sinful lifestyle). It is likely that Jesus thought of women less as potential wives and future mothers than as partners (like his male disciples) in the proclamation of the kingdom.

---

26. According to the earliest Gospel, all of Jesus's disciples fled at his arrest (Mark 14:50) except Peter (note that Mark's Gospel originally ended at 16:8—in the verses that follow, Jesus's disciples return; those verses, however, were not part of the original Gospel). Following Peter's denial of Jesus (Mark 14:66–72), the text does not explicitly mention his flight but he nevertheless disappears from the story.

27. Our earliest source, Paul, knows of Peter as the earliest witness (1 Cor 15:5).

28. This story is similar to the story of the woman who anointed Jesus in Mark 14:3 and Matt 26:6–7.

29. The fact that she was present at a formal dinner suggests that she was a prostitute; prostitutes were known to appear at such events in order to ply their trade during the course of the symposium (drinking party) that followed the dinner.

Family and Gender in the Jesus Movement following the Death of Its Founder

Family of Origin

It will probably come as no surprise to learn that Jesus's radical stance toward family of origin was not uniformly preserved as the movement progressed. In some quarters, that radical position endured, at least for a while. For example, since both the Q document and the Gospel of Thomas preserved the saying without qualification about "hating" the members of one's family of origin, it is likely that those communities continued the radical legacy of Jesus regarding family. That is to say, all of the members of those communities were, like the original followers of Jesus, expected to completely detach themselves from their families.

But in other communities of Jesus followers, Jesus's attitude toward family was overlooked. This was probably due to the involvement of Jesus's own family members in the movement after his death. Although it seems likely that Jesus's followers were originally led by Peter, Jesus's brother James ultimately became an important leader in the movement, as did some of Jesus's other brothers.[30] Indeed, in one of his letters, Paul repeats a very early tradition that indicates that James was one of the people (alongside Peter and the twelve) who experienced Jesus's resurrection (1 Cor 15:4–7).[31] Another source, Acts, includes Jesus's mother and brothers in the first gathering of the disciples in Jerusalem (Acts 1:12–14). Although we have no details about the incorporation of Jesus's family members into the movement, the 1 Corinthians and Acts passages suggest that it happened very early, shortly after Jesus's death.

Regardless, within a brief period of time, Jesus's brothers became very influential. Paul mentions James, the brother of Jesus, as one of the leaders of the

---

30. Paul, writing approximately two decades after Jesus's death, mentioned "the brothers of the Lord" (plural) as missionaries (1 Cor 9:5). The involvement of Jesus's relatives in the movement continued for some time. The historian Eusebius reported that the Roman emperor Domitian (ruled 81–96 CE) interrogated the great-nephews of Jesus (grandsons of his brother Jude). Domitian was concerned that they were revolutionaries. However, Eusebius reported that, after realizing that they were mere laborers and on being told that the kingdom was not earthly but heavenly, Domitian released them (Eusebius, *Hist. eccl.* 3.20).

31. Since we know that Jesus's family was not sympathetic to his mission during his lifetime (cf. Mark 3:21; John 7:5), it is possible that James's experience of Jesus's resurrection (whatever that experience might have been—Paul's text does not elaborate) caused James to become a member of the movement after Jesus's death.

Jerusalem assembly (Gal 2:1–14). While the Pauline passage indicates that there were three leaders of that assembly—James, Jesus's brother; Peter; and John, possibly the son of Zebedee, another important follower of Jesus during his lifetime—the context suggests that James wielded most of the power (cf. Gal 2:12).[32]

Because of the involvement of Jesus's family members in the movement, the majority of later texts demonstrate a very different attitude toward Jesus's family of origin than Jesus did while alive. For example, only Mark's Gospel reports the story of Jesus's family's attempt to seize him at Capernaum. Even though both knew the story (both used Mark as a source), the authors of Matthew and Luke's Gospels omitted this troubling episode. Furthermore, the command found in Q (and the Gospel of Thomas) that Jesus's followers were to "hate" the members of their own families was likewise softened. As we have already seen, both Matthew's and Luke's versions of the saying emphasize the importance of putting discipleship *first* but neither insisted that Jesus followers *reject* their families of origin. Although the notion that Jesus followers were members of a metaphorical family persisted, by the time that Matthew and Luke's Gospels were written, it was no longer believed that the "family" of Jesus followers was meant to *replace* one's family of origin. But these Gospels did not just omit or soften these troubling passages; they also began to describe Jesus's parents in very positive terms.

In Matthew's Gospel, for instance, Jesus's father Joseph (who did not appear in Mark's Gospel) was depicted as a model of piety and obedience. He was called "a righteous man" (1:19), and on several occasions received heavenly communication by way of his dreams (1:20–23; 2:13; 2:19–20). Mary, Jesus's mother, although playing a less dominant role at the beginning of Matthew's Gospel than did her husband, was nonetheless portrayed as an admirable figure, a virgin who conceived by the Holy Spirit (Matt 1:20). On the other hand, Luke's Gospel spotlighted not Jesus's father, but his mother. In this Gospel, the angel Gabriel appeared to her to announce that she would conceive, despite her virginity. Mary, although somewhat puzzled, nevertheless responded obediently, "Here am I, the servant of the Lord; let it be with me according to your word" (1:38). Unlike Jesus's mother in Mark's Gospel—a woman who believed her son to be mentally ill—the mother depicted in Luke's Gospel "treasure[d]" the events of Jesus's birth and childhood "in her heart" (2:19, 51).

---

32. There are also two letters in the New Testament attributed to men named James and Jude. Although the letters do not further identify the authors, readers were likely supposed to believe that the authors were Jesus's brothers. However, it is unlikely that either was authored by one of Jesus's brothers.

John's Gospel likewise portrayed Jesus's mother in a very positive light. She was even involved in Jesus's ministry, urging her somewhat reluctant son to perform his first miracle (John 2:3–11). She was also present at the crucifixion, "near the cross," something that we do not see in the other Gospels.[33] The glorification of Jesus's parents was carried to extremes in the noncanonical *Infancy Gospel of James,* a work that was likely written in the late second century CE. In that text both Joseph's righteousness and Mary's purity were repeatedly emphasized.

But the Jesus movement's attitude toward family of origin probably did not change simply because of the involvement of Jesus's family members. It also likely changed as a result of the importance of family networks in the movement's growth. When the Jesus movement reached the hellenized cities of the eastern empire, it first took root in individual households. Paul, for example, tells us that shortly after he first arrived in Corinth, he baptized the household of Stephanas (1 Cor 1:16). Stephanas's household would have included Stephanas himself, his wife, their children, and any slaves that he owned (or possibly any slaves that he had previously freed).[34]

Did Paul preach to all of the members of the household and then subsequently baptize them or did he simply convert Stephanas, the head of the household, expecting the others to simply follow his lead and receive baptism? Unfortunately, we cannot be sure. The second option is certainly a viable possibility since, at that time, one's entire household was expected to follow the religious practices of its head. In the New Testament, we have several other examples of whole households that were baptized along with the household's head, suggesting that the dependents' conversion may not have been voluntary (Acts 11:14; 16:15; 18:8; cf. Rom 16:10–11).

Although Paul tells us that those in Stephanas's household "were the first converts in Achaia," he also gives us some more information about them: "they have devoted themselves to the service of the saints." It is unclear what exactly this service was but the context makes clear that this household was important in the early years of the Corinthian assembly. It is likely that its members brought others into the movement by reaching out to their

33. In Mark, Matthew, and Luke, there are women who view the crucifixion from afar. According to Mark and Matthew, two of them are named Mary; one is Mary of Magdala and the other is identified as the mother of James the younger, Joses, and Salome in Mark's account (15:40) and the mother of James and Joseph in Matthew's Gospel (27:56). Clearly, neither of these Marys is Jesus's mother.

34. Slaves who had been manumitted were still closely connected to their former owners as we will see in the next chapter.

friends and associates.[35] As a result of Stephanas's household's labor for the community, Paul urged the rest of the Corinthians to put themselves "at the service of such people, and of everyone who works and toils with them" (1 Cor 16:15–16).

In sum, in the years following Jesus's death, the significant role played by Jesus's brothers—particularly James—made the rejection of family, preached by the historical Jesus, untenable. Furthermore, the importance of the household in the cities into which the movement quickly spread actually gave new impetus to the importance of family within the movement. Parents were not to be hated. Rather, they were to be honored. This can be fittingly illustrated by two documents written in the latter half of the first century, the letter to the Colossians and the letter to the Ephesians, each attributed (almost certainly incorrectly) to the apostle Paul.

In the New Testament letter to the Colossians, possibly composed in the late 60s or early 70s, the author counsels, "Children, obey your parents in everything, for this is your acceptable duty in the Lord. Fathers, do not provoke your children, or they may lose heart" (Col 3:20–21). Unlike in Jesus's time, followers were *not* commanded to hate their parents. Rather, obedience to one's parents was seen to be a child's "acceptable duty in the Lord." It is noteworthy that no exception is made here for an unbelieving father. Was it believed to be the acceptable duty for a believing child to obey even an unbelieving father?

A similar command to obey one's parents appeared in the letter to the Ephesians, but there it was put into the context of Moses's commandment: "Children, obey your parents in the Lord, for this is right. 'Honor your father and mother'—this is the first commandment with a promise: 'so that it may be well with you and you may live long on the earth.' And, fathers, do not provoke your children to anger, but bring them up in the discipline and instruction of the Lord" (Eph 6:1–4 quoting Deut 5:16; cf. Exod 20:12). As the passages from Colossians and Ephesians demonstrate, toward the end of the first century, Jesus's command "to hate one's father and mother" had not only disappeared, it had been reversed. The movement had come full circle; more traditional Greco-Roman values concerning the relationship between

---

35. Stephanas may have also continued to provide a meeting place for members once the population of Jesus followers in Corinth expanded beyond the confines of his immediate household. Rom 16:23 tells us that Gaius was host to "the whole assembly" in Corinth. But the reference to the whole assembly suggests that Gaius hosted when the various smaller assemblies in Corinth (i.e., household assemblies) met together as a whole. Stephanas may have hosted one of the smaller assemblies.

parents and children took precedence over Jesus's command to renounce one's family.

Marriage and Divorce

If one's family of origin once again gained importance within the movement following Jesus's death, what about the families of Jesus followers created by marriage? Were members of the movement still encouraged to remain celibate, to become "eunuchs for the sake of the kingdom"? In the middle of the first century, it seems as if the whole idea of marriage (and particularly sex) was under attack within the Corinthian assembly, an assembly founded by Paul. Some single people were asking whether they should marry or remain celibate; widows were asking if they should remain celibate or remarry; and some married believers were wondering if they should live celibate lives, despite their marital status. Curiously, the Corinthians were not wondering about marriage versus celibacy because of Jesus's saying about "eunuchs for the kingdom." They were almost certainly unaware of it.[36] Rather, marriage versus celibacy was a matter of some debate in the Greco-Roman world at large. The Corinthians' concerns probably arose from discussions taking place in the popular culture of the time.[37]

Paul counseled the unmarried in Corinth to remain so, if possible: "I think that, in view of the impending crisis, it is well for you to remain as you are. . . . those who marry will experience distress in this life, and I would spare you that" (1 Cor 7:26–28). Marriage, Paul insisted here, could cause distress:

The unmarried man is anxious about the affairs of the Lord, how to please the Lord; but the married man is anxious about the affairs of the world, how to please his wife, and his interests are divided. And the unmarried woman and the virgin are anxious about the affairs of the Lord, so that they may be holy in body and spirit; but the married woman is anxious about the affairs of the world, how to please her husband. (1 Cor 7:32–34)

36. Paul does not reflect much knowledge of Jesus's life or sayings. See below, note 51.

37. It is also possible that the baptismal phrase, "there is no longer male and female" (Gal 3:28), coupled with expectations of the end, fueled a leveling of gender differences, which in turn made celibacy attractive.

From Paul's perspective, pleasing one's spouse could get in the way of pleasing God.

Paul's advice about divided interests conformed somewhat to philosophical thinking of the time, especially that of the Cynics. The Cynics eschewed marriage because, like material possessions, it put constraints on one and made it difficult to live the philosophical life. The philosopher Epictetus, for example, described the Cynic philosopher as one sent by Zeus to show people how to live well with neither possessions nor family: "'Look at me,' he says, 'I am without a home, without a city, without property, without a slave; I sleep on the ground; I have neither wife nor children, no miserable governor's mansion, but only earth, and sky, and one rough cloak. Yet, what do I lack? Am I not free from pain and fear, am I not free?'" (*Disc.* 3.22.45–48). As Epictetus made clear, wives (among other things) were, at best, unnecessary, at worst, they interfered with the Cynic philosopher's freedom.[38] The same author elsewhere emphasized the lack of freedom possessed by the married man: "he must show certain services to his father-in-law, to the rest of his wife's relatives, to his wife herself. . . . He must get a kettle to heat water for the baby, for washing it in a bath-tub; wool for his wife when she has a child, oil, a cot, a cup (the vessels get more and more numerous); not to speak of the rest of his business . . ." (*Disc.* 3.22.70–72). In short, for a married man, life with a wife (and the children that inevitably follow) would become little more than a series of distractions. With such distractions, no time would be left for what was really important.

It is, however, important to recognize two important differences between Paul's stance on marriage as a distraction and the attitude of the Cynics. First, Paul's advice came in the context of the movement's apocalyptic expectations. One should not be distracted, he argued, by one's spouse "in view of the impending crisis." Here, Paul clearly pointed to the end of the present age: "I mean, brothers and sisters, the appointed time has grown short" (1 Cor 7:29). The Cynics had no expectation of any such "impending crisis."

---

38. A Cynic epistle, falsely attributed to the famous philosopher Diogenes, likewise advises against marriage: "One should not wed nor raise children, since our race is weak and marriage and children burden human weakness with troubles. Therefore, those who move toward wedlock and the rearing of children because of the support that these promise, later experience a change of heart when they come to know that they are characterized by even greater hardships. But it is possible to escape right from the start. Now the person insensitive to passion, who considers his own possessions to be sufficient for patient endurance, declines to marry and produce children (*Epistle* 47, 1–9. Translation by Benjamin Fiore, S. J. [slightly emended] in Abraham J. Malherbe, *The Cynic Epistles: A Study Edition*, SBLSBS 12 [Missoula, MT: Scholars Press, 1977]).

The second difference between Paul's advice and that of the Cynics was that Paul was more egalitarian in his approach. Unlike the Cynic philosopher described by Epictetus, the apostle addressed the issue of marriage from the point of view of both husband and wife. While the Cynic philosophers worried that a wife could bring trouble to a man, Paul (more equitably) claimed that husbands could also cause anxiety for their wives. He urged, in response, that each partner (both husband and wife) show consideration for the other (cf. 1 Cor 7:3-5).[39]

But the questions raised in Corinth focused not only on marriage. They were also concerned with sex, including sex within marriage. Some wondered if celibacy represented the proper state for those in the movement. The Corinthians wrote to Paul to ask his opinion. He responded: "Now concerning the matters about which you wrote: 'It is well for a man not to touch a woman.' But because of cases of sexual immorality, each man should have his own wife and each woman her own husband. The husband should give to his wife her conjugal rights, and likewise the wife to her husband. For the wife does not have authority over her own body, but the husband does; likewise the husband does not have authority over his own body, but the wife does. Do not deprive one another except perhaps by agreement for a set time, to devote yourselves to prayer, and then come together again, so that Satan may not tempt you because of your lack of self-control" (1 Cor 7:1-5).

Paul began his response by quoting what was probably a slogan of the Corinthians: "It is good for a man not to touch a woman." The phrase "to touch a woman" functions here, as elsewhere in Greek literature, as a euphemism for sexual intercourse. Some people in Corinth were obviously promoting a celibate existence. Since Paul mentioned divorce a few verses later, it is possible that some members of the community had abandoned their spouses in order to live a celibate life.

For some philosophically and physiologically minded people of Paul's time, sex was considered problematic. There were a couple of reasons for this. First, some philosophers argued that sex, like marriage, left little time for the philosophical life. Along the lines of Epictetus's disdain for marriage, a Cynic philosopher insisted in a letter that "immoderate intercourse with women . . . demands a lot of spare time" (Diogenes, *Epistle* 44, 7-8).[40] Others believed

---

39. Here Paul sounded more like some of the Stoic philosophers of his day who saw marriage in terms of friendship and mutuality.

40. This letter was ascribed, falsely, to the famous philosopher Diogenes.

that the pleasures of the body, sex in particular, could actually interfere with one's spiritual development.[41]

But apart from being a distraction or an obstacle to spiritual accomplishment, many assumed that sex could present an actual physical threat, particularly to a male; too much sex could drain his masculinity and bring about weakness. Such a fear caused an ancient physician, Rufus of Ephesus, to warn that "those who engage in sexual relations, and particularly those who do so without restraint, must take greater care of themselves than others, so that by ensuring that their bodies are in the best possible condition they may suffer less from the harmful effects of sexual activity" (Oribasius, *Med. Coll.* 6.22.2).[42] Because of such physical concerns about sex, both physicians and philosophers touted self-control as an important virtue that all men should continually nurture.

Although in some ways Paul's positive response to the suggestion that "it is good for a man not to touch a woman" falls in line with much of the philosophical thinking of his day, in other ways it does not. Most philosophers would have argued that any man could (and should) discipline himself so as not to be ruled by his desire.[43] Paul, however, conceived of sexual control (or lack thereof) differently. Such was not, in Paul's eyes, a matter of disciplining oneself; rather, it was a *charisma*. In everyday Greek, the term *charisma* meant something like "a favor." But for Paul, a *charisma* was a gift from God.[44]

At one point in his argument, Paul asserted, "I wish that all men were as I myself am." By this he meant that he wished all men had the God-given *charisma* to remain celibate. But, as Paul understood things, such was not the case. In his words, "each [person] has a particular gift (*charisma*) from

41. Philo, for example, wrote the following about a certain group of Jewish ascetic women: "The [Sabbath] feast is shared by [these] women also, most of them aged virgins who have kept their chastity not under compulsion like some of the Greek priestesses, but of their own free will in their ardent yearning for wisdom. Eager to have her for their life mate they have spurned the pleasures of the body and desire no mortal offspring but those immortal children [whom] only the soul that is dear to God can bring to birth unaided because the father has sown in her spiritual rays enabling her to behold the verities of wisdom" (*Contempl. Life* 68 [Colson]).

42. The translation is from Aline Rouselle, *Porneia: On Desire and the Body in Antiquity* (Oxford: Blackwell, 1988), 18.

43. Having disciplined himself, a man could thereby either choose to remain celibate or engage in moderate sexual activity for the purpose of creating children. While many philosophers agreed that marriage was a distraction, they nevertheless deemed it necessary for the production of children.

44. It is worth noting that this is the same term that Paul used in 1 Cor 12:4–10 for the gifts of the Spirit.

God, one having one kind and another a different kind" (1 Cor 7:7). For those individuals who did not have the *charisma* to remain celibate, Paul thought that marriage was the best option. For them, it was "better to marry than to be aflame with passion" (1 Cor 7:9).

Paul believed that it would be dangerous for those who lacked the *charisma* for celibacy to try to live a celibate life. He viewed the state of being "aflame with passion" as hazardous because it could lead one into immoral acts, acts like frequenting prostitutes or committing incest, both of which Paul had addressed earlier in the same letter (1 Cor 5:1–13; 1 Cor 6:12–20). Unlike the physicians of his time, Paul believed that the peril was spiritual rather than physical. If a person did not have the *charisma* to live celibately, then marriage could direct his or her passion appropriately and so that person could avoid sin.

But still another way that Paul's thinking differed from the philosophers of his time had to do with presuppositions about gender. Paul's advice about sex and marriage was directed to both men and women. Most philosophers of the time would have thought it fruitless to give such advice to women because the society of the time believed that women were incapable of controlling their passions.[45] But Paul seemed to believe that the *charisma* of celibacy was given to people of both genders: some men had it while others did not and in the same way, some women had it while others did not.

To sum up thus far, Corinthian attitudes toward celibacy were, for the most part, in line with those of the historical Jesus who taught that one should be a "eunuch for the sake of the kingdom," even though the attitudes in Corinth had likely been shaped by Greco-Roman cultural forces. These forces, philosophical and physiological opinions in particular, also influenced Paul's response. However, as we have seen, he displayed a certain amount of independence from them. For example, he believed that celibacy was a *charisma*, not something that one could achieve by self-discipline.

As time went on, however, other cultural forces began to influence attitudes toward celibacy and marriage. By the end of the first century, as Christianity struggled to move into the mainstream of Greco-Roman society, opinions in the movement began to change. While Paul favored celibacy, the Pastoral Epistles—1 Timothy, 2 Timothy, and Titus, letters attributed to Paul but written several decades after his death—disparaged it. The author of one

---

45. The Stoic philosopher Musonius Rufus was an exception. He believed that women could also be trained to control their passions: Cora E. Lutz, *Musonius Rufus: "The Roman Socrates,"* Yale Classical Studies 10 (New Haven: Yale University Press, 1947), frag. 3 (40.17–20).

of those letters, 1 Timothy, warned readers against the *false teaching* of some who promoted an ascetic lifestyle, namely, those who "forbid marriage and demand abstinence from foods" (1 Tim 4:3). For this author, sexual asceticism was to be rejected. Marriage was to be the norm. Indeed, as we see elsewhere in the same letter, the author insisted that young widows should remarry (1 Tim 5:14). He also asserted that the bishop of the assembly should be a married man who had "[managed] his household well" (1 Tim 3:2–4).[46]

Why was marriage so important to this author? It is undoubtedly because he had a more traditional understanding of the sexes. It is unlikely that he believed, as did Paul, that women, like men, could have the God-given *charisma* to live celibately. Rather, the author was probably more aligned with the predominant Greco-Roman views of his time: namely that most women were physiologically incapable of self-control; rather, they were governed by their desires and emotions.[47] Since, by nature, they could not control their passions, it was considered the duty of men to do it for them. Consequently, marriage was necessary. The author's use of the biblical story of Adam and Eve plainly demonstrates his cultural bias: "For Adam was formed first, then Eve; and Adam was not deceived [by the serpent], but the woman was deceived and became a transgressor" (1 Tim 2:13–14, referring to Gen 3:1–6).[48] The implication is that, had Adam been at Eve's side when the serpent tempted her, she would not have been deceived.[49]

Although societal forces brought a change of opinion about celibacy in some parts of the movement, in others, the preference for the celibate life expressed by Jesus and Paul persisted. In a second-century work, the Acts of Paul and Thecla, readers encounter a young heroine who, after she heard Paul preach, resolved to follow him and live a celibate life. According to this later

46. It should be noted that at this time each assembly had its own bishop. It was only later that bishops became administrators of larger areas.

47. Nevertheless, this author seems to have not believed that *all* women were enslaved to their passions; some women, he believed, had the capability of living rational lives. He says with regard to women deacons (an office about which we know very little) that they "must be serious, not slanderers, but temperate, faithful in all things" (1 Tim 3:11).

48. This is somewhat at odds with the Genesis story. Adam was indeed deceived. Eve was first deceived by the serpent but Adam followed Eve's lead. Nevertheless, the later Christian writer Tertullian concurred with this author's characterization of women. In one of his writings, he asked his "sisters in Christ," "Do you not know that every one of you is an Eve?" (*Appar. Wom.* 1.11).

49. Note the difference between this author and Paul, who interpreted the same passage but laid the blame on Adam: "Therefore, just as sin came into the world through one man, and death came through sin, and so death spread to all because all have sinned" (Rom 5:12).

story, Thecla ultimately persevered, despite numerous threats to her virginity and her life. The Acts of Paul and Thecla represents only one of the many Christian works extolling celibacy that were produced from the second century on.[50]

While a celibate life was preferred by some and condemned by others in the century following Jesus's death, what was the thinking about those in the movement who were already married? Paul maintained Jesus's radical prohibition of divorce, at least for the most part. In 1 Corinthians, he appealed directly to Jesus's command: "To the married I give this command—not I but the Lord—that the wife should not separate from her husband (but if she does separate, let her remain unmarried or else be reconciled to her husband), and that the husband should not divorce his wife" (1 Cor 7:10–11).[51] Although Paul prohibited divorce, he nevertheless inserted some flexibility into that prohibition. He seemed to allow for a couple's separation as long as they did not remarry, as the parenthetical statement in the above quotation indicates. He also encouraged those married to pagans to preserve their marriages if possible, a topic that we will return to in chapter 8.

The author of Matthew's Gospel likewise upheld Jesus's ban on divorce, although he adjusted Jesus's saying to say: "But I say to you that anyone who divorces his wife, *except on the ground of unchastity,* causes her to commit adultery; and whoever marries a divorced woman commits adultery" (Matt 5:32; cf. Matt 19:9, emphasis added). Although Jesus's prohibition of divorce was retained in principle here, the addition of the phrase "except on the ground of unchastity" altered the original command significantly; it allowed a man whose wife had been unfaithful to divorce her. Note here that no provision was made for the woman whose husband had committed adultery. By making an exception to the prohibition of divorce for the man only, the author of Matthew's Gospel adapted Jesus's original command to reflect the dominant culture's values: women were expected to be faithful to their husbands but no such fidelity was expected of men. To the contrary, a married man's extramarital sexual relationships were, if not expected, at least tolerated by society.

---

50. The Acts of Thomas, for example, portrayed a sort of male equivalent to Thecla. In that work, the apostle Thomas was depicted preaching and performing miracles on his missionary journey to India. He converted many people both to Christianity and, just as importantly, to celibacy. Ultimately, the story depicted Thomas martyred by an angry king whose wife and relatives had converted to Christianity.

51. The fact that Paul referred here to Jesus's prohibition of divorce—which he called "the Lord's command"—is significant; this is one of the very few places where Paul appeals to the teachings of Jesus. Besides here, the only other references to Jesus's teaching appear in 1 Cor 9:14 and possibly 1 Thess 4:15–17.

Nevertheless, despite some moderation of Jesus's radical stance against divorce in the writings or Paul and Matthew, the movement continued to insist—in opposition to the common mores of Greco-Roman society—that marriage was permanent; divorce was to be avoided.

The Role of Women in the Movement Following the Death of Jesus

As mentioned earlier, the baptismal ritual probably arose not very long after Jesus's death, when Jesus followers ventured outside of Jewish territory and began preaching to non-Jews. Indeed, it likely appeared first in Antioch where, according to Acts, Jewish members of the movement began preaching to gentiles (Acts 11:19–21). The phrase from the baptismal ritual, "there is no longer male and female," suggests that women enjoyed the same status as men within the assemblies. But did they?

Unfortunately, our evidence is somewhat ambiguous. For example, according to an oft-quoted passage from 1 Corinthians, the expectation in the Corinthian community regarding women was the following: "Women should be silent in the assemblies. For they are not permitted to speak, but should be subordinate, as the law also says. If there is anything they desire to know, let them ask their husbands at home. For it is shameful for a woman to speak in church" (1 Cor 14:34–35). This hardly sounds like a community in which there was "no longer male and female." To the contrary, the command indicates quite vividly that women did not have equal standing with men within the Pauline assemblies.

However, there is a serious problem with this text; it appears to contradict something Paul had said previously in the same letter where, in a somewhat difficult passage, Paul addressed the issue of head coverings for men and women at worship.[52] At one point, Paul argued that "any woman who prays or prophesies with her head unveiled disgraces her head" (1 Cor 11:5). What is surprising about this—given what we have just seen in 1 Cor 14:34–35—is that Paul did not here condemn women for praying and prophesying in the assembly but for praying and prophesying in the assembly *with their heads unveiled*. In short, this passage indicates that Paul accepted the

---

52. This passage is particularly difficult because it is not exactly clear what Paul is talking about; his language is ambiguous and can be read several ways. Some scholars have argued that the discussion has to do with whether or not women should have worn veils in the assembly. But others have insisted that the passage had to do with hairstyles (i.e., women wearing their hair down rather than up).

practice of women speaking (i.e., praying and prophesying) during worship. What he objected to was their doing so *unveiled*. Because of the difficulty of reconciling these two passages, many scholars have concluded that the passage in which Paul exhorts women to be silent (14:34–35) represents an interpolation, a text added later by someone other than Paul. If this was the case (and it seems likely that it was) then we can conclude that women did actively participate in worship in Paul's assemblies. But, did they play any other roles in the early movement? Although our evidence is limited, we can draw some cautious conclusions.

One notable woman mentioned by Paul in another letter was a certain Phoebe from Cenchreae, the eastern port of the city of Corinth (Rom 16:1–2). In his letter to the Romans, Paul asked the Roman community to "welcome [Phoebe] in the Lord as is fitting for the saints, and help her in whatever she may require from you." The reason for Paul's recommendation, he claimed, was that Phoebe had been "a benefactor of many and of myself as well." Paul's label of "benefactor" (the term could also be translated "patron") suggests that Phoebe at some point financially supported Paul and others in the community. It is, however, also worth noting that Paul referred to Phoebe in the same passage as a *diakonos*, a term meaning something like "servant" or even "envoy." Remarkably, Paul sometimes described his own role with this word (1 Cor 3:5; 2 Cor 3:6). In connection with Phoebe then, the term *diakonos* probably indicated some kind of position of responsibility within the Cenchreaen community, perhaps some kind of leadership role. So it is likely that she not only funded the ministries of Paul and others, but that she also held a position of responsibility in the assembly at Cenchreae.

Another woman mentioned by Paul is a certain Chloe. Toward the beginning of 1 Corinthians, Paul wrote: "it has been reported to me by Chloe's people that there are quarrels among you, my brothers and sisters" (1:11). Unfortunately, this is all we hear about this woman. Nonetheless, from this statement, some tentative inferences can be made about her. First of all, Chloe was obviously the head of a household; this was a somewhat unusual position for a woman. Perhaps she was a widow. Or perhaps she was an unmarried freedperson (i.e., former slave).[53] Second, Chloe had "people." These people were probably her slaves or perhaps freedpersons who worked for her. The fact that they had traveled to Ephesus, the location from which Paul wrote 1 Corinthians (as 1 Cor 16:8 indicates), suggests that they had been sent there

---

53. We will look at the latter possibility in the next chapter.

for some reason, probably on some kind of business.[54] So it is likely that Chloe ran a business, although we have no indication of its type. Did she hold some kind of leadership role in the community as well, perhaps like that of Phoebe in Cenchreae? It is possible.

Another woman that we hear of, connected to Paul, surfaces not in Paul's letters but in Acts.[55] Her name was Lydia. Paul encountered her when he arrived at the city of Philippi, in Macedonia:

> On the Sabbath day we went outside the gate by the river, where we supposed there was a place of prayer; and we sat down and spoke to the women who had gathered there. A certain woman named Lydia, a worshiper of God, was listening to us; she was from the city of Thyatira and a dealer in purple cloth. The Lord opened her heart to listen eagerly to what was said by Paul. When she and her household were baptized, she urged us, saying, "If you have judged me to be faithful to the Lord, come and stay at my home." And she prevailed upon us. (Acts 16:13–15)

Here we see a female "worshiper of God" (i.e., a "Godfearer") who, like Chloe of Corinth, owned her own business; she sold cloth that had been dyed purple. She hailed originally from Thyatira, a medium-sized city in western Asia Minor. It is likely that her wares came from there as well. Like Chloe, Lydia herself was the head of her household, whose members probably included slaves.[56] Like Phoebe of Cenchreae, Lydia acted as a patron to the apostle. She put him up and fed him (and likely did the same for his companions).

Another woman mentioned in both Paul's letters and Acts is Prisca (referred to as Priscilla in Acts), whose husband was named Aquila (1 Cor 16:19; Rom 16:3–4; Acts 18:2–3, 18, 26). Like Chloe and Lydia, Prisca was a business-

---

54. It is also possible that Chloe lived in Ephesus (where Paul was at the time) and that her "people" had traveled to Corinth. They reported the Corinthian situation to Chloe upon their return to Ephesus and Chloe, in turn, relayed it to Paul. However, the fact that Paul mentions Chloe's name in 1 Corinthians indicates that the Corinthians knew her. That makes it more likely that she resided in Corinth rather than Ephesus.

55. Since we did not hear about Lydia in Paul's letters, it is possible that she was a fictional character, created by the author of Acts. But, even if that were the case, Acts's description of her merits attention; the people who read that work would have recognized a woman who probably resembled others that they had encountered in the movement.

56. Although the text does not mention it, she likely sent slaves to Asia periodically to procure the purple cloth.

woman. She, however, was married and both she and her husband worked at a trade; like Paul they were tentmakers. Prisca resembles Phoebe and Lydia somewhat because she (and her husband) acted as patrons for Paul; according to Acts 18, they sheltered him when he first arrived in Corinth and they also gave him a place to work. But, Prisca also played an active role in the movement by hosting the assembly at her and her husband's home (Rom 16:5). However, one might ask how active Prisca's role really was; perhaps she was simply assisting her husband. Nevertheless, the fact that her name is sometimes mentioned before that of her husband is suggestive. While some have proposed that her name sometimes received top billing because she possessed a higher status than that of her husband, it is also possible that she was mentioned first because she was a more effective missionary than Aquila. Regardless, it seems reasonable to assume her direct participation in the movement and in the assembly at her home.

Other women of note in the early years of the Jesus movement included a certain Mary, described by Paul as someone who "worked very hard" among the Jesus followers of Rome (Rom 16:6), and the woman Junia, mentioned earlier, who also "worked hard in the Lord" (Rom 16:7). Both of these women were probably influential leaders within the Roman assembly. Likewise mentioned in connection with the Roman assembly were Tryphaena and Tryphosa, possibly sisters, and Persis (Rom 16:12). Like Mary and Junia, they too labored "in the Lord." The fact that each of them was singled out by Paul in his letter suggests that they performed significant duties in the assembly.

Although Paul gives us very few names in connection with the Philippian church, he does mention two women, Euodia and Syntyche (Phil 4:2–3). They had, Paul averred, "struggled in the Gospel" with him. Although he also mentioned a certain Clement as well as other unnamed coworkers, the two women were mentioned first and their work was highlighted. This description suggests that they were the true leaders in the community. Perhaps they were among the earliest converts in that city; perhaps one of them hosted the assembly in her home.

Toward the end of the first century, we also encounter a prophetess in the Jesus movement who held considerable sway in the town of Thyatira (the city connected with Lydia in Asia Minor). Unfortunately, all the information that we have about this woman is polemical; it came from a rival male prophet, a certain John, the author of the book of Revelation.[57] We do not even know the

57. By the middle of the second century, the John of Revelation was identified with the

woman's name, for John disparagingly referred to her as "Jezebel," the name of an infamous Israelite queen from the ninth century BCE.[58] John accused this rival prophetess, "Jezebel," of leading astray the members of the assembly (Rev 2:20). If we look at the woman in Thyatira without John's polemical lenses, however, it seems likely that "Jezebel" was merely promoting a more liberal form of the Jesus movement than John. Regardless, she was a well-regarded prophetess in Thyatira (and perhaps elsewhere in western Asia Minor) toward the end of the first century. We will again look at her and the accusations that John made against her in chapter 8.

At around the same time that "Jezebel" was active in Thyatira, a letter we know as 2 John was written to a certain "elect lady and her children, those whom I love in truth." The author described himself only as "the elder."[59] Although it is clear that the "children" mentioned in the address points to the members of the assembly addressed by "the elder," it is not obvious to whom or to what the "elect lady" refers. Many scholars understand the "elect lady" to refer to the assembly itself.[60]

Alternatively, a few scholars have recommended that the "lady" points to an actual woman. The term that is translated "lady" is *kyria*. Although it can mean "lady" (along the lines of the woman-in-charge), it also functioned as a name in the Greco-Roman world.[61] Consequently, it is *possible* to translate the opening of 2 John as, "The elder to the elect [woman] Kyria and her children, whom I love in truth." Understood in this way, 2 John would then represent a letter written to an assembly headed by a woman, specifically, one named Kyria.[62] In that case, her "children" would be the members of the assembly. But, although some texts like the book of Revelation and possibly 2 John give

---

author of the fourth Gospel. Nevertheless, scholars are convinced that the two texts were written by different people.

58. The original Jezebel was a princess of Tyre who married Ahab, the king of Israel. Jezebel promoted the cult of Ba'al, a deity worshipped by the Tyrians. She and her husband are described in 1 Kgs 16–22 as some of the most wicked rulers in the history of Israel.

59. Besides the Gospel of John, there are three letters in the New Testament that are attributed to the same author. Although these letters almost certainly came from the same circle of Jesus followers as the Gospel, when they were written (before or after the Gospel) and by whom (the same author or a different author or authors) is disputed.

60. Such a metaphor is not unknown in the New Testament. Both 2 Cor 11:2 and Eph 5:22–23 describe the assembly as a woman, specifically as the bride of Christ.

61. The Aramaic name "Martha" and the Latin name "Domina" also mean "lady." Like Kyria, both refer to the woman-in-charge.

62. Ross Kraemer, *Her Share of the Blessings: Women's Religions among Pagans, Jews, and Christians in the Graeco-Roman World* (New York: Oxford University Press, 1992), 175–76.

evidence of women holding significant leadership roles in the Jesus movement at the end of the first century, two other texts from roughly the same time indicate that some women played quite a different, active role in the movement.

The author of 1 Timothy, a letter mentioned earlier, gave the following command: "If any believing woman has relatives who are really widows, let her assist them; let the assembly not be burdened, so that it can assist those who are real widows" (1 Tim 5:16). The meaning of this passage is puzzling. What did the author mean when he spoke about a "believing woman" assisting "those who are real widows"? The believing woman must have been a female member of the assembly who had money. Otherwise, she would have been incapable of assisting others. The fact that no husband is mentioned suggests that she would have been a single woman, likely a widow herself. This woman, the author instructed, should assist "real widows."

But what is the difference between a "widow" and a "real widow" in this author's eyes? There are two possible ways to understand "real widow." Since, elsewhere in the same letter, the author prohibited putting a widow on the "list" (presumably, a list of widows to be supported by the assembly) who was under sixty (5:9), perhaps the author considered only those widows above that age to be "real widows." Alternatively, perhaps some unmarried women who wished to remain single were calling themselves "widows," a status that the author did not acknowledge. Support for the latter interpretation comes from a letter of Ignatius of Antioch, written at about the same time. In that letter, Ignatius greets "the virgins who are called widows" (*To the Smyrnaens* 13.1). But, regardless of its precise meaning, this passage suggests that in some cases, women with resources (likely widows themselves) were expected to take in and care for other widows.[63]

But despite that expectation, it nevertheless seems that the author of 1 Timothy was still somewhat troubled by the active role that women, and especially widows, were playing in the assembly.[64] When speaking elsewhere of young widows, he described them as fickle: one day they want to be single, the next they want to marry. He further claimed that they were "idle, gadding

---

63. For other passages that suggest that widows cared for one another, see Ignatius, *Smyrn.* 13.1 and Herm. Vis. 2.4.3 (8.3). See also Margaret Y. MacDonald, "Was Celsus Right? The Role of Women in the Expansion of Early Christianity," in *Early Christian Families in Context: An Interdisciplinary Dialogue*, ed. David L. Balch and Carolyn Osiek (Grand Rapids: Eerdmans, 2003), 168–72.

64. Perhaps the author was willing to allow for such an active role in this case because it would relieve the rest of the assembly of a considerable financial burden. The assembly would presumably support widows over sixty if other women with means did not step up and do it instead.

about from house to house . . . [and] also gossips and busybodies, saying what they should not say" (5:11–13). As this author saw things, single women were weak-willed, idle, nosy, and indiscreet. The author's solution? They should "marry, bear children, and manage their households" (5:14). Elsewhere in the letter, the author's traditional view of women comes through loud and clear: "Let a woman learn in silence with full submission. I permit no woman to teach or to have authority over a man; she is to keep silent" (1 Tim 2:11–12).[65] The best a woman could do, according to this author, was to be a good mother: "she will be saved through childbearing" (1 Tim 2:15).[66]

We see a similar attitude toward women in 2 Timothy, another later work falsely attributed to Paul. According to that document, women presented a danger to the movement because of their inability to distinguish truth from falsehood. Consequently, they became easy prey for those promoting false teachings. Such false teachers "make their way into households and captivate silly women [who are] overwhelmed by their sins and swayed by all kinds of desires, who are always being instructed and can never arrive at a knowledge of the truth" (2 Tim 3:6–7). Here the author's label of them as "silly women" says it all: women, he believed, were incapable of serious thought and therefore gullible. They needed guidance so as not to be led astray.

In both 1 and 2 Timothy, we see the values of the dominant society beginning to take over within the Jesus movement. Women, according to these documents, should not play too active a role in the assembly.[67] They certainly should not lead assemblies. At this time, the gender roles of the dominant society are beginning to emerge in the assemblies; women were thought to be incapable of both independent thought and self-control. Consequently, the assemblies must be managed by men, particularly men who have demonstrated that they can control their wives and children: "For if [a man] does not know how to manage his own household, how can he take care of God's assembly?" (1 Tim 3:5).

---

65. Note the similarity of this passage to the likely interpolated passage in 1 Cor 14:34–35: "Women should be silent in the assemblies. For they are not permitted to speak, but should be subordinate, as the law also says. If there is anything they desire to know, let them ask their husbands at home. For it is shameful for a woman to speak in the assembly."

66. We can also see something like this in the book of Revelation. In that work, the author condemns "Jezebel" because she does not conform to the proper female stereotypes of the larger culture.

67. As noted earlier, however, the author seems not to have objected to women "deacons" (cf. 1 Tim 3:11) although we do not know what role these figures played in the assemblies at the time.

Although many, and possibly most, assemblies went the way of 1 and 2 Timothy in the second and third centuries, others still allowed women to play significant roles. Two women, Prisca (not the Prisca mentioned in Paul's letters and Acts) and Maximilla, were important figures in a second-century prophetic movement in Asia Minor (sometimes known as Montanism, after its founder, Montanus). Furthermore, among gnostics—various groups in the second and third centuries who focused on knowledge (*gnosis*) as the means to salvation—women also seem to have played an important role. Indeed, the *Gospel of Mary*, a Gospel produced by a gnostic assembly, featured Mary of Magdala as Jesus's only true disciple.[68]

Summary and Conclusion

Jesus himself emphasized the rejection of one's family of origin and its replacement with the metaphorical family of Jesus followers. Fathers, mothers, brothers, and sisters were no longer considered relatives; rather, whoever "[did] the will of God" became "brother and sister and mother" (Mark 3:35). Although families created by marriage were not to be dissolved (because of Jesus's prohibition of divorce), members of the movement were expected to cut other family ties. Insofar as we can tell, married followers of Jesus were encouraged to celibacy. They were to strive to be "eunuchs for the kingdom." Following Jesus's death, however, some things quickly changed; members of the family of Jesus, particularly his brother James, quickly rose to prominence in the movement; the importance of family and family connections in the early assemblies of Jesus followers in the Hellenistic cities could not be ignored. In response, Jesus's command to reject one's family was downplayed. On the other hand, Jesus's rejection of divorce continued to hold sway and the support for celibacy was also upheld, encouraged by concerns about marriage and celibacy within Greco-Roman culture.

Gender roles were also flattened out somewhat when the movement began. It was not only men who followed Jesus in his travels, women did as well, most notably Mary of Magdala. Following Jesus's death, women continued to play an active role in the movement. Although men seem to have dominated the leadership, women were not totally excluded. Unfortunately, our sources

---

68. Whether or not the assembly that produced the *Gospel of Mary* was actually gnostic is disputed. Nevertheless, it is fair to say that it was gnostic at least insofar as it believed salvation to come through knowledge.

tell us little about the important women in the assemblies. Sometimes, all we have is their names. Nevertheless, it is clear that figures like Lydia, Euodia, and Syntyche played an important part in the assembly at Philippi, as did Chloe and Prisca in Corinth, Phoebe in Cenchreae, and Junia, Tryphaena, Tryphosa, and Persis in Rome.[69] A number of well-to-do women (including Phoebe and Lydia) funded missionaries so they could spread the movement; well-off women also acted as benefactors for impoverished widows (and likely also orphans, 1 Tim 5:16). At the end of the first century, we know of a prominent prophetess in western Asia Minor ("Jezebel") and it is possible that a woman named Kyria led an assembly connected with the community that produced the Johannine letters. Although in the late first or early second century some assemblies began to pigeonhole women into more traditional roles (as wives and mothers), among other groups women continued to play key roles.

69. Prisca and her husband also seem to have played important roles in Rome (Rom 16:3) and Ephesus (1 Cor 16:19), the place from which Paul wrote that letter.

CHAPTER 6

No Longer Slave or Free

The Jesus movement began among the peasantry in Judea, people with minimal economic resources and very low status. Such peasants were often desperately poor, sometimes even starving while the fruits of their labor were carried away to feed city dwellers. In terms of status, a peasant was considered "an unmannerly, ignorant being, in bondage to sordid and wretched labor, and so uncivilized that he could not be called upon for the full duties of citizenship."[1] Such were the people Jesus featured in his parables: a farmer whose crops had failed three times out of four (Mark 4:3–9; Matt 13:3–9; Luke 8:4–15), a shepherd who had lost his prized sheep (Matt 18:12–14; Luke 15:4–7; Gos. Thom. 107), and a farmer whose fruit tree no longer produced (Luke 13:6–9).

Nevertheless, according to the preaching of Jesus, these poor, hungry, unhappy, and generally despised peasants were to be heirs of the kingdom, as were other outcasts like tax collectors and prostitutes. The normal social distinctions that dominated Greco-Roman society, Jesus promised, would be upended: "You know that among the Gentiles those whom they recognize as their rulers lord it over them, and their great ones are tyrants over them. But it is not so among you; but whoever wishes to become great among you must be your servant, and whoever wishes to be first among you must be slave of all" (Mark 10:42–44).

But, as we have seen, the movement that began in the rural area of the Galilee did not remain there for long. It soon moved into the city of Jerusalem. From there it spread to non-Jewish territory, and eventually it found a home in the cities of the empire, a domain where—as described by Jesus—rulers

---

1. Ramsay MacMullen, *Roman Social Relations: 50 B.C. to A.D. 280* (New Haven: Yale University Press, 1974), 32.

lorded it over the people, and the great ones were tyrants over them. In the urban assemblies established in the large, pagan cities, did Jesus's vision of an overturned economic and social structure endure? In this chapter, we will try to answer that question. We will examine what we know about the assemblies of early Jesus followers in the context of the larger urban society.

Being Free in Society and in the Assembly

The title of this chapter, "No Longer Slave or Free," describes the most basic social division in Greco-Roman society. A bright line ran between these two categories that those in the inferior one could never cross. Even if freed by their masters, slaves could never attain the status of the free inhabitants of the empire. Rather, until their deaths, they would remain freedpersons, living a liminal existence suspended somewhere between that of the free and the enslaved.

Although being counted as one of the free inhabitants of the empire may have seemed ideal to a slave or a freedperson, life was not easy for most of those who were free. While some were very well off, most were not. Just as with the entire populace, the free population of the empire could be divided into two, those typically labeled the "honorable" (the *honestiores*) and those called the "humble" (*humiliores*). Obviously, the labels were created by those in the former group. Those who comprised the "honorable" group constituted a very small fraction of the empire's population; it consisted of what might be called that society's gentry or aristocracy. Of course, as we might expect, the "honorable" were wealthy, often very wealthy. They were also wellborn.[2]

The aristocrats or the "honorable" members of society (*honestiores*) consisted of three distinct group: senators, equestrians, and decurions. During the time of the Roman Republic (up until 27 BCE), these groups, with the senators at the top of the pyramid, ruled Rome and her conquered territories. But following the demise of the republic, they were superseded by the emperor, the members of the imperial household and the emperor's administrative staff in

---

2. In Greco-Roman society, status was tied not only to one's lineage but also to one's wealth. As in today's world, wealth was important and the state of one's finances to some extent dictated where one stood on the social ladder. However, if one were not wellborn, no amount of money would allow one into the top tiers of society. Unlike us, the Romans did not admire the self-made individual who rose from rags to riches by the sweat of his or her brow. Such an individual would be forever shut out of the upper social ranks. Money raised one's status but alone, it could only get one so far.

Rome.[3] Senators stood, status-wise, just beneath the emperor, his family, and his staff. Beneath them came the equestrians, followed by the decurions. These three groups were legally defined, established by the state.

The most exclusive group of the three was that of the senators, the smallest of the three populations. In total, there were only about 600 senators in the empire. The exclusivity of this group can be demonstrated by comparing it to the larger empire's population. During the reign of Augustus (27 BCE–14 CE) the empire's population approached 60 million. The senators therefore represented no more than a tiny fraction of the empire's overall population. It was an exclusive club indeed. Senators advised the emperor, commanded the empire's armies, and administered its provinces. They were incredibly wealthy; in fact, there was a minimum amount of money required to be a senator.[4] Senators would be comparable to the billionaires of our time. But wealth was not all that was required to be a senator; one also needed a spotless pedigree. These were the bluebloods of Roman society.

Equestrians also had to be wealthy but not nearly as wealthy as senators. If senators were comparable to billionaires today, equestrians would be analogous to our multimillionaires. Of course equestrians, like senators, had to be of reputable birth. They did not, however, have to possess the impeccable pedigree of those in the senatorial class. While there were many more equestrians than senators, this group was still small, comparatively speaking; it made up less than one tenth of a percent of the empire.

The next group, the decurions, represented the local aristocracy of the various cities and towns of the empire; decurions made up the councils that ran the different municipalities. Although there were requirements for these individuals, they were somewhat flexible, depending on local circumstances.[5] However, regardless of wealth, freedpersons (those who had previously been enslaved) could not serve and neither could those whose wealth had come from some kinds of unsuitable employment (such as collecting taxes).

Although some in the lowest ranks of the *honestiores* worked for a living, for the most part, those in this category did not. This group of people typically despised labor. Even laborers with a significant amount of wealth could not

---

3. The Roman Republic came to an end when the Senate ceded extraordinary powers to Octavian (Julius Caesar's nephew and adopted son), following Caesar's assassination in 44 BCE and the subsequent civil wars. Although Octavian, henceforth titled Augustus, kept the outward forms of the republic, in reality he held absolute power.

4. At the time of Augustus, a senator had to be worth at least one million sesterces.

5. Some smaller cities may not have had enough of the "leisure class" to fill their needs for decurions. In such cases, these cities would look for wealthy laborers.

escape the stigma attached to work. The orator Cicero stated this prejudice well: "all workers are engaged in sordid professions" *(On Duties* 1.42). The respectable way to make money for those in the upper classes was to invest in land. Pliny the Younger, for example, who was enormously wealthy, worth many times the amount needed for admission to the Roman Senate, made virtually all of it from his land holdings.

The aristocrats of the empire were not only wealthy, they also had special privileges, which they carefully protected. They were entitled to wear symbols marking their status; they received a greater portion of publically distributed food (at festivals, for example); and they laid claim to the best seats in theaters and stadiums. Furthermore, they were favored by the law. They could not be sued by their inferiors; they were tried by separate courts; and they almost always received lighter sentences for their crimes than would someone from among the *humiliores*.

In its early years, we know of no members of the Jesus movement that came from among this group of aristocrats. Even by the end of the first century, when there was some rise in economic and social status within the movement, it is unlikely that any *honestiores* entered the assemblies of Jesus followers. The senator T. Flavius Clemens and his wife Domitilla were accused of atheism and subsequently executed by the emperor Domitian toward the end of the first century. As a result of that charge, it has sometimes been claimed that they were members of the Jesus movement. But it is much more plausible that the "atheism" with which they were charged was really Judaism.[6] It was probably not until the late second or early third centuries that Christians began to penetrate the ranks of the empire's gentry.

The majority of the free population of the empire consisted of the *humiliores*. They were despised by the aristocrats for a number of reasons, some of them seemingly irreconcilable. First and foremost, they were uncultured. The *humiliores* worked for a living and, as we have already noted, labor was considered demeaning by the aristocracy; only the coarse and uncultured would engage in such. Second, the *humiliores* were also loathed (surprisingly enough) because they did not work hard enough; they were considered lazy. Third, they were thought to be, on the whole, dishonest. But these are clearly stereotypes. They tell us little about the people described as *humiliores* themselves. Consequently, we need to ask: what were these people really like? What did those who made up this class do for a living and how did they fare?

---

6. Both Jews and Jesus followers/Christians were typically considered atheists because they did not believe in the traditional gods.

In the large cities of the empire (like Antioch, Ephesus, or Corinth), one could expect to find a huge and varied workforce. Inscriptions from Asia Minor give evidence of clubs or associations composed of laborers who worked with fabric (e.g., hemp, linen, wool) or leather; prepared food (e.g., bakers, farmers, fishmongers, wine tasters); or manufactured objects (e.g., potters, coppersmiths, silversmiths, goldsmiths). We also have inscriptions from associations of builders, bankers, doctors, or merchants as well as various kinds of entertainers (e.g., acrobats, actors, athletes, gladiators, and musicians).[7]

In contrast to our society, where there is a large and comfortable "middle class," most *humiliores* were, by our standards, impoverished. The great majority of them would have lived at or close to subsistence level. Some of course fell below subsistence level; for them life was both bleak and short. Continually weakened by hunger, they were more prone to disease and much more likely to suffer an early death. Nevertheless, with hard work, frugality, and time, some *humiliores* could manage not only to make ends meet but to also put aside a bit of money. With a bit of luck, a hardworking merchant, craftsman, or shop owner could provide an adequate supply of food for his or her family. Such an individual might even purchase a place to live.

A series of first-century papyri tell of a certain Trypho, a weaver in the Egyptian town of Oxyrhynchus who, after many years of work and saving, was able to put aside enough money to buy a loom, possibly for himself (assuming he had leased one previously) or possibly for his son Apion (assuming that Trypho already owned his own loom). If the loom was purchased for his son, it would be used to supplement the family income. Eventually, Trypho was able to purchase half a house for his family, likely with the help of the money brought in by his wife Saraeus (P.Oxy. 1.99 and P.Oxy. 2.264).

A shopkeeper or craftsperson like Trypho, successful enough to acquire a place to live, could make dual use of the house. Part of it could be used for business and the rest of it for housing his family. Someone like Trypho could weave and meet customers in one part of his house while the rest of the home would serve as living quarters. A number of such dual-use homes have been excavated in Pompeii and Herculaneum (near present-day Naples, Italy). There shops are connected directly to living areas.[8] Some of the shops excavated were

---

7. A more comprehensive list can be found in Philip A. Harland, *Associations, Synagogues, and Congregations: Claiming a Place in Mediterranean Society* (Minneapolis: Fortress, 2003), 40–41.

8. Nearly half of the houses excavated in Pompeii and Herculaneum were connected to living space.

quite small, about one hundred square meters. Others were quite a bit larger, up to seven hundred square meters.[9]

Alternatively, the whole space could be used for business during the day and converted to living space at night. Some of the smaller shops excavated in Pompeii and Herculaneum probably functioned in this way. During the day, someone like Trypho could both weave in the room and display the products of his labor there (and possibly the products of other craftspersons who had less space). Although someone like Trypho would normally weave throughout the day, he could pause if a prospective customer came in to order something or to browse the other products. At the end of the workday, the woven products could be put away, the loom moved aside, and the entire space converted to living space for him and his family.

Although we cannot be certain of the amount of money earned or the level of status of members of the early Jesus movement, we can be certain that most were of the laboring class (i.e., the *humiliores*). One piece of evidence regarding their status appears in one of Paul's letters to the Corinthians. There he said to the members of that community: "Consider your own call, brothers and sisters: not many of you were wise by human standards, not many were powerful, not many were of noble birth. But God chose what is foolish in the world to shame the wise; God chose what is weak in the world to shame the strong; God chose what is low and despised in the world, things that are not, to reduce to nothing things that are, so that no one might boast in the presence of God" (1 Cor 1:26–29).

A good indicator of the wealth of most in the community appears elsewhere in the same letter, where Paul gave instructions to the Corinthians regarding their participation in a collection of money destined for the poor in the Jerusalem assembly: "On the first day of every week, each of you is to put aside and save whatever extra you earn, so that collections need not be taken when I come. And when I arrive, I will send any whom you approve with letters to take your gift to Jerusalem" (1 Cor 16:2–3). These instructions indicate that spare money would be meager among most in the community; clearly, many were just scraping by. Consequently, a one-time collection would likely have yielded very little. Paul therefore advised the members of the community to put aside a little money every week; when he arrived to gather the money, the funds for the collection would then be sufficient.

In another letter, Paul encouraged his readers "to aspire to live quietly,

9. Carolyn Osiek and David L. Balch, *Families in the New Testament World: Households and House Churches* (Louisville: Westminster John Knox, 1997), 14–17.

to mind your own affairs, and to work with your hands, as we directed you" (1 Thess 4:11). The fact that he encouraged them to work with their hands tells us that those in the community (or at least most of them) were artisans like Paul himself. Although, as we have already seen, such labor would have been despised by the aristocracy, Paul obviously thought that manual labor was appropriate for those in his communities. Even a century later, things had apparently not changed much for most; the Greek philosopher Celsus could still characterize members of the movement as "wool-workers, cobblers, laundry-workers, and the most illiterate and bucolic yokels" (Origen, *Against Celsus* 3.55).[10] While Celsus's remarks were meant sarcastically, there must have been some truth to them or his mockery would have been in vain.

Is there anything else that we can learn about the economic level of the early Jesus followers? We can cautiously derive some additional information from the New Testament. We can note, for instance, a few individuals in the New Testament who seem to have either owned their own homes or at least had some space to spare in rented quarters. Paul tells us of a certain Gaius who hosted him (i.e., put him up) while he labored in Corinth, presumably for a significant amount of time (Rom 16:23). Paul also mentions that Gaius had been host to the "whole assembly" in Corinth, presumably when they assembled for their ritual meal, the "Lord's Supper." The "whole assembly" probably refers to a gathering of a number of smaller house communities. The smaller units would have met together regularly, perhaps weekly, and then periodically (perhaps monthly?) the smaller assemblies would have gathered together for worship.[11] If we assume that the total number of Jesus followers in Corinth numbered somewhere around fifty or sixty, then Gaius's place must have been relatively spacious. Indeed, it had previously been proposed that Gaius owned a villa that he used to host the assembly. This, however, seems unlikely. Of course, it is possible that the "whole assembly" did not meet in Gaius's home but rather in a different space, perhaps the workspace where Gaius made his living.[12] But regardless of

10. The translation is by Henry Chadwick, *Origen: Contra Celsum; Translated with an Introduction & Notes* (Cambridge: Cambridge University Press, 1980).

11. We have no direct information about these household assemblies. However, it has been suggested that there may have been assemblies in Corinth attached to the following individuals: Prisca and Aquila (1 Cor 16:19), Titius Justus (Acts 18:7), Stephanas (1 Cor 1:16), Crispus (1 Cor 1:14), Chloe (1 Cor 1:11), and Phoebe at Cenchreae (Rom 16:1–2).

12. The issue of meeting space for assemblies in the first century CE is a complicated one. Unfortunately, we have very little to go on. It is possible that a fairly large assembly (like the one in Corinth) might have met in a warehouse, an insula (what we would call an apartment house), or even in rented space.

where the assembly met, Gaius had enough income to own (or perhaps rent) a home at least large enough to put up Paul (and perhaps coworkers like Timothy).

From Acts, we hear a somewhat different story of Paul's lodgings in Corinth. According to that work, when the apostle arrived in Corinth, he encountered Prisca and Aquila, a couple mentioned in the previous chapter: "[In Corinth, Paul] found a Jew named Aquila, a native of Pontus, who had recently come from Italy with his wife [Prisca], because Claudius had ordered all Jews to leave Rome. Paul went to see them and, because he was of the same trade, he stayed with them, and they worked together—by trade they were tentmakers" (18:2–3).[13] This passage indicates that Aquila and Prisca not only put Paul up, they allowed him to work with them. It is possible and perhaps even likely that Aquila and Prisca had a dual-use house like those mentioned above. Aquila, Prisca, and Paul possibly worked in the shop/house during the day and slept in the same space at night.[14] It is important to note that the Acts story and Paul's statement about Gaius as his host are not necessarily in conflict with one another. Perhaps Paul began his stay in Corinth in Prisca and Aquila's dual-use house and then later moved elsewhere. Indeed, since Paul seems to have spent a lot of time in Corinth, such a scenario is probable. Various people likely shared the burden of housing the apostle. Others who seem to have possessed some disposable income in Paul's communities would have included Chloe (mentioned in the previous chapter), Philemon in whose home Paul also stayed (Phlm 22), and Phoebe, the *diakonos* from Cenchreae (also referred to in the previous chapter). But these individuals seem to have been exceptions in the early Jesus movement.[15]

13. The Acts account refers to Prisca as Priscilla, a diminutive of Prisca. For the sake of clarity, I have substituted Prisca for Priscilla in the quotation.

14. Since workers of the same trade typically clustered together either on the same street or at least in the same area of the city, it seems more likely that the couple would live where they worked rather than work in one place and live elsewhere or work from their home isolated from others of the same trade.

15. In somewhat later times, however, more people with wealth entered the movement. For example, the author of 1 Timothy, writing a half century or more after Paul, urged the women in his community to "dress themselves modestly and decently in suitable clothing, not with their hair braided, or with gold, pearls, or expensive clothes" (1 Tim 2:9; cf. 1 Pet 3:3). Elsewhere, he told "Timothy" (the alleged recipient of the letter): "As for those who in the present age are rich, command them not to be haughty, or to set their hopes on the uncertainty of riches, but rather on God who richly provides us with everything for our enjoyment" (6:17). These commands would have made little sense in a community that held less than a significant number of relatively well-off people. We also see evidence of some wealth in the book of Revelation. There the risen Jesus condemns the people of the Laodicea assembly:

But even those individuals who were well off, at least relatively speaking, would hardly have been wealthy by our standards. Someone like Gaius would have had enough surplus income to render himself and his family relatively secure. But others, including Prisca and Aquila, probably lived just a little bit above subsistence level. Despite long hours and hard work as artisans, day laborers, merchants, or small shop owners, probably most people in the assemblies barely made ends meet. Even Paul himself must have lived at or barely above subsistence level.

A work of the second-century satirist, Lucian of Samosata, can shed some light on Paul's life as an artisan. In a work known as *The Downward Journey*, or *the Tyrant*, Lucian depicts a shoemaker named Micyllus as cold, perpetually hungry, shoddily clad and, in the end, eager for death (15, 20). Since, as Acts tells us, Paul was a tentmaker (Acts 18:1–3), he was, like Micyllus, probably a leatherworker. He was, therefore, probably also hard-pressed like Micyllus. Paul was probably not exaggerating when he described his intense "labor and toil," or when he claimed to have worked night and day (1 Thess 2:9) to support himself. In other places, where he portrays himself as "hungry and thirsty," "cold," "inadequately clothed" (1 Cor 4:11; 2 Cor 11:27), and going without sleep (2 Cor 6:5; 11:27), he is probably describing his life as a subsistence-level artisan as much as that of a missionary for the Jesus movement.[16]

Up until this point, we have focused primarily on money, not status. What would the status of the artisans, merchants, or small shop owners in the movement have been? We have already seen that the aristocracy despised the working folk; from the point of view of the former, all labor was demeaning and

---

"For you say, 'I am rich, I have prospered, and I need nothing.' You do not realize that you are wretched, pitiable, poor, blind, and naked" (3:17). Finally, there also seems to have been some wealth in the community that produced the Gospel of Matthew for in that work, Jesus's radical sayings about wealth are toned down, likely to make them more palatable to people with some money. First, the beatitude that originally blessed the (literal) poor (cf. Luke 6:20) becomes in Matthew's Gospel a blessing on those who are not necessarily destitute: "Blessed are the poor in spirit" (Matt 5:3). In that same Gospel, the famous saying that it is easier for a camel to go through the eye of a needle than a rich person to enter the kingdom is concluded with the following dialogue between the disciples and Jesus: "When the disciples heard this, they were greatly astounded and said, 'Then who can be saved?' But Jesus looked at them and said, 'For mortals it is impossible, but for God all things are possible'" (Matt 19:25–26). The disciples' astonishment and Jesus's final response to their question let those in Matthew's community with money off the hook: despite their wealth, their salvation could nevertheless be brought about by God.

16. See Ronald F. Hock, *The Social Context of Paul's Ministry: Tentmaking and Apostleship* (Minneapolis: Fortress, 1980), 26–49.

all workers contemptible. But the workers themselves would have seen things differently. They would have perceived differences in status among the laboring class. Some professions were considered more respectable than others.

It seems that those occupations requiring more intelligence were respected much more than professions that relied just on backbreaking physical labor. So among the working class, physicians, teachers, architects, and the like would rank higher in status than others. On the other hand, artisans and day laborers, those who relied more on brawn than brain, would rank lower. At approximately the same level as artisans and common laborers would be merchants and shop owners. Their status was lower because they were generally considered untrustworthy; they were suspected of both chicanery and dishonesty in their business dealings. Tanners and those who cleaned clothing would have had an even lower status because of the conditions under which they labored; tanning leather produced foul odors and the process for cleaning clothes involved both urine and burnt sulphur.

Where would the members of the early Jesus movement fit into the pecking order? With few exceptions (e.g., Lydia, Aquila, and Prisca), we do not know how the Jesus followers in Paul's assemblies earned their living. But those who had some wealth seem to have claimed a certain status. Paul's references to Stephanas, for example, suggest that he was well respected in the community. Was that because he possessed some wealth or was it because he was Paul's first convert? It is hard to say. It is likely that Gaius was well respected as well. His standing in the community may have been based solely on his wealth (meager though it may have been by our standards). But we cannot know for sure.

Most of the rest of the people in Paul's communities were probably from fairly low-status professions: artisans, shopkeepers, day laborers, and the like. There seems to be some evidence of a few Jesus followers of a somewhat higher status in Corinth besides those individuals already mentioned. We have no specific information about them and it is unlikely that they can be identified with any of the names that Paul has given us. But we can be relatively sure of their existence because of their attacks on Paul. For these people, Paul's profession as an artisan may have been an issue. One scholar, comparing Paul the leatherworker to Lucian's shoemaker Micyllus (mentioned above), has made the following suggestion: "[In] the social world of a city like Corinth, Paul would have been a weak figure, without power, prestige, and privilege. We recall the shoemaker Micyllus, depicted by Lucian as penniless and powerless—poor, hungry, wearing an unsightly cloak, granted no status and victimized. . . . To Corinthians who, relative to Paul, appeared to be rich, wise, and respected . . . their lowly apostle had seemed to have enslaved himself with his plying a trade."[17]

But, it was not just Paul's status as a seemingly unrefined artisan that bothered these snobbish people in Corinth. His overall physical presentation also troubled them. As his letters indicate, he was of humble appearance and not particularly well-spoken (2 Cor 10:10). Although he clearly had an education and some religious expertise, he may not have come across as a particularly cultured person. With his relatively low-status job, his poor appearance, and "contemptible" speech, Paul seemed despicable to some in the community.

But even though Paul and many others in the community were of fairly low economic and social status, there were also those in the community who were worse off. In terms of status, there were slaves and freedpersons, both of which we will look at shortly. Economically, there also were some who were likely in constant crisis; these would have included widows and their children. Although in our time many societies provide a safety net for such people, such was not the case in the ancient world. Widows in particular, as well as their offspring, were extremely vulnerable.

Lucian of Samosata, from whom we have already heard several times, told of the plight of one such woman. She had originally been the wife of a smith; he had been able to provide a decent living for the family. But following his untimely death, his wife had difficulty caring for herself and her daughter. She sold her husband's tools and with the money she received from that sale, she and her daughter were able to support themselves for half a year. After that she tried spinning and weaving. Unfortunately, she was unable to make enough to sustain the two of them in that way. As a result, she was forced to set her daughter up as a prostitute (*Dial. Court.* 6.293–95). As Lucian's narrative indicates, some widows, especially widows of laborers who had previously been scraping by, could have easily starved to death.

But it seems that, in the assemblies of Jesus followers, impoverished widows and other vulnerable people (such as orphans) were—at least in some cases—supported by the other members of the assembly. Various texts indicate that this was expected of them. The New Testament letter of James, for instance, asserted that one of the two measures of "pure and undefiled religion" was "to care for orphans and widows in their distress" (1:27). Likewise, the early-second-century documents, the Shepherd of Hermas (Herm. Sim. 1.8 [50.8]; Herm. Mand. 8.10 [38.8]) and a letter of Ignatius to Polycarp (4.1) both insisted that their readers take care of the widows in their communities.

17. Hock, *Social Context*, 60.

Sometimes, as in the case of 1 Timothy, widows with financial means were themselves encouraged to care for other widows, likely to relieve the other members of the assembly of the financial burden.

Besides caring for widows (and orphans), other texts enjoined Jesus followers to care for anyone in their assembly who was in distress. Jesus, in the Gospel of Matthew, speaking of the day of judgment, told his followers:

> Then the king will say to those at his right hand, "Come, you that are blessed by my Father, inherit the kingdom prepared for you from the foundation of the world; for I was hungry and you gave me food, I was thirsty and you gave me something to drink, I was a stranger and you welcomed me, I was naked and you gave me clothing, I was sick and you took care of me, I was in prison and you visited me." Then the righteous will answer him, "Lord, when was it that we saw you hungry and gave you food, or thirsty and gave you something to drink? And when was it that we saw you a stranger and welcomed you, or naked and gave you clothing? And when was it that we saw you sick or in prison and visited you?" And the king will answer them, "Truly I tell you, just as you did it to one of the least of these who are members of my family, you did it to me." (Matt 25:34–40)

As these different texts all demonstrate, those in the assemblies were expected to provide some kind of safety net for the most destitute of the free Jesus followers.[18]

Slaves in Ancient Society and in the Assemblies

Slaves and freedpersons also belonged to the assemblies of the Jesus movement. What would their lives have been like? When we think of slaves today, we typically imagine slaves of the antebellum American South: impoverished, overworked people of African descent who worked the plantations of their masters. While it would certainly be inaccurate to say that *no* comparisons could be drawn between the phenomena of American slavery and slavery in the Greco-Roman world, it is fair to say that the latter was significantly more diverse.

---

18. See also Matt 10:42; Luke 3:11; 6:38. The letter of James, already mentioned, asked the question: "If a brother or sister is naked and lacks daily food, and one of you says to them, 'Go in peace; keep warm and eat your fill,' and yet you do not supply their bodily needs, what is the good of that?" (Jas 2:15–16; cf. 1 John 3:17). Some texts even enjoined Jesus followers to care for outsiders, e.g., Matt 5:42; Luke 10:25–37.

To begin with, in America, only one group of people was enslaved: Africans and their descendants. In the Greco-Roman world, to the contrary, slaves came from many different places. Furthermore, in antebellum America, slaves were uneducated and often prohibited by law from learning to read or write. But in the Greco-Roman world, many slaves were educated; some received their education prior to their enslavement, but others while slaves. Another contrast concerns the kind of labor that slaves performed. In the American South, the vast majority of slaves were either agricultural or domestic workers. In the Greco-Roman world, slave occupations were much more varied.

Describing slavery in the ancient world is particularly difficult. Other than its ubiquity, there are few unequivocal claims that can be made about the phenomenon. Ancient slaves worked in the fields and as domestics as they did in the American South. But they also worked as artisans: bakers, potters, weavers, linen workers, wool workers, seamstresses, metal workers, and cobblers. Sometimes they labored in small shops alongside their masters; at other times, they worked in larger factories. But slaves held other occupations as well. Some worked as entertainers: as prostitutes, musicians, and painters. Others were physicians. The book of Acts even tells of a very profitable slave girl who had the gift of prophecy. Interestingly enough, she was owned by a consortium of businessmen (Acts 16:16). Like this young girl who had no single master, other slaves were also owned by communities, employed as constables, garbage collectors, or workers who kept the roads in good repair.

Perhaps the best way to talk about ancient slavery is to divide slaves into two different types by occupation. The first type could be called the common slave. This type encompassed a wide variety of slave occupations; it would include virtually all of the slaves in the occupations mentioned above. The second type included slaves in administrative positions; these could be labeled managerial slaves. These slaves would administer businesses, agricultural estates, or oversee large households. They were often well-educated or at least schooled in a particular task (such as accounting). Because of their education, managerial slaves could easily carve out a career if freed.

A discrete class of slaves within the managerial category were the imperial slaves, the property of the emperor himself. It was by means of the thousands of such slaves spread across the Mediterranean that the emperor managed his domain. In effect, they functioned as the empire's civil service. They differed from other managerial slaves by degree rather than kind. They wielded considerable power, sometimes even over free people. They could even own their own slaves; a first-century-CE inscription tells of an imperial slave who owned more than fifteen slaves (*ILS* 1514). Imperial slaves typically lived better lives than most slaves (and even better than many free people). They also possessed a higher status than most slaves. Once freed, imperial slaves had the knowledge and the connection to prosper economically. Many of them even married freeborn wives.

But with the possible exception of some imperial slaves, the life of an enslaved person was hardly enviable. Slaves had no control over their fate. Legally, they could not own property (although some did); they could not officially marry. Even if a slave were to enter into an unofficial marriage with another slave, either partner could be sold at the master's whim. Furthermore, female domestic slaves were frequently the sexual victims of their masters. But a young slave woman not only had to endure routine sexual assaults by her male master, she also had to put up with the jealous anger of the master's wife.

Although ancient slavery was widespread, it is difficult to know with any precision the number of slaves that occupied the empire. The physician Galen (second century CE) claimed that in his native city of Pergamum, there was one slave for every free person. This may be an exaggeration but, if not, it could mean as many as forty thousand slaves in that city. On the other hand, a modern scholar has estimated that at the end of the first century BCE (i.e., roughly at the time of Jesus's birth), 35 percent of the population of Italy was enslaved.[19] Regardless, although we cannot be sure of exact numbers, a rough estimate of the slave population in the first century would put it at approximately one-third of the total population of the empire, somewhere between fifteen and twenty million people.

Where did all these slaves come from? Originally, most were captives taken in war. Josephus, for example, tells us that during the Jewish revolt against Rome (66–73 CE), ninety-seven thousand prisoners were taken (*Jewish War* 6.420). Most of these were sold as slaves. Prisoners of war were not necessarily soldiers; any member of the general population who had survived an attack would typically be killed or sold into slavery. The incessant warfare of the first century BCE provided the Romans with a seemingly endless supply of slaves. Of course, things changed with the *Pax Romana,* the long period of peace that began under the rule of the emperor Augustus. With few exceptions (like the Jewish revolt mentioned above), the supply of slaves captured in war came to an end. From that point on, the slave population came to consist primarily of the children of slaves or children who had been abandoned by their birth parents.[20]

19. Keith Hopkins, *Conquerors and Slaves,* SSRH (Cambridge: Cambridge University Press, 1981), 9.
20. By law, foundlings could be raised as slaves. Unwanted children were regularly "ex-

What do we know about the presence of slaves in the Jesus movement? In Paul's letter to an individual named Philemon, we learn the name of one of the slaves in the Jesus movement. In that letter, Paul encouraged Philemon to accept Onesimus, his wayward slave (whom Paul had since converted), back into his household without punishing him, indeed, in a kindly manner (16).[21] But Onesimus would not have been the only slave in the early assemblies. As mentioned above, Chloe's "people"—i.e., those who delivered the news to Paul that the Corinthian community had become factionalized—were likely slaves.[22] We also know of imperial slaves in the Philippian community (Paul mentioned people "from the household of Caesar," Phil 4:22) who were presumably converted by him.[23] Unfortunately, we do not know how many of these imperial slaves were in the Philippian assembly, nor do we know what their duties were. They may have only been domestic slaves (who worked in the imperial offices); alternatively, they may have been important bureaucrats.[24]

Although we do not have other names of slaves in the assemblies, we can infer their presence. As we saw above, in 1 Corinthians, Paul indicated that he had baptized the household of Stephanas (1 Cor 1:16). This would have included Stephanas's slaves. Although Paul himself tells us of no other entire households converted by him or anyone else, Acts presents a number of such cases. As we have already seen, Acts tells us that Paul baptized Lydia and her whole household at Philippi (Acts 16:14–15); he also baptized his jailer and the latter's household in the same city (Acts 16:27–34). Finally, Acts tells of Paul baptizing the entire household of Crispus in Corinth (Acts 18:8). Even if we acknowledge that Acts is not necessarily historically accurate in all of these instances, the fact that the work mentions so many instances of whole households being baptized with the head of the family indicates that such a

---

posed" to either die or be picked up by another. A first-century-BCE papyrus letter from a certain Hilarion to his pregnant wife instructs her to "throw out" (i.e., expose) their child if it is a girl (P.Oxy. 744).

21. Although it is often assumed that Onesimus was a runaway slave who sought out Paul, there is no real evidence for this. It is more likely that Onesimus had done something to offend his master, Philemon, and sought out Paul to intercede on his behalf (knowing that Paul was respected by Philemon).

22. In 1 Corinthians, Paul also gives advice to slaves (7:21), although this may be merely rhetorical.

23. It is also possible that these were imperial freedmen rather than imperial slaves.

24. We are not even sure of the location of these slaves because we do not know where Paul was when he wrote Philippians. The possibilities are Caesarea, Ephesus, or (most likely) Rome.

practice would not have been unusual.[25] One can only wonder how the slaves of such households felt about their conversions.

The presence of slaves in the movement (willingly or not) raises some interesting questions. Consider, for example, Paul's teaching regarding sexual behavior in Corinth. In chapter 7 of 1 Corinthians, he counseled marriage or celibacy for those like himself who had the God-given *charisma* for it (1 Cor 7:7–9). But what could a community like Corinth do about slaves who had no control over their sexual activity, particularly slaves of non-believing masters?[26] Either the community had to, according to one scholar, "[exclude] slaves whose sexual behavior could not conform to the norms mandated . . . or [tolerate] the membership of some who did not confine their sexual activities to marriage. The first possibility challenges the [common] assumption that slavery did not jeopardize the standing of individuals in the . . . assembly; the second possibility suggests that Pauline communities viewed some sexual activities as morally neutral."[27] Although we cannot say for sure, it seems more likely that the assemblies opted for the latter possibility.

A particularly interesting inscription of a pagan cultic association from the city of Philadelphia in Asia Minor may help shed some light on this issue in the assemblies, that is, the sexual abuse of female slaves. The Philadelphia inscription dates from the second or first century BCE and is relevant because this particular association, like the assemblies of Jesus followers, welcomed "men and women, free people and household slaves."[28] Like the assemblies of Jesus followers, the cultic association also expected moral behavior of its members. Among other prohibitions, the Philadelphia inscription required the following: "Beyond his own wife, a man is not to seduce someone else's wife, whether free or slave, nor a boy, nor a virgin girl. . . . A free woman is to be pure and not know the bed of another man, nor have intercourse with anyone except her own husband" (lines 26–27, 35–36).[29] On the surface, the

---

25. It is noteworthy that Paul did not baptize the entire household of Philemon for, as we have already seen, Paul himself tells us that he later converted Onesimus, Philemon's slave (15–16).

26. Presumably, the community could pressure *believing* masters to refrain from subjecting their slaves to their sexual whims.

27. Jennifer A. Glancy, *Slavery in Early Christianity* (Oxford: Oxford University Press, 2002), 49–50.

28. *LSAM* 20 = *SIG*³ 985 = Barton and Horsley, 1981. The quotation comes from line 15 of the inscription. A translation of the complete inscription appears in Richard S. Ascough, Philip A. Harland, and John S. Kloppenborg, *Associations in the Ancient World: A Sourcebook* (Waco, TX: Baylor University Press, 2012), 82–84.

29. Note that the text prohibited a man from seducing "someone else's wife, whether

instructions concerning the sexual activity of the pagan cultic association's members sound remarkably similar to Paul's instructions to the Corinthians in 1 Corinthians 7.

Nevertheless, the inscription acknowledged a reality that Paul ignored. Note that the Philadelphia inscription insisted only that "a *free* woman . . . be pure and not know the bed of another man, nor have intercourse with anyone except her own husband." Although the inscription did not explicitly address the reality of slaves as sexual objects, it nevertheless recognized that female slaves had no control over their own sexual activities. Consequently, it only insisted on the sexual purity of the *free* woman; because slave women were vulnerable to sexual abuse by their masters, the inscription implicitly viewed the unwanted sex experienced by enslaved females as morally neutral. Based on what we see in this group—a group that welcomed both "free people and household slaves"—it seems reasonable to assume that in Paul's assemblies, which also welcomed slaves and free people (cf. Gal 3:28), the sexual abuse endured by female slaves (by a pagan master, for example) would likewise have been considered morally neutral.

Among Jesus followers, another thorny issue likely emerged within assemblies where *believing* slaves participated alongside their *believing* masters. An enslaved Jesus follower could have easily reasoned—based on the baptismal phrase "there is no longer slave or free"—that he or she was no longer subject to the authority of his or her master (who was also a Jesus follower). Paul's advice to Philemon (cited above) that he receive his errant slave Onesimus back into his household "no longer as a slave but as more than a slave, a beloved brother" (16) would have encouraged thinking along these lines.

The texts of the New Testament, however, consistently guarded against such reasoning. We see something of this kind from Paul himself in 1 Corinthians; there the apostle encouraged members of the Corinthian community to retain their present status: "In whatever condition you were called, brothers and sisters, there remain with God" (1 Cor 7:24). Most notably, for our

---

free or slave, [or] a boy, [or] a virgin girl." It did *not* prohibit a man from having sex with one of his female slaves as long as she was not "someone else's wife" (i.e., the unofficial spouse of another slave). In other words, this inscription illustrates that sex with an unattached female slave was not considered adulterous behavior in Roman times. One wonders if some in the assemblies of Jesus followers felt that they could likewise engage in sex with their slave women without feeling as if they had committed adultery. For this suggestion, I am indebted to Jennifer Glancy's paper, "Domestic vs. Conjugal Sexual Ethics: Implications for Understanding Jesus's Teachings on Adultery in the Gospel of Matthew" (paper presented at the Annual Meeting of the Studiorum Novi Testamenti Societas, Montreal, Canada, August 2–5, 2016).

purposes, he addressed the situation faced by slaves: "Were you a slave when called? Do not be concerned about it. Even if you can gain your freedom, make use of your present condition now more than ever (or possibly: if you can gain your freedom, avail yourself of the opportunity). For whoever was called in the Lord as a slave is a freed person belonging to the Lord, just as whoever was free when called is a slave of Christ" (1 Cor 7:21–22).

As the two translation possibilities in the middle of this quotation make clear, this verse presents the reader with a significant problem. Did Paul suggest that slaves who were offered the possibility of freedom should take advantage of it? Or did he assert that they should remain slaves, that is, make use of their present (enslaved) condition now more than ever. The Greek can be translated either way and so the proper translation must be based upon the phrase's context. Unfortunately, since there is ambiguity in the context as well, scholars are divided on how this passage should be understood.[30] But if the NRSV translation is the correct one ("Were you a slave when called? Do not be concerned about it. Even if you can gain your freedom, make use of your present condition now more than ever"), then the entirety of the passage suggests that from Paul's point of view the distinction between a Jesus-following slave and a Jesus-following free person, although no longer significant within the context of the believing assembly, was to be maintained in day-to-day life; a slave was to remain a slave. Presumably, in the assembly the slave would have been treated by the master more as a "brother" or "sister," but in the household the slave would be treated as a slave.

Although Paul's position on this is unclear because of the ambiguity in the text, the position of the author of the pseudepigraphic letter to the Colossians is crystal clear. He simply commands: "Slaves, obey your earthly masters in everything, not only while being watched and in order to please them, but wholeheartedly, fearing the Lord. Whatever your task, put yourselves into it, as done for the Lord and not for your masters, since you know that from the Lord you will receive the inheritance as your reward; you serve the Lord Christ" (Col 3:22–24). The author of 1 Timothy gave similar advice to slaves: "Let all who are under the yoke of slavery regard their masters as worthy of all honor, so that the name of God and the teaching may not be blasphemed. Those who have believing masters must not be disrespectful to them on the

30. On the one hand, Paul insists that those in the assembly remain as they were when they were called (7:17, 20). That would suggest that Paul encouraged slaves to remain in slavery, even if they had the opportunity to be freed. On the other hand, in several places Paul allows for exceptions to his rule (vv. 8–9, 10–11, 12–15). This in turn could suggest that Paul encouraged slaves to take advantage of an opportunity to gain their freedom.

ground that they are members of the assembly; rather they must serve them all the more, since those who benefit by their service are believers and beloved" (1 Tim 6:1–2; cf. 1 Pet 2:18–25). The author of the letter to the Ephesians, on the other hand, while delivering comparable instructions to slaves in the assemblies (Eph 6:5–8), also saw fit to direct instructions to the slaves' masters: "Stop threatening them, for you know that both of you have the same master in heaven, and with him there is no partiality" (Eph 6:9; cf. Did. 4.10–11).

An interesting passage from the early second century provides us with a different insight into slavery and the Jesus movement. In the aforementioned letter of Ignatius to Polycarp, the Syrian bishop recommended to slave owners: "Do not be arrogant toward male or female slaves." He then addressed the situation of slaves: "but neither let them become haughty, rather, let them serve even more as slaves for the glory of God, that they may receive a greater freedom from God." So far, this advice does not sound all that much different from what we have already seen. But the next command from Ignatius tells us something new: "And they should not long to be set free through the common fund, lest they be found slaves of passion" (*To Polycarp* 4.3). This command presumes that some assemblies had collected money to buy the freedom of a Jesus-following slave. Ignatius obviously did not approve of such a practice, perhaps because it had been divisive in his home assembly in Antioch.

Two passages from another text, the Shepherd of Hermas, written at about the same time as Ignatius's letter, may also refer to the practice of buying slaves' freedom. In the first, the author counseled charitable behavior, including caring for widows, orphans, and others in need. But he also advocated "redeeming the slaves of God from their calamities (Herm. Mand. 8.10 [38.10]). If, by the phrase "slaves of God," the author meant believers who were literally enslaved, then this passage would also point to the practice of buying Jesus followers out of slavery. Elsewhere in the same text, the author encouraged his readers to use their money, not to purchase land but "purchase souls that have been afflicted" (Herm. Sim. 1.8 [50.8]). This passage may also point to the practice of buying the freedom of slaves. Unfortunately, however, we cannot be sure because both of these passages could be interpreted differently.[31]

---

31. The author may have used the phrase "slaves of God" in the first passage to refer metaphorically to believers who were not slaves in the same way that Paul claimed that "whoever was free when called is a slave of Christ" (1 Cor 7:22). In the case of the latter interpretation, the text merely enjoined its readers to help believers who were in some kind of distress. The second passage could likewise be interpreted to encourage people to help anyone in difficulty.

Freedpersons

Former slaves who had been freed, freedpersons, present us with another group in the assemblies to consider. In some ways, it is fair to say that this group was neither slave nor free. This is because a freedperson continued to be obligated to his or her former master. A freedperson would forever owe his or her master obedience and respect and could not, for instance, sue or even insult that former owner. In addition, the freedperson also owed his or her former master a certain amount of annual work. Such work usually comprised a set number of days of free labor. If both master and former slave were in the same profession—if they were physicians, for example—the former master could, by law, prevent the freedperson from even practicing in the same town. In short, the freedperson was only somewhat free; he or she always had to defer to the master.

If, despite these restrictions, a freedperson enjoyed a financially successful career—and many did—the freedperson would still never escape the stigma of having once been a slave; the dishonor of slavery followed that individual to his or her grave. Society at large viewed freedpersons much as they viewed slaves; a change of status from slave to freedperson often meant little to most. When viewed by one's social betters, the perspective was this: once a slave, always a slave! The best a freedperson could hope for would be for his or her children to escape the shame of slavery and be accepted into "polite society."[32]

However, from the vantage point of a slave, the status of a freedperson was something to be desired. How might a slave gain his or her freedom? There were three primary avenues for manumission. One could be freed by one's master, one could buy one's way out of slavery, or one could be bought out by someone else (a possibility that Ignatius's letter already demonstrated). Sometimes a master would free a slave out of affection. We know from tombstone inscriptions that female slaves were sometimes freed and then married by their former masters. Other such inscriptions tell of the affection that developed between a master and a slave who had been a foundling; some foundling slaves came to be viewed almost as children by their masters. But sometimes affection had nothing to do with it. At times, wealthy people freed one or more of their slaves just to demonstrate how much wealth and power they had at

32. An inscription from Pompeii tells of a six-year-old child of a wealthy freedperson who was elected to the town council (*CIL* 10.846). Although the father was ineligible for the decurionate, his son could serve. In this case, the father was able to "buy" the son a status that had been denied to himself.

their disposal. Giving up such valuable property as one's slaves dramatically exhibited the true extent of an individual's affluence.

Buying one's freedom was another way, although it was expensive. Inscriptions from Delphi inform us that in the first century BCE, the average price of freedom for an adult male was between 550 and 650 drachmae. For an adult female it was between 400 and 500 drachmae.[33] Although it is difficult to convert the value of ancient currency to today's money, we can nevertheless get some idea of its worth from Matt 20:1–15, which informs us that one denarius (roughly equivalent to one drachma) represented a full day's wage for an unskilled laborer. Obviously, it would have been very difficult for a slave to procure more than 400 drachmae. But, as the Delphi inscriptions attest, some slaves were somehow able to do it. But, as we have already seen, a slave's freedom could also have been purchased by someone else (or by a group of people). Sometimes a former slave would buy his wife and children out of slavery.[34]

Unfortunately, we have no *direct* evidence of freedpersons in the early assemblies. But there are some indirect signs that they were present. For example, both Chloe (1 Cor 1:11) and Phoebe (Rom 16:1–2) had names that were derived from mythology. Since mythological names were often given to slaves, it is likely that these women had been slaves earlier in their lives. Obviously, they were no longer slaves at Paul's time; Chloe was the head of a household and Phoebe's former dedication to her assembly (and the travel on which she was about to embark)[35] would hardly have been possible for a slave. Both women were likely freedpersons who were able to succeed financially following their manumission. They also played significant roles in the movement. It is likely that Chloe hosted a small assembly in her home.

The merchant of purple cloth, Lydia, mentioned in Acts (16:14–15), was also probably a freedperson. Her name is really the name of a place (Lydia was an area in western Asia Minor) and, as such, may have been "a relic of servile

---

33. Hopkins, *Conquerors and Slaves*, 159 (table 3.3).

34. It is worth noting that Paul uses imagery of manumission in two places. In 1 Cor 6:20 he tells the Corinthians, "you were bought with a price!" In this passage, he means that they have been freed from (i.e., bought out of) the slavery of sin. In 7:22 he tells those who were literally enslaved that they have been bought out of slavery and, in the context of the assembly, are now free ("For whoever was called in the Lord as a slave is a freed person belonging to the Lord").

35. Rom 16:1–2 is a recommendation for Phoebe, written by Paul. Such a recommendation would not be needed unless one were traveling; it would be carried by a traveler so that he or she would be welcomed by friends of the author of the recommendation (in this case, Paul).

origins."[36] Possibly the same could be said for the man, Achaicus, mentioned in 1 Cor 16:17 (since Achaia was also a geographical region).[37] Persis, who Paul described as both "beloved" and one "who has worked hard in the Lord" at the end of his letter to the Romans (Rom 16:12) was probably also a freedperson; her name, Persis, was apparently a popular one for female slaves. Epaenetus (Rom 16:5) and Ampliatus (Rom 16:8) were also common slave names and so it is possible that these Roman Jesus followers were also freedpersons.[38]

Finally, we come to the figure of Erastus of Corinth, whose story is somewhat complicated. Erastus was mentioned by Paul in Rom 16:23. In that passage, Paul passed on the greetings of two Corinthians to the members of the assembly in Rome. One was Gaius (mentioned above) and the other was Erastus, labeled the *oikonomos* (translated by the NRSV and others as "treasurer") of the city. Because of this label, many scholars concluded that Erastus was an important Corinthian bureaucrat, the city treasurer.

Furthermore, an inscription from Corinth (originally dated to the first century CE), discovered in the twentieth century, credited a certain Erastus with paving a public plaza in the city at his own expense. Clearly, this Erastus would have been a wealthy man. Since the inscription, although broken, would not have originally allowed room for a patronymic (i.e., a surname), it was further believed that the Erastus of the inscription was probably a freedperson. But the story does not end there. The inscription further indicated that Erastus donated the pavement "in return for his aedileship," an important public office. Scholars naturally assumed that this Erastus must have been the person from whom Paul sent greetings to the Romans. Consequently, they concluded that Paul's Erastus was a wealthy freedperson who was, at the same time, one of the most important people in the city government of Corinth.

Unfortunately, recent scrutiny has called much of this into question. First of all, the precise meaning of the term *oikonomos* is unclear. While it had previously been assumed that the *oikonomos* of the city was the equivalent of a *quaestor*, a high-ranking civic official, more recently it has been argued that an *oikonomos* was a mid- to low-level financial administrator and possibly a slave.[39] Second,

---

36. Wayne A. Meeks, *The First Urban Christians: The Social World of the Apostle Paul*, 2nd ed. (New Haven: Yale University Press, 2003), 203 n. 93.

37. Achaicus was a Latin name indicating that one was from Achaia. Because Achaicus actually lived in Achaia (in Corinth), he could not have received the name there. It is possible that he or his father (who originated from Achaia) lived in Italy as a slave and then traveled back to Achaia after manumission (Meeks, *First Urban Christians*, 56).

38. Meeks, *First Urban Christians*, 57.

39. For the former, see Gerd Theissen, *The Social Setting of Pauline Christianity: Essays on*

the identification of the Erastus in the inscription and the person in Paul's letter is also uncertain due to questions about the inscription's date. In the words of one scholar: "[The] Erastus of Corinth and the Erastus of Paul's letter were two different individuals. Several aspects of the archaeological record were recorded inaccurately: the plaza does not come from the mid-first century, the inscription is not in its original location, and the inscription was probably commissioned in the middle of the second century CE."[40] So the Erastus mentioned in Romans was likely not a wealthy and influential freedperson as was previously supposed. Rather, he may have been a slave.

Summary and Conclusion

The Jesus movement began among the rural peasantry of Judea. Its adherents were of very low social and economic status: agricultural laborers, shepherds, fishermen, and the like; the movement also included tax collectors, prostitutes, and others of ill repute. When it migrated to the cities of the Greco-Roman world, its makeup changed along with the landscape. Assemblies came to be populated with artisans, laborers, and shopkeepers rather than agricultural workers and shepherds. While most in the assemblies were of fairly low economic and social status, a few—like Gaius of Corinth—had some economic resources to spare and likely held a somewhat higher social status. Besides artisans and laborers, the assemblies also included freedpersons and slaves. Some freedpersons, like Phoebe and Lydia, functioned as patrons for missionaries like Paul; others, people like Chloe, probably held unofficial leadership roles—perhaps because they hosted regular gatherings at their dwellings. Unfortunately, it is difficult to say much about the slaves in the Jesus movement. We do not know how many there were and we only have the name of one Jesus-following slave, Onesimus, mentioned in Paul's letter to Philemon (although it is possible that Erastus of Corinth was also a slave). We also do not know the roles that slaves played in the assemblies. To the best of our knowledge, no slave held a leadership position in any of the early assemblies.

Corinth (Philadelphia: Fortress, 1982), 82–83. For the latter, see Steven J. Friesen, "The Wrong Erastus: Ideology, Archaeology, and Exegesis," in *Corinth in Context: Comparative Studies on Religion and Society*, ed. Steven J. Friesen, Daniel N. Schowalter, and James C. Walters (Leiden: Brill, 2010), 245–49.

40. Friesen, "Wrong Erastus," 255.

ACCOMMODATION AND RESISTANCE

CHAPTER 7

One in Christ Jesus

W hen we consider the core of the baptismal formula ("there is no longer Jew or Greek, there is no longer slave or free, there is no longer male and female") in light of what we have discovered in the previous three chapters, we are forced to concede that the formula cannot simply be taken at face value. Rather, it represented an ideal that only partially reflected reality. Most of the assemblies in the empire's cities were composed of non-Jews (although there may have been a few Jews in some assemblies). Although women had some responsibilities in the assemblies, men dominated the leadership, and the slaves in the assemblies are mostly invisible in the literature that we have. Nevertheless, even though the mid–first century assemblies may not have completely measured up to their ideal, there seems to have been a lessening of gender and social distinctions in some communities; furthermore, there was at least an openness to ethnic diversity within the assemblies (e.g., there seem to have been a few Jews in the assembly at Corinth).

But what kept these groups together? In the dominant society, hierarchical structures provided stability. Designated (high-status, male) leaders led and everyone else (including men of lower status, women, freedpersons, and slaves) followed. In the Jesus movement, leadership was likely ad hoc or informal. With no such structure (or at least a largely attenuated structure), how did the Jesus assemblies function? What was the glue that held them together? From what we know, there seem to have been two essential things: first, the worship of a common deity and particularly his son (to the exclusion of all other gods) and, second, a sense of fellowship and belonging. The final phrase of the baptismal formula—which serves as the title of the current chapter—captures these two elements: "All . . . are one in Christ Jesus." The notion of fellowship and belonging is obviously evident in the phrase "all are one." The worship of the common deity and his son can be detected in the phrase "in Christ Jesus," the latter being the son who made possible reconciliation with Jesus's father, the one "living and true God" (1 Thess 1:9).

Remarkably, the assemblies of Jesus followers resembled other groups in the ancient world, groups that contemporary scholars identify by the label of *voluntary associations*. While these associations were many and varied considerably, they all had a couple of things in common. They all possessed a cultic as well as a social dimension. One scholar has illustrated these two primary concerns with the phrases "honoring the gods" and "feasting with friends."[1] Such a description is in line with the primary objectives of the assemblies of Jesus followers. The dedication of the latter to the Jewish God and his son corresponds to the associations' concern for "honoring the gods"; the sense of fellowship within the assemblies likewise corresponds to the "feasting with friends" within the pagan associations. Indeed, as we will see, the assemblies of Jesus followers not only met to worship together, that worship was usually conducted in the context of a meal. In light of this fact, "feasting with friends" could easily describe what happened when Jesus followers gathered to honor their God and his son.

Other parallels between voluntary associations and the assemblies of Jesus followers are likewise noteworthy. Familial labels for fellow members (e.g., "brother," "sister") were found within both voluntary associations and the assemblies of Jesus followers. Even the term "assembly" (*ekklēsia*), the self-designation for the gatherings of Jesus followers, was used by some associations to describe themselves. Because of the number of likenesses between pagan associations and assemblies of Jesus followers, a description of the practices of the former will help us better understand the Jesus movement's early assemblies.

The Assembly as a Voluntary Association

What do we know about Greco-Roman voluntary associations? First of all, as previously mentioned, there were different types. They were created for any number of reasons. Sometimes artisans from the same field (e.g., silversmiths) or laborers who worked the same kinds of jobs (e.g., stevedores) formed an association. At other times, people who had emigrated from the same homeland

---

1. Philip A. Harland, *Associations, Synagogues, and Congregations: Claiming a Place in Ancient Mediterranean Society* (Minneapolis: Fortress, 2003), 55.

would form an association. In still other cases, those who favored one particular deity put together an association. In fact, voluntary associations have been categorized into five different types: 1) household associations; 2) ethnic or geographic associations; 3) neighborhood associations; 4) occupational associations; and 5) cultic associations.[2]

Of these, the first mentioned, the household association, consisted of people connected by family. It would have been made up not only of blood relatives but also slaves of the household, freedpersons (formerly enslaved in that household), as well as other people with some kind of connection to the household (perhaps close friends or business associates). The ethnic or geographic association included resident aliens originating from the same place. A synagogue could be considered a good example of this type of association.[3] Although, in Greco-Roman times, synagogues were places of prayer (as they are in our time), they also functioned as community centers for Judeans. Neighborhood associations were, as the name indicates, made up of people from the same part of town. Such groups might have gathered together to improve their situation in one way or another, or they may have met primarily to socialize. Occupational associations allowed people of the same trade to network. Such networking might have enabled a laborer to expand his or her business, to share tools or techniques, to make connections with persons or families in power, or simply to commiserate. We know of many such groups, including associations of bakers, linen workers, dyers, carpenters, musicians, physicians, potters, and merchants, to name only a few.[4] The final type was the cultic association, typically dedicated to the worship of one particular deity. For our purposes, this is the most significant type of association, since it bears the closest resemblance to assemblies of Jesus followers.

Nevertheless, there were very often significant overlaps among the different kinds of associations. For example, on the Greek island of Delos, an association dedicated to the worship of Poseidon was made up of merchants, shippers, and warehouse workers from Berytus (modern Beirut).[5] So this would

---

2. The five different types have been categorized by Harland, *Associations*, 28–52.

3. Indeed, the Greek word *synagōgē* simply means "assembly" or "association." It is unclear when *synagōgē* became a technical term for a Jewish place of worship. However, in the book of Revelation, the term *synagōgē* (Rev 2:9; 3:9) is clearly distinguished from the word *ekklēsia*, "assembly" (Rev 2:8 and 3:7), the former standing for a Jewish gathering place, the latter for an assembly of Jesus followers.

4. There was often some overlap between neighborhood associations and occupational associations since workers of a particular type often tended to live in the same area.

5. For translations of inscriptions by this group, see Richard S. Ascough, Philip A. Har-

qualify as a cultic, an occupational, and an ethnic association; its members all favored a common deity (Poseidon), they all shared the same or similar professions (having to do with goods transported by sea), and they all hailed from the same place (Berytus).

Related to the notion of overlap is the fact that virtually all associations possessed a significant cultic dimension; as mentioned above, they all "honored the gods" in one way or another. The household association worshipped the household gods and any deity favored by the head of the family. Ethnic associations often worshipped the gods of their people (e.g., Jewish synagogues worshipped the Judean God). Occupational guilds of physicians typically worshipped Asclepius, the god of healing; similarly, associations of actors and musicians were usually devoted to Dionysus, the patron deity of the theater. The aforementioned association of merchants, shippers, and warehouse workers from Berytus, worshipped the deity Poseidon, because they all relied on seafaring for their livelihood.

Besides the cultic dimension, there was also a significant social component to every association. Many possessed a strong sense of belonging. In the inscription from a group called the Iobacchoi, an Athenian group dedicated to Dionysus, the following expression of the group's pride was recorded: "Now we are the best of all Bacchic societies!"[6] The sense of belonging that one gained from an association can be compared to the kind of role played in contemporary times by a fraternity or sorority at a large public university. In such a group, a student overwhelmed by an enormous and seemingly impersonal and uncaring institution can find a welcoming group of friends. In the same way, in an ancient association, whatever one's status in the dominant society, one had "brothers" and "sisters" in the association. Meals together with these brothers and sisters, when friends "feasted with friends," regularly affirmed such fraternal feelings.

Associations usually met regularly. According to an inscription put up by the aforementioned Iobacchoi, that association gathered together every month (on the ninth day) and on special days devoted to Dionysus, both regular, annual festivals and occasional festivals. All members were expected to attend (*IG* II^2 1368.42–44). Associations met in a variety of places. Household associations obviously met in the home. Some prosperous associations (like the Iobacchoi)

---

land, and John S. Kloppenborg, *Associations in the Ancient World: A Sourcebook* (Waco: Baylor University Press, 2012), 136–140 (nos. 224–228).

6. *IG* II^2 1368.26–27. For a translation of the entire inscription, see Ascough, Harland, and Kloppenborg, *Associations*, 13–16.

had their own assembly halls; less affluent ones had to find other venues. Some convened in the dining facilities of one temple or another; others rented space. An association might have also met in a warehouse or in the workshop of one of its members, assuming one spacious enough could be found.

The early Jesus assemblies probably all began as household associations. In 1 Cor 1:16, Paul mentions that he baptized the household of Stephanas. Following that, the assembly probably met in Stephanas's house. By the time that Paul wrote 1 Corinthians, however, the group had expanded considerably. In 1 Cor 14:23, Paul writes of the "whole assembly" gathering "in the same place" as if this were somewhat exceptional. From his statement we can infer that the increased numbers eventually made the frequent gathering of *all* Corinthian Jesus followers cumbersome, and so the individual household assemblies likely gathered on their own fairly regularly (perhaps weekly) and then the whole assembly would gather less frequently (perhaps monthly) for the Lord's Supper. Paul's comments obviously refer to the latter, larger assembly.

Throughout his letters, Paul's comments indicate that he was not only concerned about the periodic gatherings in which the members of his assemblies would worship. He was also focused on the personal transformation of every member of the assembly. Did other voluntary associations expect a similar transformation of their members? Although one might suspect that such an attitude was unique to the Jesus movement, the inscription from Philadelphia in western Asia Minor (which was briefly discussed in the previous chapter in connection to slavery) indicates that such was not the case.

This particular inscription is from an association that met at the home of a certain man named Dionysios. The association was originally dedicated to the Asia Minor goddess Agdistis, but as the inscription tells us, Dionysios had at some point been instructed in a dream to add altars for a number of other deities. Consequently: "In [the] house [of Dionysios] altars have been set up for Zeus Eumenes and Hestia his consort, for the other Savior gods, and for Eudaimonia ("Prosperity"), Ploutos ("Wealth"), Arete ("Virtue"), Hygeia ("Health"), Agathe Tyche ("Good Fortune"), Agathos Daimon ("Good Spirit"), Mneme ("Memory"), the Charitae ("the Graces"), and Nike ("Victory")."[7] Despite the difference between the monotheism of the household assemblies of the Jesus followers and the polytheism of Dionysios's association, some striking parallels between the groups nevertheless emerge later in the inscription, having to do with morality and ritual.

---

7. *LSAM* 20 = *SIG*³ 985 = Barton and Horsley 1981. The lines quoted are 5–11. The translation is from Ascough, Harland, and Kloppenborg, *Associations*, 82–84.

Like the assemblies of Jesus followers, Dionysios's household association expected moral behavior of its members in their day-to-day lives. In the last chapter, we saw that it prohibited adultery. But the inscription also insisted: "When entering this house, let men and women, free people and household slaves, swear by all the gods that they do not know about any deceptive action against a man or a woman or about any drug harmful to people and that they neither know nor use harmful spells, a love charm, an abortive drug, or a contraceptive" (lines 15–20; cf. 25–28, 35–36). The inscription clearly prohibited entry to anyone who was dishonest, who used harmful drugs, magical incantations to aid abortion or to encourage love, or contraception (as well as adultery, as we saw previously).

We can compare these prohibitions to Paul's warning about wrongdoers who will not gain entry to the kingdom of God: "Live by the Spirit, I say, and do not gratify the desires of the flesh. . . . Now the works of the flesh are obvious: fornication, impurity, licentiousness, idolatry, sorcery, enmities, strife, jealousy, anger, quarrels, dissensions, factions, envy, drunkenness, carousing, and things like these. I am warning you, as I warned you before: those who do such things will not inherit the kingdom of God" (Gal 5:16, 19–21; cf. 1 Cor 6:9–10). While there are some obvious differences in the details of the moral instructions given by Dionysios versus those given by Paul, there are also some similarities. Note that both prohibit sexual immorality and both forbid the use of magic. Obviously, Paul also warns against idolatry, something that we would not expect to see in the Philadelphia inscription.

But besides their commands having to do with day-to-day morality, there is a striking similarity having to do with the worship services of the two different groups. The Philadelphia inscription commands that: "During the monthly and annual sacrifices, may those men and women who have confidence in themselves touch this stone on which the instructions of the god have been written, so that those who obey these instructions and those who do not become evident" (lines 55–58). The act of touching the monument at the monthly and annual sacrifices was intended to separate those who had followed the moral commands articulated on the stone from those who had transgressed them. Although not stated explicitly, the text strongly suggested that the very act of touching the stone would bring some kind of punishment to the transgressors.[8]

We see something similar concerning the assembly of Jesus followers at Corinth. In 1 Corinthians, Paul also focuses on the regular gathering, and specifically the Lord's Supper (on which we will focus shortly): "Whoever,

---

8. Of course, it is likely that those people would not touch the stone or would possibly avoid the gathering altogether.

therefore, eats the bread or drinks the cup of the Lord in an unworthy manner will be answerable for the body and blood of the Lord. Examine yourselves, and only then eat of the bread and drink of the cup. For all who eat and drink without discerning the body, eat and drink judgment against themselves. For this reason many of you are weak and ill, and some have died" (1 Cor 11:27–30). In this passage Paul wrote about participating in the ritual of the Lord's Supper "in an unworthy manner." Paul here did not mean those who had committed some moral infraction since the last time the group had come together. Instead, here he focused on inappropriate behavior at the meal itself. So, there is an obvious difference between Paul's warning and that on the Dionysios inscription. Nevertheless, both writings worried about the possibility that evildoers would contaminate the sacred gatherings. In Paul's case, the evildoer would have been someone who had acted inappropriately at the gathering; in the case of Dionysios's inscription, it would have been someone who had committed an infraction prior to attending the gathering.

Regardless, the sacrality of the gathering itself was of utmost importance. In each case, a sacred meal was involved. This resemblance brings us to what is possibly the most striking similarity between the assemblies of Jesus followers and those of pagan associations, their rituals. The two primary rituals of the Jesus movement were baptism, a rite that every convert underwent only once, and a ritual meal, known as the Eucharist (e.g., Did. 9.1) or the "Lord's Supper" (1 Cor 11:20), a ritual that was practiced regularly.

Baptism and Initiation as Entrance Rituals

Baptism, the entrance rite for members of the Jesus movement, consisted of the immersion of an individual in water; if possible, in water that was both cold and running (Did. 7:1–4). The rite itself owed its existence to Judaism, and in particular to John the Baptist. In ancient Judea, both temple priests and the laity had used immersion in water as a means of ritual purification (cf. Exod 30; Lev 13–15). In Jesus's time, John the Baptist employed water to symbolize not ritual but spiritual purification; immersion in the Jordan River signified both the forgiveness of sins and moral rejuvenation in the face of God's imminent judgment (Mark 1:4; Josephus, *Jewish Antiquities* 18.117). As mentioned in chapter 2, Jesus had been baptized by John and, likely as a result of that, his followers appropriated John's ritual.[9]

9. Our New Testament sources tell us almost nothing about the ritual during Jesus's

Nevertheless, even though the rite of baptism owed its origin to John, it was not totally without parallel in Greco-Roman associations. While there were not specific similarities between the ritual of the Jesus followers and association rituals, the fact that the Jesus movement possessed an entrance rite at all parallels the fact that some associations also had entrance rituals. Some cultic associations, especially those dedicated to the deities Dionysus, Demeter, Isis, or Serapis, required *initiation* into the deity's mysteries as a condition of entrance. So, just as initiation functioned as the entrance rite to those cultic associations, baptism functioned as the entrance rite for the members of the assemblies of Jesus followers.

Sacred Meals as Community Rituals

Virtually all voluntary associations held regular meals that were both social occasions and acts of worship, particularly in connection to the meetings of cultic associations. When a cultic association met, it would typically honor its patron deity or deities with sacrifices and then partake in a common meal during which time the meat from the sacrifices would be consumed. But, it was not only *cultic* societies that featured sacrifices performed to honor the gods. Sacrifice played a role in other types of association meals as well. In an inscription from Ephesus, an association of doctors (i.e., an occupational association) described itself as "the physicians who sacrifice to ancestor Asclepius."[10] Presumably at the beginning of their gatherings they would offer sacrifice to their patron, the god of healing. Following that sacrifice would come the meal, consisting primarily of the meat of the sacrificed animal. The meal would typically be a fairly lengthy affair, lasting several hours. Most of the diners would recline on couches to eat.[11] An association meal followed the same pattern that was shared by most formal

---

time. Consequently, some scholars believe that Jesus did not baptize. There are, however, two intriguing passages in John's Gospel that mention Jesus baptizing (3:22 and 4:1).

10. IEph 719 = PHI 249247. For a translation of the inscription, see Ascough, Harland, and Kloppenborg, *Associations*, 105. The inscription actually reads, "The physicians who sacrifice to ancestor Asclepius and to the *Sebastoi*." It is hardly surprising that the physicians of this club sacrificed to Asclepius, the deified healer that the group refers to as its ancestor. But it is noteworthy that the group also sacrificed to the *Sebastoi* ("the revered ones"), the honorific title ascribed to the deified Roman emperors.

11. There were some exceptions. Slaves usually did not recline but rather sat. In earlier times, women had also sat, but by Greco-Roman times, they typically reclined as well.

meals in the Greco-Roman world; it consisted of three parts: the supper, the libation, and the symposium.

The typical formal meal began with the supper (*deipnon* in Greek),[12] during which time the main course (e.g., the meat of the sacrifice) was served; slaves or other designated members of the association took the food from the tables in the center of the room and set it in front of those reclining on dining couches that ran along the outer walls of the room. All diners, however, were not necessarily served the same amount of food. Some inscriptions indicate that former association officers, for example, would receive a larger portion. The arrangement of guests, that is, who reclined where and next to whom, was also significant. Some individuals, often officers or former officers, were honored with more desirable places on the dining couches than others.[13]

After the food was consumed, the tables holding the food were taken away and the wine was mixed (in the Greco-Roman world, wine was never drunk unadulterated; it was always mixed with water). Then the person leading the event—typically an officer of the association—performed a libation (i.e., a drink offering): a cup filled with wine was held up, the name of the relevant deity was pronounced, and a few drops of the wine were dribbled onto the floor. After taking a sip of the wine, the leader would pass the cup around to all of the diners, each of whom would in turn pronounce the name of the deity and drink from the cup.

The libation separated the end of the supper from the beginning of the symposium. While we typically think of a symposium as a rather formal meeting during which serious intellectual topics would be discussed, the Greek word *symposion* literally meant a "drinking party." And, indeed that is what took place after formal meals. At social meals, the symposium featured not only drinking but also conversation and entertainment. The entertainment may have included music and dances performed by entertainers hired for the event. Alternatively, the diners themselves might entertain one another with conversation, songs, and drinking games.

At the meals of religious associations, however, the symposium would provide the opportunity for honoring the deity in one way or another. Depend-

---

12. Here and in the pages that follow, I will use the Greek word *deipnon* in conjunction with the English word, "supper" to remind us that the supper was only part of the meal (as opposed to in our usage where supper typically refers to the entire meal).

13. Because some places were more desirable than others, association regulations sometimes specifically outlawed moving into another person's reclining space. The offending person could be fined.

ing on the association and the god(s) being honored, any number of things could have happened at this time. Sometimes hymns were sung, either by members of the association or a choir hired for the purpose.[14] At other times, a sermon would be delivered. Or the diners may have viewed a theatrical performance. Such a performance happened at the meal of the Iobacchoi at the time of the Great Dionysia, a major Athenian civic festival in honor of Dionysus (the Iobacchoi's patron deity); in that theatrical performance, which may have included the acting out of mythological stories about Dionysus, various members of the association played the different roles (*IG* II² 1368.123–24). Such a performance would likely be comparable to the pageants put on at Christmas by some Christian congregations.

In other cases, the symposium would have featured a sacred dance. An image of such a performance has been preserved on an ancient monument. Engraved on that monument are six diners reclining on couches. On the floor before them appear four figures. One, off to the side, mixes wine for the symposium. The other three are obviously the performers; two are musicians and the third is a dancer. One musician plays a flute while the other holds sticks, probably to provide some kind of percussive accompaniment to the flute music. In between the musicians a woman stands, with legs crossed and arms outstretched beside her; she is clearly dancing, probably in honor of the gods Zeus, Artemis, and Apollo, three much larger figures carved into the monument above the heads of the reclining diners. Alternatively, the dance may have been in honor of Zeus Hypsistos, the deity to whom the monument was dedicated (*GIBM* IV.2 1007).[15]

We can see strong parallels between the meals of the cultic association and the ritual meals of the first-century assemblies of Jesus followers. We can be certain that such meals took place in virtually all of the early assemblies for the author of Acts maintains that the earliest converts to the movement "devoted themselves to the apostles' teaching and fellowship, to the breaking of bread and the prayers" (Acts 2:42). The earliest discussion of such a meal appears in 1 Corinthians. Unfortunately, Paul does not give us a particularly detailed description of the meal; he only wrote about it because he was displeased with the way that the Corinthians had been celebrating it. Indeed, he began his discussion with the following reprimand: "Now in the following instructions I do

---

14. In inscriptions, we sometimes see *hymnōdoi* ("hymn singers") mentioned. At other times, we see *hymnodidaskaloi* ("hymn teachers") or *chorēgos* ("choral leader").

15. The monument is from Panormos, near Kyzikos in what is now northwest Turkey. For a reproduction, see Harland, *Associations*, 57.

not commend you, because when you come together [for the Lord's Supper] it is not for the better but for the worse" (1 Cor 11:17).

In the course of his discussion, Paul presented a narrative of Jesus's last meal. He introduced that narrative with the comment, "For I received from the Lord what I also handed on to you." His phrase "what I also handed on to you" obviously refers to the past; he was not giving the Corinthians new information here. Rather, he was *repeating* a narrative that they had already heard. Because of this, it seems safe to assume that the Corinthian meal would have corresponded to the narrative previously given by Paul.

It seems that Paul repeated the narrative in order to emphasize Jesus's selfless behavior (in contrast to what he saw as selfish behavior among the Corinthians). Obviously, he hoped to change the Corinthians' conduct so that they could properly enact their own meal "in remembrance of [Jesus]." In any case, the narrative reads as follows: "For I received from the Lord what I also handed on to you, that the Lord Jesus on the night when he was betrayed took a loaf of bread, and when he had given thanks, he broke it and said, 'This is my body that is for you. Do this in remembrance of me.' In the same way he took the cup also, after supper, saying, 'This cup is the new covenant in my blood. Do this, as often as you drink it, in remembrance of me'" (11:23–25).[16]

According to Paul, Jesus's last meal began with a blessing over the bread, followed by its distribution and consumption. Although an initial blessing of (or prayer over) the food was not necessarily a standard way to begin a meal, a prayer at the commencement of a formal meal would not have been unheard of.[17] The blessing, distribution, and consumption of the bread during Jesus's last meal as described by Paul would have corresponded to the first portion of the typical banquet, the *deipnon* ("supper"). Although we might be puzzled by a main course consisting of only bread, such fare would not have been at all unusual in the ancient world. It would probably have been accompanied by side dishes of seasoned vegetables, cheese, oil, or fish. Nevertheless, the bread would have represented the main dish. Meat was a luxury, consumed only on special occasions.

The next act in Paul's narrative was Jesus's blessing over the cup. Although contemporary readers might assume that this blessing came immediately after the blessing over the bread (as is typical of the Eucharist in many contemporary Christian congregations), a close look at Paul's text indicates something different. The text indicates that Jesus took up the cup "*after supper*" (literally,

16. This account is similar to that found in Mark 14:22–25.

17. If a sacrifice took place, it would have happened prior to the meal. Obviously, a sacrifice would count, if not as prayer, certainly as a kind of worship.

"after the *deipnon*"). Jesus's act of taking up the cup, blessing it, and passing it around to the other diners would have been understood by Paul's readers as the libation, that which formally brought the supper portion of the banquet (i.e., the *deipnon*) to a close.[18] Consequently, assuming the Corinthians were following the pattern laid down by Jesus, it is reasonable to assume that the ritual meal of the Corinthian assembly consisted at least of the normal supper (*deipnon*) and libation, two of the three typical components of a Greco-Roman meal. The *deipnon* followed by the libation, of course, would also have been the pattern that the cultic associations followed. But cultic association meals would have included a symposium following the libation, a symposium that would feature both wine and acts of worship.

Did the meal of the Jesus followers at Corinth include such a symposium? There are a number of reasons to believe that it did. First, in Paul's criticism of the Lord's Supper, he chastised the Corinthians because "one goes hungry and another becomes drunk" (11:21). Wine was not mentioned in connection with the *deipnon* of Jesus's meal (the template that Paul had laid out for the Corinthians at an earlier time); it only made its appearance at the libation. Assuming that the Corinthians were following the pattern of Jesus's meal, the offending Corinthians therefore would have become intoxicated not while eating the supper (*deipnon*) itself but only *after* the libation, that is, at a symposium when the wine began to flow.

Second, when he focused on the supper (*deipnon*) itself in 1 Corinthians 11, Paul employed the language of the Corinthians "coming together" several times ("when you come together" [11:17]; "when you come together as an assembly" [11:18]; "when you come together" [11:20]; "when you come together to eat" [11:33]). In his later discussion of their worship service in chapter 14, he used the same language (1 Cor 14:26), suggesting that the worship service likewise took place when they "came together" to eat.[19] The best opportunity for such worship to take place in connection to a meal (as the meals of other associations have shown us) would have been at a symposium, that which normally followed the meal's libation.

Third, there is a curious passage in the letter to the Ephesians that specifically tied acts of worship to wine-drinking (which, in turn, suggests that

18. Although the passing around of the cup to those at the meal is not specifically mentioned in 1 Cor 11:25, it is nevertheless presumed by Paul's comments that follow ("Do this, as often as you drink [the cup], in remembrance of me"); furthermore, Paul repeatedly summarizes the meal as eating the bread and drinking the cup (11:26, 27–29).

19. Andrew B. McGowan, *Ancient Christian Worship: Early Church Practices in Social, Historical, and Theological Perspective* (Grand Rapids: Baker, 2014), 30.

Eucharistic meals included symposia). The passage states: "Do not get drunk with wine, for that is debauchery; but be filled with the Spirit, as you sing psalms and hymns and spiritual songs among yourselves, singing and making melody to the Lord in your hearts, giving thanks to God the Father at all times and for everything in the name of our Lord Jesus Christ" (Eph 5:18–20; cf. Col 3:16). This passage hints that some worshipers focused on drinking wine (to the point of drunkenness) rather than on acts of devotion during the worship service of the assembly. Although Ephesians came from a later time than 1 Corinthians (and was written by a different author), the connection that we find in Ephesians suggests that the earliest worship services occurred during a symposium, following the common meal.[20]

Do we have any indication of the type of devotional activities that happened during the Corinthian symposium? From Paul we hear that it would have included "hymns, lessons, revelations, [speaking in] tongues, and [the] interpretation [of that which was spoken in tongues]" (1 Cor 14:26). Of these activities, we have already seen that the symposia of cultic association meals would sometime feature hymns sung in honor of the gods. At the symposium of the Lord's Supper, hymns were probably sung in praise of Jesus. While we do not know anything about the melodies to such hymns, words from some early hymns can be recovered from the New Testament. For example, in Paul's letter to the Philippians, the apostle quotes a hymn in honor of Jesus that was likely sung at the Philippian worship service (and possibly in the symposia of Paul's other communities):

> Christ Jesus,
> Who being in the form of God,
> Did not count equality with God
> Something to be held on to,
> But he emptied himself,
> Taking on the form of a slave,
> Becoming as humans are,
> And being in all ways like a human
> Was even more humble,
> Accepting even death, death on a cross.
> And for this God raised him up
> And gave him the name
> Which is above all other names,

20. MacGowan, *Ancient Christian Worship*, 113.

> So that all things
> In the heavens,
> On earth, and under the earth
> Should bend the knee at the name of Jesus
> And that every tongue should acknowledge
> Jesus Christ as Lord
> To the glory of God the Father. (Phil 2:6–11)[21]

Other important hymns of the early Jesus movement appear, among other places, in the pseudepigraphic letter to the Colossians (1:15–20) and at the beginning of John's Gospel (1:1–18, probably excluding vv. 5–7 and 15).

In the passage from 1 Cor 14 quoted above, Paul also mentioned "lessons" delivered at the symposium. It is not exactly clear what Paul meant by this. It may have been ethical exhortation or it may have been some kind of narrative. We know that a symposium of the Iobacchoi, a cultic association dedicated to Dionysus, featured something called a *theologia*. This probably meant some kind of speech delivered in praise of Dionysus (*IG* II² 1368.115). Perhaps the "lesson" mentioned by Paul would have been a similar kind of speech, in praise of Jesus or God. The other activities mentioned by Paul, delivering "revelations" (by which he probably meant prophesying), speaking in tongues, and the interpretation of speech delivered in tongues—all activities associated with the Spirit—were perhaps unique to the symposia of the Jesus movement.

Regardless, it appears that the ritual meals of the Jesus assemblies, consisting of a supper (*deipnon*), libation, and symposium (worship service), strongly resembled the regular ritual meals held by other cultic associations. But the meal not only resembled that of ancient associations in form, it seems to have also corresponded (at least somewhat) in its purpose and meaning.

In terms of its purpose, the regular, ritual meals of both voluntary associations and assemblies of Jesus followers functioned to affirm the importance of each community. That is to say, the very act of communal eating by those in each group implicitly acknowledged the boundary between those within (i.e., the diners of the association or assembly) and those outside. More importantly, it reinforced for the diner in each community what it meant to belong to a group of like-minded individuals.

Indeed, Paul's quotation of Jesus's words over the bread, "this is my body that is *for you* (plural)," affirmed both the significance and the unity of the

---

21. The translation is from Hal Taussig, *In the Beginning Was the Meal: Social Experimentation and Early Christian Identity* (Minneapolis: Fortress, 2009), 106.

community. The significance of the group was made evident by the phrase "for you." Christ, Paul insisted, had given his life for the creation of the community. But although a stronger connection between the bread and the unity of the community is not immediately evident to us in this particular passage, it would have been to the Corinthians because of what Paul had told them earlier in the same letter (chapter 10).

In that earlier chapter, the apostle had made the claim: "Because there is one bread, we who are many are one body, for we partake of the same bread" (1 Cor 10:17). With this statement, Paul correlated the dining community itself with the bread it consumed and thereby insisted that the many people eating the one loaf should be understood as "one body," that is to say, one community. In short, for Paul, *one* loaf symbolized *one* community.[22] Surprisingly, such an idea was not a Pauline invention. We can see something very similar in connection with an association of Pythagoreans, a philosophical-religious group that traced its origin to the sixth-century-BCE philosopher Pythagoras. At their meal, the Pythagoreans shared one loaf of bread as a symbol of their communal unity.[23]

22. It is noteworthy that the loaf not only symbolized the community, it also symbolized Christ's body as the words "this is my body" in 1 Cor 11:24 clearly indicate. Another passage in 1 Corinthians that connected Christ's body with the community appears in 1 Corinthians 12 where Paul described the assembly by using the image of the "body of Christ" (12:12–30). He contended that the assembly—made up of people with various spiritual gifts—resembled a body in which each different limb and organ was indispensable. That is to say, the diversity among the members of the association did not nullify the unity of the group. Indeed, it strengthened it. Like the image of the single loaf representing one group, the notion of a diverse group as a body was not Paul's creation. It was also borrowed from the surrounding culture (Cf. Livy, *History of Rome* 2.32; Dionysius of Halicarnassus, *Ant. rom.* 6.86).

23. The one loaf as symbolic of the unity of the group is from Diogenes Laertius, *Lives* 8.35. Unity at meals was important for many associations. Indeed, many prohibited any kind of antisocial behavior at their meals that could contribute to disunity. A cultic association devoted to Zeus Hypsistos, for example, wrote in its regulations: "It shall not be permissible for any [members] to . . . establish divisions . . . or for men to argue about one another's genealogies at the banquet or to abuse one another verbally at the banquet, or to chatter or indict or accuse one another" . . . (P.Lond. 7.2193.10–17; the text and the translation—which I have slightly emended—is from Ascough, Harland, and Kloppenborg, *Associations*, 176–77). The Iobacchoi, mentioned above, similarly legislated against antisocial behavior at their meals (*IG* II2 1368.63–90, translated in Ascough, Harland, and Kloppenborg, *Associations*, 13–16; the relevant lines appear on 15). The regulations of the worshipers of Diana and Antinoüs at Lanuvium (southeast of Rome) were similar. They, like those of the Iobacchoi, proposed a fine for abusive language or for moving from one place to another (*CIL* 15.2112, translated in Ascough, Harland, and Kloppenborg, *Associations*, 194–198; the relevant lines are found on 197–98).

Jesus's words following the blessing over the bread, "Do this in remembrance of me" (1 Cor 11:24), signal that the Lord's Supper functioned for early Jesus followers as a type of memorial meal. In this regard, the Lord's Supper also resembled the meals of certain associations, specifically memorial meals held by them. An association of Epicureans, for example, held a monthly memorial banquet in honor of their founder, Epicurus. Like the Lord's Supper, established by Jesus, the Epicurean banquet was presumed to have been started by the philosopher Epicurus himself.[24] Both meals, the Epicurean banquet and the Lord's Supper, celebrated the founder of each respective community.[25]

In Paul's account of the last supper, Jesus's words over the cup (i.e., the words spoken at the meal's libation), "This cup is the new covenant in my blood" (1 Cor 11:25), add yet another dimension to our understanding the significance of the meal for the members of the assembly of Jesus followers. The phrase "new covenant" on the surface shows significant divergence from the meals of pagan cultic associations. This is because the idea of a "new covenant" presupposes the notion of an earlier covenant, specifically, the original covenant between the deity and Israel.

According to the Scriptures, that original covenant was established by means of a blood sacrifice:

> [Moses] sent young men of the people of Israel, who offered burnt-offerings and sacrificed oxen as offerings of well-being to the Lord. Moses took half of the blood and put it in basins, and half of the blood he dashed against the altar. Then he took the book of the covenant, and read it in the hearing of the people; and they said, "All that the Lord has spoken we will do, and we will be obedient." Moses took the blood and dashed it on the people, and said, "See the blood of the covenant that the Lord has made with you in accordance with all these words." (Exod 24:5–8)

The use of the terms "blood" and "covenant" in Jesus's words over the cup almost certainly pointed to this passage. Consequently, the words spoken over the wine (i.e., the words spoken during the libation) were clearly intended to express the similarity between the sacrifice of oxen in the Exodus passage (note especially the emphasis on the role of the blood of the oxen) and the sacrificial

---

24. Epicurus lived from 341 to 270 BCE. On the banquet as established by Epicurus himself, see Diogenes Laertius, *Lives* 10.17.

25. Another example comes from Lucian of Samosata, who tells of sacrifices (naturally followed by a common meal) made in memory of the suffering of the deity Adonis (*Goddess* 6).

death (i.e., the blood) of Jesus. Just as the blood of the sacrificed oxen signaled (and to some extent, initiated) the covenant between God and Israel, so too the death of Jesus (i.e., his blood, recalled by the meal's libation) inaugurated a new covenant between the deity and the members of the Jesus movement.

The command to drink the cup "in remembrance of Jesus" would suggest that the Lord's Supper be understood by the members of the assembly as a *remembrance* of the sacrificial establishment of a new covenant. But it is also important to note that, as Paul describes things in 1 Corinthians, the Lord's Supper was not only to be understood as a meal *commemorating* Jesus's sacrificial act; the meal itself also *functioned* as a kind of sacrifice.

Evidence for a sacrificial understanding of the meal appears in 1 Cor 10:16, where Paul asked, "The cup of blessing that we bless, is it not a sharing in the blood of Christ?" Shortly thereafter, the apostle commanded the Corinthians to "consider the people of Israel" (meaning here the Jews of his time) and then asked, "Are not those [people] who eat the sacrifices partners in the altar?" (1 Cor 10:18). The connection made here between the consumption of the Eucharistic wine and the consumption of meat sacrificed at the Jerusalem temple suggests that Paul viewed the Eucharist as in some way acting like a sacrifice. Paul affirmed this sacrificial understanding of the Eucharist a few verses later when he made the claim: "You cannot partake of the table of the Lord [i.e., the Lord's Supper] and the table of demons [i.e., pagan sacrifice]" (1 Cor 10:21). This juxtaposition also casts the Eucharist as a sacrifice of sorts.

The idea of the Lord's Supper as a kind of sacrifice brings us back to the meals of other associations for, as mentioned above, those meals often began with a sacrifice; the sacrificial animal, after it was slaughtered and cooked, provided the fare for the association's meal. The interpretation of Jesus's death as a sacrifice may have made the celebration of the Lord's Supper more comprehensible to a Greco-Roman audience. As with those other associations, the Lord's Supper was understood as a kind of sacrificial meal, although in the case of the assemblies of Jesus followers, the bread consumed stood in place of the sacrificial victim.

Summary and Conclusion

In this chapter, we have compared the assemblies of Jesus followers to Greco-Roman voluntary associations. Although Jesus assemblies most resembled the cultic type association, that similarity was not absolute. Indeed, smaller Jesus assemblies, such as the one that met in the home of Prisca and Aquila in Rome

(Rom 16:4–5), probably looked much more like small household associations than large cultic ones.

Both Jesus assemblies and voluntary associations possessed a cultic dimension. Associations typically honored one or more deities; professional associations usually focused on a deity connected to their professions while ethnic organizations tied themselves to one or more gods from their homeland. The urban assemblies of Jesus followers, although primarily made up of non-Jews, focused their attention on the God of the Jews and his son, Jesus.

But besides their cultic dimension, both voluntary associations and assemblies of Jesus followers provided important social benefits to those who had joined. Each gave their members a sense of belonging and treated them as in some sense "set apart" from the rest of society. An inscription from one association in Philadelphia, an association that included "men and women, free people and household slaves" (cf. Gal 3:28), required its members to live an ethical existence. In this regard, it closely resembled the assemblies of Jesus followers, which likewise insisted on the moral transformation of their members.

Voluntary associations and assemblies of Jesus followers also resembled one another in their ritual practices, especially their regularly celebrated common meals. Association meals, like all formal banquets at the time, were comprised of three parts, a supper (*deipnon*) during which the meal itself was served, a libation, which brought the supper to a close, and a symposium, during which time wine was served. Cultic associations typically combined the symposium with some sort of worship service. Featured would be sacred hymns, orations in honor of a deity, sacred drama, or even sacred dances. The cultic meal of the Lord's Supper, as it was practiced in Corinth in the mid–first century, also tied its worship service to the symposium of its meal. It typically included hymns, lessons, revelations, and speaking in tongues. The quasi-sacrificial character of the Lord's Supper, at least as it was understood by Paul, also resembled the association meals, for the latter frequently featured the sacrifice of an animal whose meat served as the main course of the meal's *deipnon*.

CHAPTER 8

Unstained by the World

How did committing oneself to the Jesus movement affect one's relationships with pagan friends and associates? Did members of the movement have to set themselves totally apart from the larger society? Or could they, for the most part, continue their lives as before? The author of the New Testament letter of James suggested that proper behavior (what he called "religion that is pure and undefiled before God") consisted of two things: "to care for widows and orphans" and "to keep oneself unstained by the world" (Jas 1:27).[1] It is the latter phrase that is of primary importance in this chapter. How would one "keep [him or herself] unstained by the world"? What would that entail?[2] As

1. The letter of James was purportedly written by James, the brother of Jesus. This would be the same James that Paul mentions as one of the pillars in the Jerusalem church in the mid–first century. But based upon the author's excellent command of the Greek language and the seeming late date of the letter (James himself died in 62 CE), most scholars believe that the letter is pseudepigraphical.

2. In some ways, the situation of those in the movement was comparable to that of Jews living in the diaspora. Both groups were monotheistic and both rejected the worship of the traditional gods. Each group also rejected the imperial cult. That is to say, each group rejected the idea that the emperor, the members of his family, and his ancestors were divine beings. But the situation of non-Jewish Jesus followers was different from that of the Jews in a couple of different ways. First, Judaism was an ancient religion and, as such, it was tolerated by pagan society. To put it bluntly, the "odd" behavior of the Jews (i.e., their refusal to participate in some societal events) was accepted. Although the Jesus movement had some things in common with Judaism (e.g., the belief in the Jewish God and respect for the Jewish Scriptures), the movement itself was not ancient, and many of its members were not Jews. Consequently, the "odd" behavior of non-Jews in the movement puzzled outsiders. Second, most Jews living in the diaspora were the children of Jews; they had been raised Jewish and had lived all of their lives as Jews. Furthermore, they lived in communities of Jews with whom they had grown up. To the contrary, in its early years, the members of the Jesus movement had all converted. They

we will see, not everyone in the Jesus movement pursued the same strategy for negotiating the world. Keeping oneself "unstained by the world" meant different things to different people.

Monotheism and the Problem of Idolatry

Because of Judaism's commitment to absolute monotheism, it had long considered idolatry a particularly odious offense. Indeed, the first of the Ten Commandments insisted that God alone be worshipped:

> I am the Lord your God, who brought you out of the land of Egypt, out of the house of slavery; you shall have no other gods before me. You shall not make for yourself an idol, whether in the form of anything that is in heaven above, or that is on the earth beneath, or that is in the water under the earth. You shall not bow down to them or worship them; for I the Lord your God am a jealous God. (Exod 20:2–5a; cf. Deut 5:6–9a)

The Scriptures insisted that the violation of this essential commandment had been responsible for most of ancient Israel's misfortunes. The destruction of the Northern Kingdom (Israel) at the hands of the Assyrians in the late eighth century BCE was blamed on Israel's idolatrous behavior (e.g., 2 Kings 17:15–18; Ezek 23:5–10). The catastrophic end of the Southern Kingdom, and the Babylonian exile that followed (early sixth century BCE), was likewise attributed to the idolatry both of its rulers and its people (e.g., 2 Kgs 21:2–7, 10–14; Ezek 23:11–35). It is noteworthy that in the Scriptures both the people of the Northern and Southern Kingdoms were charged with following the practices of others, variously described as "the nations that were all around them," "the Amorites," and "the nations that the Lord drove out before the people of Israel." The message of the Scriptures was very clear: the God of Israel demands that he alone be worshipped; his people should not worship the gods of their neighbors.

In the Hellenistic and Roman periods, Jewish concern over idolatry continued; it became a particularly important issue among those living in the di-

---

were all children of pagans who had lived as pagans up until the point of their conversion. As a result, converts had divided loyalties. They still held strong connections to the larger (pagan) culture in which they were raised but they had also become members of a new subculture that made demands on them.

aspora. Diaspora Jews were faced with two choices: assimilating, that is to say, worshipping the gods of their neighbors (which some Jews did) or finding a way to preserve their monotheistic heritage while, at the same time, not living in total isolation. Given the Jewish origin of the Jesus movement (as well as the latter's acceptance of the Jewish God and the Jewish Scriptures), it is hardly surprising that concern over idolatry became important in the assemblies that had sprung up in the hellenized cities of the empire. Jesus followers, who had turned to "the one, true God" found themselves, like the diaspora Jews, surrounded by "so-called gods" (1 Cor 8:5), "beings that by nature [were] not gods" (Gal 4:8), and "dumb idols" (1 Cor 12:2).

It is somewhat difficult for us to grasp how challenging it was to lead a monotheistic existence in a polytheistic society. In our society, religion is considered a private matter; religion and civic life belong to separate realms. This, however, was not the case in the first century. Religion—that is to say, the traditional polytheistic religion of the empire—was both public and pervasive; it was woven into the very fabric of the culture. We would be surprised if a public concert, play, or professional sporting event that we attended began with some form of worship. But in the ancient world, it was expected. Religion was ever-present at public events. Even at a private dinner with pagan friends, a libation would have been dedicated to the *agathos daimon* (the "good spirit" that protected the household) and to the divine emperor.

Wherever he or she turned, the Jesus follower was hedged in by idolatrous practices; it was virtually impossible to avoid them. Choices had to be made continually about what could or could not be done in any number of situations. In the pages that follow, we will look at some events and circumstances where most members of the Jesus movement would have found it challenging to keep themselves "unstained by the world."

Participation in Civic Life and the Problem of Idolatry

One obvious venue where an encounter with pagan gods was unavoidable was the civic festival. Since the distinction between sacred and secular did not exist in the ancient world, we could just as easily refer to them as *religious* celebrations as *civic* festivals. Although some festivals were common throughout the cities of the Greek East, each city also had its own. For instance, festivals like the Panathenaia or Artemis's birthday celebration happened only in the cities of Athens and Ephesus respectively; each gave its inhabitants the opportunity to express pride in their cities.

Virtually all festivals focused on deities. The Athenian Panathenaia honored Athena, that city's patroness. The aforementioned Ephesian festival obviously featured Artemis, the patron of that city. Even civic festivals that celebrated the change of seasons featured gods. The Anthesteria, a three-day Athenian festival held in the spring, featured the drinking of the new wine from the grapes harvested the previous fall. Not surprisingly, this festival was dedicated to Dionysus, the god of wine. A spring event in Corinth that celebrated the opening of the navigation season, centered on Isis.[3] It was entitled the *Isidis navigium* ("ship of Isis") festival. It included a procession honoring the deity and it featured a decorated ship that was paraded through the streets of the city and ultimately launched at Cenchreae, Corinth's southern port.[4]

A highlight of many festivals, including most of those already mentioned, was a lavish procession that journeyed through the city. Statues of deities, crowds of devotees, herds of sacrificial animals, and even carts carrying mythological scenes were sometimes featured. Typically, the procession came to an end at the deity's temple; there sacrifices were offered. The famous frieze from the Athenian Parthenon depicts the Panathenaic procession and it shows both sacrificial cows and sheep being led through the city. They would eventually be slaughtered before the altar in front of the Parthenon. Of course, the sacrificial meat that resulted from the sacrificial beasts would have been distributed to the populace, most likely at dining facilities on the temple grounds.[5]

Although these civic festivals were indeed *religious* events, they were by no means strictly solemn affairs. In fact, they often had a carnival-like atmosphere, and looked more like a Mardi Gras celebration than a church service. Because of their carnival-like character, people would sometimes travel for miles from the surrounding areas to participate.[6] Festivals also afforded the possibility of shopping; merchants were obviously attracted to the crowds generated by the festivals and so they set up their stalls wherever they could.

But besides socializing and shopping, festivals also offered cultural events. People could hear a choir perform, see a play (possibly one written specifically

---

3. Because of the danger of winter sea travel, shipping was usually suspended from late September until early March.

4. The procession is vividly described in Apuleius, *Metam.* 11.1–16.

5. It should be noted here that, for the average urban inhabitant, meat would have been a normally out-of-reach delicacy due to its high price. Consequently, the opportunity to enjoy such a delicacy might have been difficult to pass up.

6. In fact, heralds were sometimes sent to nearby cities to invite their inhabitants to join the festivities.

for the festival), observe a dance recital, or listen to a poetry competition.[7] The subject matter of all such events would typically have been the god or goddess being celebrated. If such were a bit too highbrow for a given individual, he or she might instead attend the festival's athletic contests: track and field events, wrestling, boxing, and chariot racing, to name a few. Even sporting events like these had religious overtones. Of course, added to the above-mentioned spectacles was the lure of abundant food and drink.

Given the excitement and civic pride that adhered to such celebrations, it is hard to believe that many Jesus followers would have been uninterested in participating. Such festivals, like our national holidays, would have provided a welcome break from day-to-day life. The food, drink, entertainment, and fellowship would have been hard to pass up. Additionally, any hesitancy would probably have been countered by social pressure from friends and family. Indeed, the total avoidance of such a celebratory event had the potential to cause resentment on the part of one's friends and neighbors. An Ephesian who refused to celebrate the birthday of Artemis or an Athenian refusing to take part in the Panathenaia would be like an American repudiating the Fourth of July. Such refusal could be easily construed as both unpatriotic and blasphemous.

The type of resentment that could have been directed against those who would slight a city's patron is readily illustrated by a passage in Acts 19:23–40. There we see a riot breaking out in the streets of Ephesus because it had been believed that Paul had belittled the goddess Artemis, the city's patron. Fearing that "the temple of the great goddess Artemis will be scorned, and she will be deprived of her majesty that brought all Asia and the world to worship her," the populace—all the while chanting "Great is Artemis of the Ephesians!"— dragged Paul and his fellows to the theater, presumably to be condemned by the Ephesian assembly.[8] Although the historicity of the Acts episode is ques-

---

7. This is attested by Dio Chrysostom, who asserted: "But people also attend the [civic] festivals, some just to see the sights and the athletic contests in particular; and all those who take a very great interest in these continue doing nothing else from early dawn. Many too bring in merchandise of all sorts, the tradespeople, that is; and some display their own arts and crafts; while others show off their accomplishments, many of them declaiming poems, both tragedies and epics, and many others prose works, so that they annoy the man who has come for a rest and wishes to have a holiday. And these people seem very much like those who hum tunes and sing songs at the symposia, whom you cannot help hearing even if you do not wish it" (*Symp.* 27.5–6).

8. A comment made by an inhabitant of Ionia (western Asia Minor) likewise shows similar resentment experienced by monotheists living in a polytheistic culture. The Ionian individual represented a group who had argued to the Romans that the Jewish inhabitants of their territory should not enjoy the same privileges as the rest of the population. The unnamed

tionable, the narrative nevertheless illustrates the pride that a patron deity could inspire among her people.[9]

In light of the lure of the festivals and the potential resentment of neighbors if Jesus followers did not participate, it is reasonable to assume that some (perhaps many?) in the movement would have continued to take part in traditional civic festivals after their conversion, at least to some extent. Perhaps some thought that there was little harm in watching the myths being dramatized or presented in dance. Others probably saw little wrong with attending the athletic competitions. Still others may have thought it acceptable to observe the spectacle of the procession.

Unfortunately, we have no direct evidence from Jesus followers about the acceptability (or lack thereof) of attending such events. If some participated and others did not, we would expect to see some controversy reflected in the New Testament texts. But we do not. Can we assume from such silence that most saw little objectionable about participating? Perhaps. A glance at Jewish attitudes may offer some insight. Although we have no specific evidence about Jewish views about civic festivals on the whole, we do know something about Jewish attitudes toward a couple of the events that would have been staged at festivals, specifically, athletic events and theater performances.

Athletic events, although under the patronage of the pagan gods, were apparently attended by many Jews. Philo, the Jewish philosopher, gives evidence in his writings that he had attended games on more than one occasion. Indeed, in a single passage (*Agr.* 111–21), "he gives details about contests in running, boxing, wrestling, the *pankration* (an athletic contest invoking both boxing and wrestling), and the long jump. In some cases he has given us information we find in few other sources."[10] Furthermore, an extant letter from the Emperor Claudius to the Jews of Alexandria informs us that the Jews in that city had been lobbying for the privilege of participating in athletic events there alongside pagan Alexandrians.[11] Even in Judea, Herod introduced pagan-style

---

Ionian insisted that "if the Jews were to be their fellows, they should worship the Ionians' gods" (Josephus, *Ant.* 12.126).

9. Although a number of scholars see a source that narrated a historical event lying behind the narrative, such is not necessary. As one scholar has rightly maintained, "[the author] did not require a source to depict urban disorder, for he had no lack of practice. Mob action is quite common in Acts after all, and the works of fiction and history were replete with accounts of urban disorder" (Richard I. Pervo, *Acts: A Commentary* [Minneapolis: Fortress, 2009], 490).

10. Louis H. Feldman, *Jew and Gentile in the Ancient World* (Princeton: Princeton University Press, 1993), 60.

11. The letter is cited in Feldman, *Jew and Gentile*, 61.

games in Jerusalem (held every four years) in honor of the emperor Augustus (Josephus, *Jewish Antiquities* 15.8.1). It is hard to believe that these games were not attended by the Jerusalemites. Most Jews, it seems, had little problem attending athletic competitions, despite their pagan underpinning.

Theater attendance was a bit more controversial. Because the entertainment was explicitly performed in honor of pagan deities, Rabbi Meir (second century CE) prohibited Jews from attending (b. ʿAbod. Zar. 18b). But other evidence suggests that Jews did indeed attend theater performances. Philo tells us that he went to the theater frequently (*On Drunkenness* 177). An Alexandrian Jew named Ezekiel (sometimes known as Ezekiel the Tragedian) composed a Greek-style drama retelling the story of the Israelite Exodus from Egypt.[12] It is hard to believe that he could have written his tragedy without extensive knowledge of Greek theater. Finally, an inscription in the ancient theater of Miletus (in western Asia Minor, not far from Ephesus) marks out a "place for the Jews who are also [known as] those who fear God" (*CIJ* 2.748). Clearly, Jews in Miletus not only attended the theater, they had reserved seats. In sum, while some Jews objected to the theater because of its connection to the pagan gods, many others attended, untroubled by that association.

All of this suggests to us that the monotheistic Jesus followers likewise may have found little reason to avoid sporting events or the theater. Consequently, we can cautiously assume that many would have taken part (at least to some degree) in civic festivals.[13] But a crucial issue associated with civic festivals would have been the consumption of the food (i.e., meat) distributed following the festival sacrifices. Could people in the Jesus movement have eaten it? This, we know, was controversial.

Two New Testament writings, 1 Corinthians (written in the middle of the first century) and the book of Revelation (written at that end of the first century) demonstrate that there was significant controversy over the practice. Both texts inform us that some believed that eating such food was acceptable while others strongly disagreed. We will look at both of these texts in some detail below. But before we do, we will describe some of the other venues, primarily private events, in which one might encounter sac-

---

12. An introduction and translation can be found in James H. Charlesworth, ed., *The Old Testament Pseudepigrapha* (Garden City, NY: Doubleday, 1985), 2:803–19.

13. Tertullian, writing at the end of the second or beginning of the third century, addressed many of these issues in his work "On Idolatry" (*De idolatria*). He asserted that Christians could take part in social events such as weddings. They could not accept invitations to sacrifices but, if they were in attendance at events in which sacrifices were performed, they could remain, as long as they were only spectators and not participants.

rificial meat or other practices that could be considered idolatrous from a monotheistic perspective.

Social Gatherings with Family or Friends and the Problem of Idolatry

Private events involving family or friends could also raise the possibility of issues concerning idolatry. In many cases, sacrificial meat would also be an issue. For example, a friend seeking a cure for a disease or medical condition might offer a sacrifice to Asclepius. Or, having been cured, that same friend would probably offer a thanksgiving sacrifice to the deity. In either case, the person making the sacrifice would likely have invited close friends or relatives to attend the sacrificial ritual and participate in the meal that followed.

Other occasions could also call for sacrifice. For example, a successful sea voyage was often followed by a sacrifice to the Dioskouroi, the twin deities favored by seafarers.[14] A homecoming might also call for a thanksgiving sacrifice. The return of a long-lost son was the occasion for a feast in one of Jesus's parables (Luke 15:11–32). Although that story presumed a Jewish context, were the same event to occur in the pagan world, the killing of the calf prior to the meal would almost certainly have been a sacrificial act; the meat from the sacrifice would have constituted the main course of the meal to follow.[15] An invitation to such an event, issued by a close pagan friend or relative, could have placed a Jesus follower in a difficult position. Could he or she attend the sacrifice? What about the meal that followed?

Some other, seemingly benign family celebrations, such as birthday celebrations, could also potentially strain relations with one's polytheistic relatives and friends. While in our culture, a birthday party is usually an entirely secular event, such was not necessarily the case in the ancient world. The Roman poet Horace, writing of a birthday celebration honoring his patron, declared, "our altar, wreathed with fresh boughs, asks for the sacred blood of the lamb as victim" (Horace, *Odes* 4.11). His comments made clear that the meat to be served at the birthday dinner would be the lamb sacrificed at the wreathed altar.

A papyrus invitation from Egypt, in which a certain Diogenes requested his friends to join him to celebrate his infant daughter's birthday, added another

14. Rituals having to do with travel were popular because voyages, especially by sea, could be quite risky. Paul mentions that he was shipwrecked three times in 2 Cor 11:25. Acts 27:1–44 narrates a sea voyage of Paul that ends in shipwreck.

15. In a Jewish context, the slaughter of the animal at home would not have been sacrificial because sacrifice was only acceptable at the temple in Jerusalem.

twist: "Diogenes invites you to dinner for the first birthday of his daughter in the Serapeum tomorrow . . . from the eighth hour onward" (P.Oxy. 36.2791). Although there is no specific mention of an animal being slaughtered here, the fact that the meal takes place in the Serapeum (i. e., the temple of Serapis) suggests at least such a possibility. But even were sacrificial meat not to be offered as fare, the location could be problematic; the celebration was to take place on the grounds of a pagan temple. Could a Jesus follower even attend?

Wedding ceremonies could also present problems for a Jesus follower. In Greco-Roman times, there was no specific marriage service per se. Nor was there any written document to confirm the union. While there were marriage rituals, they usually varied by location. Regardless, wherever a wedding took place, sacrifice was central. Could a Jesus follower attend the sacrifice performed at a friend's wedding? Furthermore, since a wedding banquet would, of course, follow the sacrifice and the sacrificial meat would be served to those in attendance, could a Jesus follower participate in the meal?

Another extant papyrus invitation, this one to a coming-of-age party, provides us with a somewhat different problem than we have already seen. In this invitation, a certain Apollonius invited his guests to a meal in honor of his brothers: "Apollonius requests you to dine on the couch of the Lord Serapis on the occasion of the coming of age of his brothers in the Thoerion" (P.Oxy. 12.1484). Note that the guest here is invited to dine "on the couch of Serapis," which was on the grounds of a temple dedicated to the Egyptian deity Thoeris.[16]

Obviously, the couch mentioned was a dining couch, on which one reclined to eat. The fact that the couch in this invitation was identified as belonging to Serapis suggests that the deity was also a participant in the meal (and perhaps was considered the real host). We are not exactly sure what that means. On the island of Kos, a wedding banquet always featured the statue of Heracles as a guest at the meal.[17] Perhaps a statue of Serapis would have been present at the meal that took place "on the couch of Serapis." We can only speculate.

Again, while there is no specific mention of sacrifice in the invitation, such was a possibility. But even if sacrificial meat was not on the menu, there were two other possible problems. One we have already seen: the meal took place on the grounds of a pagan temple. The other had to do with the guests at

16. The deity Thoeris took the form of a hippopotamus.

17. Simon Price, *Religions of the Ancient Greeks*, KTAH (Cambridge: Cambridge University Press, 1999), 96.

the meal. Since the invitation referred to "the couch of Serapis," the meal was thought to be shared with that deity. All of the examples discussed so far have had to do with special occasions, either civic festivals or private celebrations of some kind. But it was not only special occasions that could cause problems for members of the Jesus movement.

A dinner with friends could also be problematic. Again, sacrificial meat could be served. Plutarch, in a work focused on dining, speaks about the poultry that had been served at a meal shared among friends: "The cock that [the cook] had set before the diners, although it has just been slaughtered as a sacrifice to Heracles, was as tender as if it had been a day old" (*Table Talk* 6.5). As far as we can tell, there was nothing particularly special about this meal. It was simply a dinner enjoyed by friends during which sacrificial meat was served. Even a meal for which an animal was not specifically sacrificed might still feature sacrificial meat. Temples sold surplus meat to local vendors who in turn sold it to the public; consequently, even meat bought at the meat markets could have been sacrificial meat.

One more issue regarding social occasions, particularly special celebrations, had to do with their location. As a few of the previous examples have shown us, celebratory meals were sometimes held at pagan temples. This was because most homes had limited dining space.[18] Even homes of the wealthy often had relatively small dining rooms. One fairly lavish villa excavated at Corinth could hold no more than nine in its dining room.[19] More humble dwellings would hold even fewer. For celebrations involving a dozen or more participants, a host obviously needed a larger venue. The natural place to look would be the local temples.

Because animal sacrifice played such an important role in ancient worship, temples sometimes had dining facilities on their grounds. These dining facilities were not usually within the temples themselves but in separate buildings within the temple's sacred precinct. These dining rooms could typically accommodate a fair number of diners. For example, those at a temple of Asclepius, at Troizen in Greece (approximately fifty miles southeast of Corinth), could easily serve more than fifty guests at a time. The temple of Demeter and Kore, on the acropolis overlooking the city of Corinth, at one time had at least forty dining rooms and could accommodate hundreds of diners.[20] Sometimes,

18. The fact that diners reclined to eat made space even more of a problem.

19. For a floor plan, see Jerome Murphy-O'Connor, *St. Paul's Corinth: Texts and Archaeology*, 3rd ed. (Collegeville, MN: Liturgical Press, 2002), 179 (fig. 7).

20. The dining facilities were no longer in existence at Corinth's temple of Demeter and Kore by Paul's time. However, it has been suggested that dining continued, either in less durable

a temple's dining facilities functioned merely as rented space, with little attention paid to the deity in the adjacent temple. But at other times, the immediacy of the deity was important.

What would all of this mean for a Jesus follower? Could he or she attend a celebratory meal held at a temple if sacrificial meat were on the menu? What if the temple was only being used as rented space? What about a dinner with friends at their home? Could one even go? If one did attend such a meal and an animal was sacrificed before the meal, could a Jesus follower eat it? What if no sacrifice was performed but the meal featured meat bought at the meat market?

Jesus Followers and Food Sacrificed to Pagan Gods

In Paul's discussion about sacrificial meat in 1 Corinthians, he touched on a few of the issues outlined above. His discussion is extensive, occupying three chapters of 1 Corinthians (chs. 8–10), and is complicated. Consequently, we will look at it in some detail. Such a detailed examination will allow us to both understand the complexity of the issue as well as the ambiguous attitude that many in the movement (including Paul himself) held about it.

Paul's argument began as follows: "Now concerning food sacrificed to idols: we know that 'all of us possess knowledge.' Knowledge puffs up, but love builds up. Anyone who claims to know something does not yet have the necessary knowledge; but anyone who loves God is known by him. Hence, as to the eating of food offered to idols, we know that 'no idol in the world really exists,' and that 'there is no God but one'" (1 Cor 8:1–4). Within these opening remarks, three statements appear within quotation marks. They are: "all of us possess knowledge," "no idol in the world really exists," and "there is no God but one."[21] No quotation marks were used by ancient Greek writers; these quotation marks were added by the translators because most scholars consider these statements to be the assertions of some within the Corinthian community.[22] Understood in the context of the discussion about "food sac-

---

buildings (of which no evidence has survived) or in tents, or possibly even in the open air. For more on these dining facilities, including illustrations of the Asclepium at Troizen, see Peter D. Gooch, *Dangerous Food: 1 Corinthians 8–10 in Its Context*, Studies in Christianity and Judaism 5 (Waterloo, ON: Wilfrid Laurier University Press, 1993), 3–4, 19–20; see also figs. 5–6 (xiii–xiv).

21. A few verses later, another statement appears in quotation marks: "food will not bring us close to God" (8:8). This also seems to be a Corinthian statement.

22. Not all translations feature the quotation marks. However, they are featured in many

rificed to idols," we can use these statements to piece together the argument that was made by some Corinthians.

Apparently, some in Corinth had decided that, since they had gained the knowledge (from Paul) that there was only one true God, then the idols did not really exist. Therefore, there would be no reason to avoid food that had been sacrificed to nonexistent deities. In light of this, it seems safe to infer that *some* members of the Corinthian assembly actually ate sacrificial food. How did Paul respond? Surprisingly, he did *not* seem to disagree with their argument; at least, he agreed with it in principle.

Nevertheless, he made a slight correction: "Indeed, even though there may be so-called gods in heaven or on earth—as in fact there are many gods and many lords—yet for us there is one God, the Father, from whom are all things and for whom we exist, and one Lord, Jesus Christ, through whom are all things and through whom we exist" (1 Cor 8:5–6). The first phrase of this statement follows up on the claim in the previous verse. If we put aside for the moment the phrase that is offset ("as in fact . . ."), Paul's logic is clear. The argument can be paraphrased as follows: "Since we know that pagan gods do not exist it is acceptable to eat sacrificial meat; even if so-called pagan gods existed, for us there is only one God."

But the phrase that we previously set aside, "as in fact there are many gods and lords," complicates matters. What did Paul mean by it? Did he mean that the pagan gods *objectively* existed, that is, they were real (even though they were only so-called gods)? Or did he mean that the pagan gods only existed *subjectively*, in the minds of those who worshipped them? Unfortunately, it is difficult to decide. For now, we can only conclude that Paul acknowledged the existence of "gods and lords" in some way, perhaps objectively, perhaps subjectively. But regardless, at this point in his argument, Paul did not insist that eating sacrificial meat was unacceptable. To the contrary, his warning shortly thereafter, which acknowledged the "liberty" of those who had made the argument, indicates that they (i.e., those with "knowledge") could indeed eat such meat (1 Cor 8:9). But Paul's argument was not yet finished.

Although he had, for the most part, conceded their point, he nevertheless tried to dissuade the Corinthians from their position by countering their first claim that "all of us possess knowledge." He contended instead that "it is not everyone . . . who has this knowledge" (1 Cor 8:7), and he warned those "who possess knowledge" (i.e., those arguing for the acceptability of eating sacrificial

---

translations, including the NRSV (that I have quoted here). Other translations that include the quotation marks are (among others): ESV, GNB, NAB, and NIV.

meat) that their actions could "become a stumbling block" to others: "Since some have become so accustomed to idols until now, they still think of the food they eat as food offered to an idol; and their conscience, being weak, is defiled. . . . For if others see you, who possess knowledge, eating in the temple of an idol, might they not, since their conscience is weak, be encouraged to the point of eating food sacrificed to idols?" (1 Cor 8:7, 10). Paul's argument here is crystal clear. Eating sacrificial meat could cause others (those whose consciences were weak) to sin.

It is noteworthy that at this point in his argument, Paul referred to some-one "eating in the temple of an idol" and the dangers that such could present to someone whose conscience was weak. What did he mean by "eating in the temple of an idol"? Did he mean eating food that resulted from a sacrifice *at that temple*? Did he mean dining in the space that *someone had rented* from the temple? Unfortunately, he did not elaborate. For Paul, what seemed to be important was not what was actually going on but what *could* be perceived as happening by the so-called weak person. Based on this, it seems that Paul could not approve of anyone "eating in the temple of an idol," regardless of the reason.

In the chapter of 1 Corinthians that follows (chapter 9), Paul, at first glance, seemed to go off in an entirely different direction; he began to talk about his "rights" as an apostle. He specifically articulated these as, first, his right to bring a wife on his missionary travels as did "the rest of the apostles and the brothers of the Lord and Cephas" (1 Cor 9:5–6) and, second, his right to be supported by the community in which he preached (1 Cor 9:4, 7–11), a point he reinforced with a scriptural quotation: "You shall not muzzle an ox while it is treading out the grain" (1 Cor 9:9). But, despite initial appearances, Paul had not in fact veered off subject in this chapter. Rather, he was still ad-dressing the issue of sacrificed meat by providing an example, specifically an example based on his own behavior, for those in the assembly. That is to say, Paul here implied that, just as he himself had given up some of his "rights" as an apostle, so too, those who believed that eating sacrificial meat was unob-jectionable should likewise give up their "right" to eat it for the good of the community (1 Cor 9:12b–23).

In chapter 10, although still focused on the topic of food sacrificed to idols, Paul made yet another turn. He opened the chapter with an allusion to the scriptural story of Israel's wilderness wandering: "I do not want you to be unaware, brothers and sisters, that our ancestors were all under the cloud, and all passed through the sea, and all were baptized into Moses in the cloud and in the sea, and all ate the same spiritual food, and all drank the same spiritual drink. For they drank from the spiritual rock that followed them, and the rock was Christ. Nevertheless, God was not pleased with most of them, and they were struck down in the wilderness" (1 Cor 10:1–5). Why did Paul tell this story? He provided the answer shortly thereafter: "These things happened to them to serve as an example, and they were written down to instruct us, on whom the ends of the ages have come" (1 Cor 10:11). Paul then returned directly to the issue of sacrificed meat. Whereas in chapter 8 he had allowed for the possibility of eating sacrificial meat (at least theoretically), here he suggested that the Corinthians totally avoid it. His reasoning is compact and needs to be carefully unpacked.

He began by pointing out that the celebration of the Lord's Supper brought the Corinthians into a relationship, a kind of communion with Christ: "The cup of blessing that we bless, is it not a sharing in the blood of Christ? The bread that we break, is it not a sharing in the body of Christ?" (1 Cor 10:16) He then implicitly compared this relationship between the Jesus follower and Christ to the kind of relationship that would emerge when Jews performed ritual sacrifice to God at the Jerusalem temple: "Consider the people of Israel; are not those who eat the sacrifices partners in the altar?" (1 Cor 10:18).

But then Paul stopped himself and asked: "What do I imply then? That food sacrificed to idols is anything, or that an idol is anything?" From the standpoint of those who defended their right to eat sacrificial meat because "no idol . . . really exists" (1 Cor 8:4), the expected answer would be something like: "since the pagan gods do not exist, no relationship between a person eating sacrificial meat and a pagan god could possibly result." By thus reasoning, they would have believed their position affirmed.

But Paul was moving in a different direction. He answered his own question in a rather surprising way: "No, I imply that what pagans sacrifice, they sacrifice to demons and not to God. I do not want you to be partners with demons" (1 Cor 10:19–20). Although Paul had earlier agreed in principle with those who had argued that the pagan deities were not gods and therefore sacrificing to nonexistent deities could do no harm (1 Cor 8:4–5), here he made the claim that although the pagan deities were not gods, they still existed. But they did not merely exist in the minds of their worshipers. They possessed an objective reality; they existed as demonic figures.

Having made his point, he then concluded this part of his argument: "You cannot drink the cup of the Lord and the cup of demons. You cannot partake of the table of the Lord and the table of demons" (1 Cor 10:19–21). In other words, for a person in the assembly to eat sacrificial meat could result, as he said in the next verse, in provoking the Lord to jealousy (1 Cor 10:22).[23] Here he pointed back to the story of Israel that he had recounted earlier in the chapter. Provoking the Lord to jealousy by sacrificing to demons could bring the same fate to the Corinthians as Israel met when they "were struck down in the wilderness" by provoking the Lord by their idolatry.

So although earlier Paul had seemed to agree with the Corinthian group that had insisted that there was nothing objectionable about eating food sacrificed to idols (1 Cor 8:1–6, 8), here he argued that such a practice should definitely be avoided because it honored demons. And honoring demons could provoke the Lord to jealousy. But by introducing this twist to his argument, Paul's answer seems, if not inconsistent, at least ambivalent. Was eating sacrificial meat acceptable or not? Can we reconcile the different positions that Paul seems to take?

In order to answer that question, we must consider the overarching problem that 1 Corinthians had intended to address. Although Paul addressed a number of specific problems in Corinth, such as eating sacrificial food, spiritual gifts, and problems at the Lord's Supper, the main problem that he was worried about was factionalism (1 Cor 1:10) within the assembly. That is to say, there were serious divisions within the community.[24] If we take this into account, I believe we can make some sense of the seeming inconsistency in Paul's advice.

In chapter 8, Paul had taken the side of those who saw the act of eating sacrificial meat as unobjectionable. In principle, Paul agreed with them, although he cautioned that their actions could hurt others in the community; he warned that they should not necessarily take advantage of their "liberty" to eat sacrificial meat. Paul reaffirmed that position in chapter 9 by presenting himself as an example: he had given up some of his rights for the sake of the community.

In chapter 10, however, Paul seemed to take the side of the "weak," those who had objected to the eating of food sacrificed to idols. He acknowledged that eating sacrificial meat could be harmful. But, just as he did not totally agree with the "stronger" members of the community in chapter 8 (arguing that they should give up their "right" to eat food sacrificed to idols for the

---

23. There is a textual problem here. Some manuscripts speak of "provoking *the Lord* to jealousy" while others refer to "provoking *Christ* to jealousy." It is difficult to determine the earlier reading. Rather than trying to solve this dilemma here, I have opted for the ambiguous term "Lord," which for Paul sometimes meant God and at other times meant Christ.

24. Margaret M. Mitchell, *Paul and the Rhetoric of Reconciliation*, HUT 28 (Tübingen: Mohr Siebeck, 1991).

good of the community), he also did not totally agree with the opinion of the "weak." While affirming their objections to eating sacrificial meat, he also acknowledged the legitimacy of the argument of the "strong" (at least to some extent): the idols were not gods. But, he also conceded that they had some kind of existence; they existed as demons. As such, Paul concluded, it was unwise to participate in the Lord's Supper and to eat the meat sacrificed to demons. It could incite the Lord's wrath.

Paul's intent, it seems, was to get both sides, those who ate sacrificial meat and those who did not, to think about this problem differently than they had previously. For Paul, the issue was less an ethical issue than a relational one. What was of fundamental concern for him was how the different members of the community related to one another. In light of this, what can we say of Paul's opinion regarding the ability of Jesus followers to participate in the kind of activity that could bring them into contact with food offered to the pagan gods? Probably the best answer to this question can be found in Paul's concluding section: "Do not seek your own advantage, but that of others" (1 Cor 10:24).

By making such a statement, Paul seems to have excluded the possibility of eating sacrificial meat. By extension, he also seems to have excluded participating in the other kinds of private events with friends and family. However, to draw such a hard and fast conclusion would be a mistake; Paul did make some concessions. He said: "Eat whatever is sold in the meat market without raising any question on the ground of conscience, for 'the earth and its fullness are the Lord's.' If an unbeliever invites you to a meal and you are disposed to go, eat whatever is set before you without raising any question on the ground of conscience" (1 Cor 10:25–27). In this statement, we see some flexibility on Paul's part. Those whose conscience would allow it could attend private dinners.

But, even this was not the last word. Paul added: "But if someone says to you, 'This has been offered in sacrifice,' then do not eat it, out of consideration for the one who informed you, and for the sake of conscience—I mean the other's conscience, not your own" (1 Cor 10:28–29). Paul here concedes that in a private dining situation, a person *could* eat sacrificial meat, *unless someone else raised the issue*. As the context makes clear, that "somebody else" would have been a fellow Jesus follower who saw the act as objectionable.

The situation in Corinth suggests to us that *some* Jesus followers, not just in Corinth but likely in other cities of the empire as well, went to the birthday parties of (pagan) family members and friends, attended their weddings, and accepted social invitations to dine with unbelievers, and likely participated in civic festivals. The problem of idolatry apparently did not overly trouble them.

On the other hand, we can also see that there were strong objections from others in the movement. Paul's discussion in 1 Corinthians 8–10 suggests that the consumption of sacrificial meat was the real sticking point. 1 Corinthians 8–10 gives no indication that any of the other activities mentioned were problematic. Like many Jews, Jesus followers seem to have believed that they could participate in civic and social events with their pagan friends and neighbors *up to a point*. Where some seem to have drawn the line was eating sacrificial meat.

Curiously, the controversy over the eating of food sacrificed to idols did not go away. At the end of the first century, people were still arguing about it. From the book of Revelation, we learn that some people in assemblies of Jesus followers in the cities of Pergamum and Thyatira (both in western Asia Minor) were eating such food. Apparently, the prophetess at Thyatira whom the author labeled "Jezebel" allowed it, and John, the author of the book of Revelation, strongly condemned the practice: "I have this against you: you tolerate that woman 'Jezebel,' who calls herself a prophet and is teaching and leading astray my servants . . . to eat food sacrificed to idols" (Rev 2:20). What can we make of John's accusation in this passage, that "Jezebel" taught people to eat food sacrificed to idols?

Unfortunately, John does not give us any more information. We have no information about the context in which "Jezebel" and her followers were consuming the sacrificial meat. We do not know if they were eating it in pagan temples, in private celebrations, at social meals, or in all of the above situations. Furthermore, we know nothing of "Jezebel's" rationale. Perhaps "Jezebel" had no objection whatsoever to eating sacrificial meat. Like those in Corinth who justified the practice based on the belief that pagan gods did not exist, perhaps she taught her followers that they should not worry at all about eating it; they could eat it under any circumstance. Or, it is possible that, like Paul, "Jezebel" did not absolutely condemn the practice but rather allowed it in certain circumstances (such as social dining with a pagan friend, cf. 1 Cor 10:25–27). Regardless, if we look at bit more closely at John's condemnation of "Jezebel," we can learn some interesting things about the community. This in turn can provide us with a bit more information about the situation.

The condemnatory passage in its larger context reads as follows:

I have this against you: you tolerate that woman "Jezebel," who calls herself a prophet and is teaching and leading astray my servants to practice fornication and to eat food sacrificed to idols. I gave her time to repent, but she refuses to repent of her fornication. Beware, I am throwing her on a bed, and those who commit adultery with her I am throwing into great distress, unless they repent of her doings; and I will strike her children dead. . . . But to the rest of you in Thyatira, who do not hold this teaching, who have not learned what some call "the deep things of Satan," to you I say, I do not lay on you any other burden; only hold fast to what you have. (Rev 2:20–25)

From this passage, we can determine that there were three factions in Thyatira.

The first group included "Jezebel" and "her children." The "children" mentioned here were those loyal to the prophetess "Jezebel." They presumably did not object to eating sacrificial food (although we know nothing of the circumstances under which they would have eaten such food). At the other extreme, we see the second group, those "who do not hold this teaching." This faction was obviously made up of those people in the community who were loyal to the prophet John. We can assume that, like him, they strongly objected to eating sacrificial meat.

But there is also another group evident, although we do not hear much about it. This third group encompassed "those who commit adultery with ['Jezebel']." These people I have elsewhere labeled the assembly's "invisible majority."[25] Although John gives us no other explicit information about them, his metaphorical depiction of them as "committing adultery" with "Jezebel" is telling. The metaphor tells us that this group did not *belong* to "Jezebel" (in the same way that people committing adultery do not *belong* to each other; they actually *belong* to their spouses). Rather, their liaison was temporary. To use a related metaphor, these people were "flirting" with "Jezebel."[26] This "invisible majority" was John's real focus of attention in the Thyatira assembly. He knew he had no hope of convincing "Jezebel" or her followers (i.e., her "children") to change their ways. He did at one point but had subsequently given up.[27] He also was not worried about those who thought the way that he did; he only wanted them to "hold fast" to their position. But John hoped to sway "those committing adultery" with "Jezebel."

The message to Thyatira suggests that the prophetess "Jezebel," with her more liberal attitude toward the consumption of sacrificial meat (among other things), was gaining influence in the assembly at Thyatira; and it was at John's expense. She not only had her core of followers (her "children") but other peo-

25. Paul B. Duff, *Who Rides the Beast? Prophetic Rivalry and the Rhetoric of Crisis in the Churches of the Apocalypse* (Oxford: Oxford University Press, 2001), 58–59.

26. It is possible that the people in this group did not want to choose sides. Perhaps they respected both the prophet John and the prophet "Jezebel."

27. Indeed, they had been condemned to death. "I will kill her children," says the risen Jesus, the purported author of the message to Thyatira.

ple (the "invisible majority") were also open to her message and were "flirting" with her. Consequently, John found himself trying to convince those in this group to reject "Jezebel's" teaching.

Our close reading of the passage in the book of Revelation suggests that consuming sacrificial meat was by no means a closed question at the end of the first century. Some in Thyatira believed the practice to be acceptable. Others in the community, it seems, were also open to it. Furthermore, the assembly in the nearby city of Pergamum was also divided over it (Rev 2:14–16). One wonders if Paul's ambiguous response to the practice in Corinth contributed to the difference of opinion in Thyatira and Pergamum. We have good evidence from a number of sources that by the end of the first century (i.e., around the time that the book of Revelation was written),[28] 1 Corinthians was circulating among some of the assemblies around the Mediterranean.[29] One wonders if "Jezebel" had access to Paul's letter and made her argument for the acceptability of eating sacrificial meat based on her reading of the apostle's ambiguous response to the Corinthians.

Regardless, the issue remained controversial. While some in Asia Minor ate sacrificial meat, a couple of other works, written at the end of the first or beginning of the second century, insist that eating sacrificial meat was strictly prohibited. In Acts, the prohibition was put into the mouth of James, Jesus's brother, "we should not trouble those gentiles who are turning to God, but we should write to them to abstain only from things polluted by idols" (Acts 15:19–20).[30] Although it is not clear that the phrase "things polluted by idols" necessarily points to sacrificial meat here, a later passage makes that connection explicit (Acts 15:29). The Didache also emphatically prohibited the consumption of meat that had been sacrificed: "Concerning food, bear whatever you are able, but keep strictly away from that which is offered to idols, for it is the worship of dead gods" (Did. 6:3 [Lake, slightly revised]).

---

28. It is difficult to date the book of Revelation with any precision but the best estimate is the last decade of the first century.

29. The author of 1 Clement (composed at Rome, probably between 90 and 100 CE) knew 1 Corinthians. Ignatius of Antioch (probably writing in the early decades of the second century) was likewise familiar with 1 Corinthians. Both assumed that their audiences would recognize their allusions to it (Clement's audience was in Corinth and Ignatius's in western Asia Minor).

30. I do not believe that James made this pronouncement at the time of his meeting with Paul in Jerusalem in the middle of the first century (although he would have almost certainly agreed with it). This is because we have an eyewitness account of the same gathering in Gal 2:1–10 (written by Paul who attended) and it does not mention it. Furthermore, Paul elsewhere seemed unaware of such a ruling.

Even a half century later, the issue had still not been resolved. In Justin Martyr's *Dialogue with Trypho*, written in the mid–second century, Justin's Jewish opponent Trypho claimed that "... many of those who say that they confess Jesus, and are called Christians, eat meats offered to idols, and declare that they are by no means injured in consequence" (*Dialogue with Trypho* 35). Justin dismisses Trypho's remark, asserting that it was not true Christians who did this. But, we should be careful about taking Justin at his word. Those mentioned by Trypho almost certainly would have considered themselves true Christians. Clearly, the controversy continued among Jesus followers a century after Paul wrote his letter to the Corinthians.

Because of its importance as well as its persistence, we have dedicated a good deal of space to the issue of "food sacrificed to idols." Nevertheless, one other particularly divisive issue—an issue that also long persisted—likewise demands our attention: marriage between Jesus followers and pagans. Like the issue of sacrificial meat, this controversy also persisted for more than a century. We know something about the controversy, in large part again due to Paul and to John, the author of the book of Revelation.

Marriages between Jesus Followers and Pagans

The earliest opinion about marriages between Jesus followers and pagans appears in 1 Corinthians 7. The issue surfaced in the context of Paul's discussion of celibacy, marriage, and divorce, issues that we looked at previously in chapter 5. The discussion followed directly from his citation of Jesus's command: "To the married I give this command—not I but the Lord—that the wife should not separate from her husband . . . and that the husband should not divorce his wife" (1 Cor 7:10–11). Immediately after this command, Paul raised the question of marriage to a pagan.

It is probable that Paul took up this issue because it was of particular concern in the community. Presumably, some in the assembly had converted but their spouses had not. If one spouse joined the Jesus movement but the other one did not, what was to be done? Should the marriage be dissolved? Paul's response to this was unambiguous: "If any believer has a wife who is an unbeliever, and she consents to live with him, he should not divorce her. And if any woman has a husband who is an unbeliever, and he consents to live with her, she should not divorce him" (1 Cor 7:12–13). It is noteworthy that Paul here addressed the issue of divorce (or non-divorce as the case may be) both from the perspective of the husband and the wife: "the wife should not separate from her husband" and "the husband should not divorce his wife" (1 Cor 7:10–11).[31]

Despite the fact that Paul addressed the situation from both the man's and the woman's points of view, it is almost certain that marriage to a pagan spouse presented a bigger problem for a woman than a man. This is because, as already noted, a wife was expected to follow the religious practices of her husband.[32] Therefore, if a husband joined the Jesus movement, his wife (and likely the rest of the household) would have been expected to follow suit. But a woman married to an unbeliever could find herself in a difficult position. If her husband insisted that she give up her belief in favor of his, she would have been expected to obey. In such a case, Paul would allow for (and possibly encourage) divorce. However, if the pagan husband of a Jesus follower was willing to tolerate his wife's religious practices and beliefs (and such would not have been unheard of),[33] then Paul would have insisted that they remain married.

According to Paul, "The unbelieving husband is sanctified through his wife" (1 Cor 7:14). Remarkably, Paul did not see marriage to an unbeliever as tainting either the spouse of the unbeliever or the believing community. This is particularly surprising in light of Paul's comments in an earlier chapter where he argued that a member of the assembly who consorted with a prostitute would ultimately corrupt the community: "Do you not know that your bodies are members of Christ? Should I therefore take the members of Christ and make them members of a prostitute? Never! Do you not know that whoever is united to a prostitute becomes one body with her? For it is said, 'The two shall be one flesh'" (1 Cor 6:15–16). In this passage, sex with a prostitute—based on Paul's reading of Gen 2:24, "the two shall be one flesh"—tainted both the offending member of the assembly and the assembly itself.

But unlike in the passage about the believer and the prostitute, Paul did not believe that the intimate relations between an unbelieving spouse and his or her Jesus-following spouse would taint the latter (and in turn the assembly). Instead, he argued that "sanctification" would flow the other way; from the Jesus-following spouse to the unbeliever. This sanctification would, in turn,

31. Paul's address of both genders here is noteworthy because in the Gospel passages on divorce, the point of view of the man is the only one that appears (as mentioned above in chapter 5).

32. In his *Advice to Bride and Groom*, Plutarch discouraged women from worshipping gods different from those of their husbands because "stealthy and secret rites performed by a woman find favor with no god" (19, [Babbitt, slightly revised]).

33. The very fact that Plutarch argued against a wife performing "stealthy and secret rites," suggests that some women did worship deities other than those of their husbands.

make the children holy.[34] It is obvious that for Paul the preservation of a marriage with an unbelieving spouse, provided that the spouse was agreeable, was preferable to countermanding Jesus's prohibition of divorce.

What about a marriage contracted between a Jesus follower and a pagan? In other words, would Paul countenance a marriage between a single person who was already a Jesus follower and a pagan? It is difficult to say. The only place in Paul's discussion of marriage that would possibly be applicable is the concluding advice that he gave regarding widows. There he asserted: "A wife is bound as long as her husband lives. But if the husband dies, she is free to marry anyone she wishes, only [let it be] in the Lord" (7:39). The key phrase in this passage is the final one, "only [let it be] in the Lord." Since for Paul to be "in Christ" or "in the Lord" typically meant to be within the assembly, this suggests that Paul believed that a marriage should only be *contracted* between a Jesus follower and another Jesus follower. But does that mean that Paul would have *forbidden* the marriage of a Jesus follower to a pagan? Unfortunately, it is difficult to answer that question. When Paul began the earlier section of this discussion—a discussion directed at those who were already married—he began with a command (of the Lord, 1 Cor 7:10). But this section—which was directed to the unmarried—he began with the statement, "I have no command of the Lord, but I give my opinion as one who by the Lord's mercy is trustworthy" (1 Cor 7:25). Obviously, Paul thought that his opinion was valuable (i.e., trustworthy by the Lord's mercy) but it is not clear that he believed his opinion to represent the final word.

The advice given by Paul about marriage to an unbeliever is similar to that given by the author of a later New Testament letter, 1 Peter; the reasoning, however, differs.[35] Although it is impossible to nail down a definitive date for 1 Peter, it was almost certainly written after 70 CE; its author was likely also influenced by Paul's letters. While in 1 Corinthians 7, Paul addressed the possibility that either believing husbands *or* believing wives had pagan spouses, the author of 1 Peter concentrated only on wives married to unbelievers. Furthermore, he not only implied that divorce should be avoided in such cases but he also counseled believing wives to excel in their traditional societal role, that is to say, they should "accept the authority of [their unbelieving] husbands."

---

34. It is impossible to know how Paul would have reconciled the passages concerning the prostitute on the one hand and marriage to an unbeliever on the other (or if he would have even attempted it).

35. There are two letters in the New Testament that are attributed to Peter, known as 1 and 2 Peter. It is very unlikely that Jesus's follower Peter wrote either of them. It is also likely that 1 and 2 Peter were written by two different people.

In that way, "[the husbands] may be won over without a word by their wives' conduct, when they see the purity and reverence of your lives" (1 Pet 3:1–2). Presumably, the author is here speaking about marriages that were contracted prior to the conversion of the spouse. Regardless, in 1 Peter, we see a different argument for preserving the marriage than we did in 1 Corinthians. While Paul insisted that the believing spouse would somehow sanctify the nonbeliever, the author of 1 Peter made no such claim. Instead, he argued that a believing wife's exemplary behavior—her purity and reverence—could *persuade* a husband to join the movement.

One wonders why this author, unlike Paul, did not address Jesus-following husbands who were married to unbelieving wives. It is of course possible that in his community, believing women were married to pagan husbands and not vice versa. But it is also possible that, given the author's traditional understanding of gender roles ("women should accept the authority of their husbands," 3:1), the author expected that men who joined the movement would demand that their entire household, especially their wives, become Jesus followers.

One more New Testament book that seems to have addressed the issue of mixed marriages is the book of Revelation. In both the assemblies of Thyatira and Pergamum, Jesus followers were accused of "eating food sacrificed to idols" (as we have already seen) and "fornication." In Thyatira, both offenses were blamed on "Jezebel's" teaching. What did the author mean by "fornication"? What were some people in Thyatira and Pergamum doing that so troubled John?

The Greek word translated by the English term "fornication," *porneia*, had a fairly broad meaning; it could point to virtually any kind of unacceptable sexual behavior. Should we imagine that some people in each of the assemblies were acting in some kind of sexually perverse (or promiscuous) manner? Such a conclusion is unlikely. The author of the book of Revelation consistently referred to sexual offenses metaphorically (14:8, 17:2, 17:4, 18:3, and 19:2). Indeed, we noted in our previous discussion that he also used the term "adultery" metaphorically. Consequently, it is safe to assume that John used the term "fornication" to describe something other than sexual perversity or promiscuity. But what would that be?

One option would be to understand it to refer to some kind of idolatrous activity. In the Scriptures, particularly the prophetic literature of the Bible, both "fornication" and "adultery" were frequently used to characterize idolatry (e.g., Hos 2:2; 4:13; Jer 3:9; 13:27).[36] But if "fornication" pointed to some kind

36. Indeed, in the Septuagint, even the crimes of the ancient Israelite queen Jezebel were

of idolatrous act in the book of Revelation, what would that be? Earlier in this chapter, we determined that the act most likely to be condemned as idolatrous by those in the Jesus movement was eating sacrificial meat. However, it is unlikely that "fornication" refers to that for the simple reason that it would make John's accusation against "Jezebel" (and some of the people in Pergamum) redundant. Consequently, it probably pointed to something else.

A better possibility would be to understand "fornication" to refer to marriage to a pagan.[37] We possess several examples of the term "fornication" (*porneia*) used to describe mixed marriages between Jews and non-Jews. One appears in the Septuagint, in the book of Tobit, where that individual advised his son: "Beware, my son, of every kind of fornication (*porneias*). Above all, marry a woman from among the descendants of your ancestors; do not marry a foreign woman, who is not of your father's tribe; for we are the descendants of the prophets. Remember, my son, that Noah, Abraham, Isaac, and Jacob, our ancestors of old, all took wives from among their kindred" (Tob 4:12; cf. T.Levi 14:6; Jub. 25:1; 30:1–17). A similar use of the term in the book of Revelation seems most likely, although in this case "fornication" would have been used to describe a marriage between a Jesus follower (rather than a Jew) and a pagan.[38]

Apparently, "Jezebel" did not condemn such marriages and perhaps she even encouraged the preservation of marriages to nonbelievers in lieu of divorce (much like Paul and the author of 1 Peter). John, however, was obviously horrified by the idea, as evidenced by the term that he used to describe it, "fornication."[39] Perhaps, like Paul—in the latter's discussion of sex with a prostitute—the author of the book of Revelation believed that intimacy between a Jesus follower and a pagan spouse would in some way contaminate the believing spouse, and so corrupt the assembly.[40]

In the second century, Justin Martyr also seemed unsympathetic to mixed

---

described as "fornications" (*porneiai*) although she was never condemned for cheating on her husband but rather for the idolatrous worship of Baal (2 Kgs 9:22).

37. The Hebrew equivalent (*zenut*) of the Greek term *porneia* was used comparably in the Roman period to describe mixed marriages (of Jews and non-Jews).

38. In an earlier work (Duff, *Who Rides the Beast?*, 56–57), I acknowledged this meaning as a possibility. In recent years, however, I have become convinced that it is the best explanation for the term.

39. In Tertullian's work, *To His Wife*, he uses the term *stuprum* ("immorality") to describe mixed marriages of Christians and pagans (*To His Wife* 2.3.1).

40. On the other hand, while Paul (and presumably the author of 1 Peter) were focused on marriages that had taken place *before* one member of the couple converted, perhaps the author of the book of Revelation was addressing the situation of *single* Jesus followers who decided to marry nonbelievers.

marriages. Although he offered no definitive pronouncement against them, he nevertheless provided a narrative that demonstrated the disastrous consequences of such. As he told the story, the depraved wife of a certain dissolute man was persuaded to convert to Christianity. After she did she reformed her life and attempted to convert her husband, but to no avail; consequently, she decided to divorce him but was dissuaded by her (presumably Christian) friends. After a while, she could no longer tolerate her husband's immoral behavior. Anxious that continuing in the relationship would result in her being dragged into her husband's sinful activities, she decided to divorce him once and for all. Her husband, however, became enraged at this and denounced her to the authorities for her Christianity (*2 Apol.* 2.1–6).[41] Justin was obviously sympathetic to the plight of the woman. The tone of his narrative clearly indicates that Justin believed that divorce was the proper course of action for this woman. Indeed, no evidence of sanctification flowing to the husband from the wife appears (as should have happened, according to Paul). Rather, Justin obviously believed that the likelihood of corruption ran the other way.

Tertullian, writing a bit later than Justin, also perceived the dangers of mixed marriages and so emphatically warned against them. He described the ways in which a pagan husband could and would inevitably try to undermine a believing wife's behavior. Such acts included planning a banquet on the day that his wife was fasting or planning other activities to prevent his wife from attending a gathering of the assembly (*To His Wife* 2.4.1–3). Curiously, Tertullian also provides us with evidence that others of his time saw nothing wrong with marriage to a pagan. He indicated that he had even heard of women who used Paul's comments about preserving mixed marriages (1 Cor 7:13–14) to justify their own marriages to pagans (*To His Wife* 2.2.1). Although Tertullian gives only vague hints of their reasoning, apparently these women were convinced by Paul's argument that sanctification would flow from them to their partners, and so their husbands (as well as their children) would be made holy by union with them.

Not surprisingly, Tertullian vigorously opposed this position. Among other arguments, he pointed to Paul's words later in the same chapter of 1 Corinthians, where he advised widows: "A wife is bound as long as her husband lives. But if the husband dies, she is free to marry anyone she wishes, only in the Lord" (1 Cor 7:39). Tertullian insisted that, with the phrase "only in the

---

41. Although there was no official empire-wide persecution at the time, local authorities could (and sometimes did) take action against Christians. Indeed, Justin himself was executed by the urban prefect of Rome, Junius Rusticus.

Lord," Paul undoubtedly meant "to a Christian." Although Tertullian did not disagree with Paul's opinion that women who converted after they had married should endeavor to preserve their marriage, he strongly opposed those who were already Christians undertaking a marriage to a nonbeliever.

Summary and Conclusion

The purpose of this chapter has been to consider the dictum found in the New Testament letter of James that directed Jesus followers to keep themselves "unstained by the world." Given the ubiquity of pagan deities in the urban environment, we asked what would have been meant by that command. In our investigation, we discussed a number of venues that could possibly have been considered idolatrous, in which Jesus followers would have been brought into close contact with the worship of pagan gods. These included civic festivals and their various components (of which we specifically looked at athletic competitions and theatrical events) and events with family and friends (including birthday parties, weddings, and other comparable social events, some of which may have taken place at pagan temples).

Surprisingly, we discovered that none of these events per se seem to have been considered particularly controversial. As a result, it seems likely that Jesus followers would not *necessarily* have refrained from participation. What was problematic, at least in the eyes of many Jesus followers, was the consumption of meat that had been sacrificed to idols, something that would likely have accompanied many of the events discussed. Nevertheless, there was not universal agreement on this. Indeed, the controversy surrounding the acceptability of the practice is vividly attested in 1 Corinthians 8–10. Since that document provides a number of different perspectives on the practice, we examined those chapters in considerable detail. We then turned to the book of Revelation, where the controversy continued a generation later. But, as we saw, no universal opinion emerged; even in the mid–second century, there was still some disagreement over the practice.

We then turned to another controversial issue, marriage to pagans. Paul argued that if such marriages had taken place prior to the conversion of one partner, such marriages should be preserved. The author of 1 Peter, it seems, followed Paul in this opinion. The author of the book of Revelation seems to have disparaged the practice. His opponent, "Jezebel," possibly under the influence of Paul's teaching in 1 Corinthians, allowed it (although we are unclear under what conditions she allowed it). Similar to John, Justin seems to have preferred divorce if only one member of a couple converted. While Tertullian favored preserving a marriage between a Christian and a pagan, he did not condone the marriage of an already converted Christian to a pagan. Nevertheless, some women of his time argued for the acceptability of mixed marriages and they based their argument on Paul's discussion in 1 Cor 7.

In sum, as we have seen from the controversies discussed in this chapter, there was no single understanding of what it meant to keep oneself "unstained by the world" in the early years of the Jesus movement. While to the best of our knowledge, Jesus followers did not avoid civic or social occasions, some of them obviously objected to taking part in any meals at which sacrificial meat would be served. Such could have happened at any number of the venues mentioned in the early pages of this chapter. Nevertheless, our sources indicate that eating sacrificial meat remained controversial even in the mid–second century. Similarly, the appropriateness of contracting or continuing mixed marriages continued to be debated into the early third century.

Conclusion

We began this work with the claim that the metaphor of the sojourner—a person who lived in an alien or foreign environment—functioned as a fitting descriptor of the Jesus follower in the middle years of the first century. In the cities of the empire, those pagans who were attracted to the movement continued to live much as they had before. Although some of their habits changed as a result of their conversion, others remained pretty much the same. Like the sojourner, they were in some ways "at home" in their native culture, but in other ways they were not.

When the movement began, however, the metaphor of the sojourner would not have been particularly applicable. This is because the historical Jesus proclaimed a Jewish message (about the kingdom of God) in Jewish territory, to a Jewish audience. We can safely assume that Jesus and his followers, like those to whom they preached, lived a Jewish lifestyle: they rested on the Sabbath, they followed Jewish dietary laws, they celebrated Jewish festivals, and they revered the Jewish Scriptures. Jesus's apocalyptic message was also Jewish, derived in part from Judean resistance to the forced hellenization of Antiochus IV in the second century BCE.

The Judeocentric focus of the movement began to shift when Jesus followers traveled beyond the bounds of Jewish territory. The book of Acts tells us that the Jesus movement made one of its earliest ventures outside of Judea when Jewish Jesus followers relocated to the large Hellenistic city of Antioch, in Syria. In all likelihood, the movement initially sought out other followers only among the Jews of that city. But at some point, for reasons unknown, Jesus followers also began to reach out to non-Jews. Surprisingly, some non-Jews responded positively.

At first glance, one might think it odd that such a Jewish message would have resonated with non-Jewish audiences. But, as we have seen, a number of things had prepared the way for its reception. For one, the translation of the Hebrew Bible into Greek—a project that had begun as early as the third century BCE—had made the Jewish Scriptures available to hellenized pagans. In addition, for this and other reasons, Judaism had come to be both known and admired by many non-Jews in Roman times. Furthermore, freelance religious experts, particularly those representing exotic eastern religious traditions—including Judaism—were valued by those interested in exploring alternative religious options. The early Jesus movement's missionaries to non-Jews, missionaries like Paul, would have been categorized as such.

Once the Jesus movement branched out into the empire's other cities, its missionaries began to establish assemblies comprised primarily if not exclusively of non-Jews. It is this group of non-Jewish Jesus followers that is best described as sojourners. They lived, in some ways, "betwixt and between." Their loyalties were divided; they no longer worshipped the gods of their cities or of the empire. Their allegiance was now to the God of the Jews, whose son's death had saved them from the soon-to-come divine wrath and whose Spirit had, in turn, proleptically connected them to the future age.

But these Jesus followers who now worshipped the God of the Jews did not convert to Judaism. Indeed, missionaries like Paul insisted that they remain non-Jews. Nevertheless, these non-Jewish Jesus followers were certainly not pagans in the sense that they had previously been. In a number of ways, they no longer resembled their friends and neighbors, those "pagans who do not know God" (1 Thess 4:5). Therefore, those non-Jews who had joined the movement ended up in neither group. To paraphrase the language of the baptismal formula, they were neither Jews nor were they "Greeks" (at least in the same sense that they had been before).[1]

The views of Jesus followers on some social or ethical issues at times contrasted sharply with the opinions of those in the dominant society. But at other times, there was alignment, at least to some extent. Curiously, in its early years, when the movement began, Jesus's followers were enjoined to reject their own families in favor of the newly formed family of "those who do the will of God" (Mark 3:31–35). Obviously, this attitude toward one's family of origin stood in stark contrast to the patriarchal outlook of the dominant culture (as well as to Jesus's Jewish subculture). Nevertheless, for a number of reasons, eventually

---

1. One scholar, Paula Fredriksen, recently referred to this group of non-Jewish Jesus followers as "ex-pagan pagans." She made the remark at the annual Society of Biblical Literature Meeting in San Antonio on November 19, 2016.

the command to "hate [one's] father and mother" was suppressed; Jesus followers' stance on loyalty toward family came to match that of the larger society.

Jesus followers' ideas about sexual matters vis-à-vis pagan society was somewhat mixed. The radical views of Jesus followers, while not absolutely alien, were uncommon. For example, the movement's promotion of celibacy, although it lined up with the thinking of some Greco-Roman philosophers, nevertheless contrasted with common attitudes about sexuality in pagan society. In that society, males were generally expected to be sexually active. Sex with prostitutes or one's slaves was rarely condemned; even within marriage, sex with anyone but another man's spouse was tolerated. But, for someone like Paul, such behavior was abhorrent. If one did not have the God-given gift to live a celibate life, the apostle insisted, that person should marry (and confine his or her sexual activities to that person's spouse). Even though, in later years, some assemblies discouraged celibacy, Jesus followers were nonetheless still enjoined to restrict their sexual activity to their spouses.

Divorce was one point on which the Jesus movement consistently opposed the attitude of the dominant society. While divorce was fairly easy to obtain and little stigma was attached to it, Jesus and his followers denounced the practice. As we have seen, in some cases the Jesus movement's beliefs and practices were eventually brought into conformity with the norms of Greco-Roman culture (such as its attitudes toward the patriarchal family); but on this topic, the movement remained firm. Over time, Jesus's absolute prohibition of divorce was slightly modified to allow for some exceptions (e.g., a pagan spouse who did not wish to remain married to a Jesus follower or cases of adultery). But the principle held.

Within the Jesus movement, gender attitudes differed somewhat from those of the larger society. From its beginnings, women played important roles. Although the baptismal phrase "there is no longer male and female" did not necessarily reflect the status of women within the assemblies (males, it seems, still held most leadership roles), women nevertheless had some opportunities to exercise leadership. Some functioned as patrons, supporting the missionary efforts of Paul or someone like him, others hosted assemblies in their homes, while still others exercised official or unofficial leadership. Although by the end of the first century, some assemblies (like that of 1 Timothy) forced women to take on more traditional roles, other assemblies continued to allow women to exercise more freedom. The unnamed woman prophet, for example, known to us only by the negative moniker "Jezebel," exerted considerable influence in western Asia Minor. The assembly addressed by the author of 2 John may have been led by a woman named Kyria.

In the mid–first century, the economic and social status of Jesus followers seems to have resembled their neighbors in most ways. Economically, the movement was comprised mostly of people living at or slightly above the subsistence level. The majority probably made their living as artisans, shopkeepers, day laborers, and the like. Even missionaries like Paul would have been included in this group. In terms of wealth (or lack thereof) and status, these people would not have differed noticeably from the majority of the population of their respective cities.

Economically, there were a few exceptions. Some people in the assemblies were better off than most others. Gaius of Corinth would have been one example. Stephanas and Chloe of that same city as well as Phoebe of Cenchreae would have been others. But there were also some on the lower end of the economic scale, those who could not manage to support themselves. In this regard, the practices of the assemblies of Jesus followers stood out from those of the dominant society. Assemblies did their best to care for the less fortunate, in particular, for widows and orphans. Indeed, in the Gospel of Matthew, Jesus insisted that the care given to a destitute brother or sister was care provided to him (Matt 25:34–40).

Remarkably, one's social rank in the larger society seems to have meant little within the assemblies. Paul, as a laborer who made his living by his hands, would not have been highly regarded in the larger society. Indeed, it is likely that some members of his congregations would have possessed higher status than he did. Yet, Paul was obviously respected within the communities that he had founded. The women Phoebe of Cenchreae and Chloe of Corinth provide us with other examples. As women who were likely freedpersons, these individuals would have normally fallen on the lower end of the status continuum. Nevertheless, they seem to have garnered significant respect within their own assemblies. Such respect may have resulted, at least in part, from their financial success. But others, like Persis of Rome, seem to have gained respect due solely to their labor on behalf of the assembly. Although we know of no slaves that exercised leadership in any of the assemblies, that may have been due less to their low social status than to the fact that, as slaves, they had little control over their own time.[2]

In terms of their worship activities, Jesus followers both resembled and differed from the pagans among whom they lived. Despite their rejection of the

---

2. Erastus of Corinth may have been an exception. Unfortunately, we cannot be sure that he was a slave nor can we be sure that he exercised leadership. However, there must have been some reason that Paul acknowledged him in Rom 16.

pagan gods, those in the assemblies continued to worship their deity in ways that would have been familiar to their pagan friends and neighbors. Although Jesus followers no longer sacrificed, the worship performed in their assemblies closely resembled that of other religious clubs or associations in the Roman Empire at the time. In particular, their ritual meals (such as the one described in 1 Corinthians) corresponded to the meals of the pagan associations. In each case, the ritual meal was comprised of three parts: a supper (*deipnon*), a libation, and a symposium that included a worship service honoring the relevant deity. In both the assemblies of Jesus followers and the associations dedicated to one or more pagan gods, prayers would have been offered and hymns sung while wine was consumed.

But not only was the worship similar, the fellowship created by the Jesus assemblies matched that found in cultic associations. In both cases, people found a welcoming group of like-minded individuals. Jesus followers referred to one another as "brother" or "sister." But this was not unique to the assemblies. The members of some pagan associations also referred to one another using familial terms. Even the term *ekklēsia* ("assembly"), the label used for the gatherings of Jesus followers, was used by some pagan organizations to refer to their own gatherings.

In conclusion, it is apparent that those who joined an assembly of Jesus followers continued to resemble their pagan friends and neighbors a great deal. But, at the same time, conversion also highlighted significant differences between Jesus followers and the rest of pagan society. Both the similarities and differences were substantial enough to justify the metaphor of sojourners to describe Jesus followers, a metaphor introduced by the author of the Letter to Diognetus.

As that author claimed, in the end Jesus followers were "no different from [the] other people in terms of their country, language, or habits" (Diogn. 5.1). They did, however, differ from their neighbors in some of their values and ethics. The patriarchy of the dominant society was challenged in many of the assemblies (at least to some degree), as was the larger culture's strict social hierarchy. Furthermore, Jesus followers believed that it was their responsibility to care for the destitute in their midst. But probably the most substantial distinction that emerged between Jesus followers and their pagan neighbors centered on the honor that was believed due to the gods. Jesus followers pledged their exclusive loyalty to the God that had heretofore only been worshipped by the Jews. From the time of their conversion, they no longer honored the gods of their city and of the empire.

Nevertheless, to the best of our knowledge, the fear of idolatry did not discourage most Jesus followers from participating in civic and cultural events with their neighbors, even those events that involved pagan deities to one degree or another. Many (perhaps most), however, drew the line at the consumption of sacrificial meat, likely choosing the negative social consequences over indulging in such idolatry. Furthermore, some (although not all) rejected the idea of marrying someone who did not belong to the assembly. However, each of these issues remained controversial for many years. Regardless, for the most part, Jesus followers adjusted to their new situation to the degree that most felt at home in their society, at least to the extent that such was possible for a sojourner.

Bibliography

Ascough, Richard S., Philip A. Harland, and John S. Kloppenborg. *Associations in the Ancient World: A Sourcebook*. Waco, TX: Baylor University Press, 2012.

Aune, David E. "Heracles and Christ: Heracles Imagery in the Christology of Early Christianity." Pages 3–19 in *Greeks, Romans, and Christians: Essays in Honor of Abraham J. Malherbe*. Edited by David L. Balch, Everrett Ferguson, and Wayne A. Meeks. Minneapolis: Fortress, 1990.

Baskin, Leonard, ed. *Gods and Heroes of the Greeks: The Library of Apollodorus; Translated with Introduction and Notes*. Amherst: University of Massachusetts Press, 1976.

Bell, Catherine. *Ritual: Perspectives and Dimensions*. Oxford: Oxford University Press, 1997.

Betz, Hans Dieter, ed. *The Greek Magical Papyri in Translation, Including the Demotic Spells*. 2nd ed. Chicago: University of Chicago Press, 1992.

Bickermann, Elias. *The God of the Maccabees*. Leiden: Brill, 1979.

Chadwick, Henry. *Origen: Contra Celsum; Translated with an Introduction & Notes*. Cambridge: Cambridge University Press, 1980.

Charlesworth, James H. *The Old Testament Pseudepigrapha*. 2 vols. Garden City, NY: Doubleday & Company, 1985.

Crossan, John Dominic. *In Parables: The Challenge of the Historical Jesus*. San Francisco: Harper & Row, 1973.

———. *Jesus: A Revolutionary Biography*. New York: HarperCollins, 1989.

Deissmann, Adolf. *Light from the Ancient East: The New Testament Illustrated by Recently Discovered Texts of the Graeco-Roman World*. Translated by Lionel R. M. Strachan. Grand Rapids, MI: Baker, 1978.

Dubois, Page. *A Million and One Gods: The Persistence of Polytheism*. Cambridge: Harvard University Press, 2014.

Duff, Paul B. *Who Rides the Beast? Prophetic Rivalry and the Rhetoric of Crisis in the Churches of the Apocalypse*. Oxford: Oxford University Press, 2001.

Feldman, Louis H. *Jew and Gentile in the Ancient World*. Princeton: Princeton University Press, 1993.

Fitzgerald, Robert. *Odyssey: Homer.* New York: Farrar, Straus, and Giroux, 1989.

Fredriksen, Paula. *Jesus of Nazareth: King of the Jews.* New York: Vintage, 1999.

————. "Why Should a 'Law-Free' Mission Mean a 'Law-Free' Apostle?" *JBL* 134 (2015): 637–50.

Friesen, Steven J. "The Wrong Erastus: Ideology, Archaeology, and Exegesis." Pages 231–56 in *Corinth in Context: Comparative Studies on Religion and Society.* Edited by Steven J. Friesen, Daniel N. Schowalter, and James C. Walters. Leiden: Brill, 2010.

Glancy, Jennifer A. "Domestic vs. Conjugal Sexual Ethics: Implications for Understanding Jesus's Teachings on Adultery in the Gospel of Matthew." Paper presented at the Annual Meeting of the Studiorum Novi Testamenti Societas. Montreal, Canada, August 5, 2016.

————. *Slavery in Early Christianity.* Oxford: Oxford University Press, 2002.

Gooch, Peter D. *Dangerous Food: 1 Corinthians 8–10 in Its Context.* Studies in Christianity and Judaism 5. Waterloo, ON: Wilfrid Laurier University Press, 1993.

Green, Peter. *Alexander the Great.* New York: Praeger, 1970.

Habertal, Moshe, and Avishai Margalit. *Idolatry.* Cambridge: Harvard University Press, 1992.

Hamilton, J. R. *Alexander the Great.* London: Hutchinson, 1973.

Harland, Philip A. *Associations, Synagogues, and Congregations: Claiming a Place in Mediterranean Society.* Minneapolis: Fortress, 2003.

Hayes, John H., and Sara R. Mandell. *The Jewish People in Classical Antiquity: From Alexander to Bar Kochba.* Louisville: Westminster John Knox, 1998.

Hock, Ronald F. *The Social Context of Paul's Ministry: Tentmaking and Apostleship.* Minneapolis: Fortress, 1980.

Hopkins, Keith. *Conquerors and Slaves.* SSRH 1. Cambridge: Cambridge University Press, 1981.

Jeremias, Joachim. *The Parables of Jesus.* New York: Scribner's Sons, 1963.

Johnson Hodge, Caroline. *If Sons, Then Heirs: A Study of Kinship and Ethnicity in the Letters of Paul.* Oxford: Oxford University Press, 2007.

Kearns, Emily. *Ancient Greek Religion: A Sourcebook.* Chichester: Wiley-Blackwell, 2010.

Kloppenborg, John S. *Q: The Earliest Gospel: An Introduction to the Original Stories and Sayings of Jesus.* Louisville: Westminster John Knox, 2008.

Kraemer, Ross. *Her Share of the Blessings: Women's Religions among Pagans, Jews, and Christians in the Graeco-Roman World.* New York: Oxford University Press, 1992.

Lane Fox, Robin. *Alexander the Great.* London: Penguin, 1986.

————. *Pagans and Christians.* New York: Knopf, 1987.

Lesher, J. H. *Xenophanes of Colophon: Fragments; Translation, Text, and Commentary.* Phoenix Supplement 30. Toronto: University of Toronto Press, 1992.

LiDonicci, Lynn R. *The Epidauran Miracle Inscriptions: Text, Translation, and Commentary.* SBLTT 36. Atlanta: Scholars Press, 1995.

Lombardo, Stanley. *Hesiod: Works and Days and Theogony.* Indianapolis: Hackett, 1993.

Lutz, Cora. "Musonius Rufus: The Roman Socrates." YCS 10 (1947): 3–147.

MacDonald, Margaret Y. "Was Celsus Right? The Role of Women in the Expansion of Early Christianity." Pages 157–84 in *Early Christian Families in Context: An Inter-*

disciplinary Dialogue. Edited by David L. Balch and Carolyn Osiek. Grand Rapids, MI: Eerdmans, 2003.

MacMullen, Ramsay. *Paganism in the Roman Empire*. New Haven: Yale University Press, 1981.

————. *Roman Social Relations: 50 B.C. to A.D. 280*. New Haven: Yale University Press. 1974.

Malherbe, Abraham J. *The Cynic Epistles: A Study Edition*. SBLSBS 12. Missoula, MT: Scholars Press, 1977.

McGowen, Andrew B. *Ancient Christian Worship: Early Church Practices in Social, Historical, and Theological Perspective*. Grand Rapids: Baker, 2014.

Meeks, Wayne A. *The First Urban Christians: The Social World of the Apostle Paul*. 2nd ed. New Haven: Yale University Press, 2003.

————. "Moses as God and King." Pages 354–71 in *Religions in Antiquity: Essays in Memory of Erwin Ramsdell Goodenough*. Edited by Jacob Neusner. Leiden: Brill, 1968.

Meier, John P. *Mentor, Message, and Miracles*. Vol. 2 of *A Marginal Jew*. ABRL. New York: Doubleday, 1994.

————. *The Roots of the Problem and the Person*. Vol. 1 of *A Marginal Jew*. ABRL. New York: Doubleday, 1991.

Mitchell, Margaret M. *Paul and the Rhetoric of Reconciliation*. HUT 28. Tübingen: Mohr Siebeck, 1991.

Mitchell, Stephen. "The Cult of Theos Hypsistos." Pages 81–148 in *Pagan Monotheism in Late Antiquity*. Edited by Polymnia Athanassiadi and Michael Frede. Oxford: Clarendon Press, 1999.

Murphy-O'Connor, Jerome. *St. Paul's Corinth: Texts and Archaeology*. 3rd ed. Collegeville, MN: Liturgical Press, 2002.

Nanos, Mark D. *The Mystery of Romans: The Jewish Context of Paul's Letter*. Minneapolis: Fortress, 1996.

Osiek, Carolyn, and David L. Balch. *Families in the New Testament World: Households and House Churches*. Louisville: Westminster John Know, 1997.

Patterson, Stephen J. *The Gospel of Thomas and Jesus*. Foundations and Facets. Sonoma, CA: Polebridge Press, 1993.

Peppard, Michael. *The Son of God in the Roman World: Divine Sonship in Its Social and Political Context*. Oxford: Oxford University Press, 2011.

Pervo, Richard. *Acts: A Commentary*. Hermeneia. Minneapolis: Fortress, 2009.

Price, Simon. *Religions of the Ancient Greeks*. KTAH. Cambridge: Cambridge University Press, 1999.

Reardon, B. P., ed. *Collected Ancient Greek Novels*. Berkeley: University of California Press, 1989.

Roetzel, Calvin J. *The Letters of Paul: Conversations in Context*. 5th ed. Louisville, KY: Westminster John Knox, 2009.

Romm, James, ed. *The Landmark Arrian: The Campaigns of Alexander*. Translated by Pamela Mensch. New York: Anchor, 2010.

Rouselle, Aline. *Porneia: On Desire and the Body in Antiquity*. Oxford: Blackwell, 1988.

Ruden, Sarah. *The Golden Ass: Apuleius*. New Haven: Yale University Press, 2011.

Sanders, E. P. *The Historical Figure of Jesus*. London: Penguin, 1993.

Schürer, Emil. *The History of the Jewish People in the Age of Jesus Christ (175 B.C. to A.D. 135)*. Revised and edited by Geza Vermes, Fergus Millar, and Martin Goodman. 3 vols. in 4 parts. Edinburgh: T&T Clark, 1986.

Stark, Rodney. *The Rise of Christianity*. New York: HarperCollins, 1997.

Stowers, Stanley K. *A Rereading of Romans: Justice, Jews, and Gentiles*. New Haven: Yale University Press, 1994.

Strassler, Robert B., ed. *The Landmark Herodotus: The Histories*. Translated by Andrea L. Purvis. New York: Pantheon, 2007.

Talbert, Charles H. "Once Again: Gospel Genre." *Semeia* 43 (1966): 53–74.

Tarn, W. W. *Alexander the Great*. 2 vols. Cambridge: Cambridge University Press, 1950.

———. *Hellenistic Civilisation*. 3rd ed. New York: New American Library, 1974.

Taussig, Hal. *In the Beginning Was the Meal: Social Experimentation and Early Christian Identity*. Minneapolis: Fortress, 2009.

Tcherikover, Victor. *Hellenistic Civilization and the Jews*. Philadelphia: Jewish Publications Society, 1966.

Theissen, Gerd. *The Social Setting of Pauline Christianity: Essays on Corinth*. Philadelphia: Fortress, 1982.

Theissen, Gerd, and Annette Merz. *The Historical Jesus: A Comprehensive Guide*. Minneapolis: Fortress, 1998.

Vermes, Geza. *The Authentic Gospel of Jesus*. London: Penguin, 2003.

Veyne, Paul. "The Roman Empire." Pages 5–205 in *From Pagan Rome to Byzantium*, vol. 1 of *A History of Private Life*. Edited by Paul Veyne. Cambridge, MA: Belknap, 1987.

Walbank, F. W. *The Hellenistic World*. Cambridge: Harvard University Press, 1981.

Wendt, Heidi. *At the Temple Gates: The Religion of Freelance Expert in the Roman Empire*. New York: Oxford University Press, 2016.

———. "*Ea Superstitione*: Christian Martyrdom and the Religion of Freelance Experts." *JRS* 105 (2015): 183–202.

———. "Iudaica Romana: A Rereading of Judean Expulsions from Rome." *Journal of Ancient Judaism* 6 (2015): 97–126.

Yarbro Collins, Adela. *Mark: A Commentary*. Hermeneia. Minneapolis: Fortress, 2007.

Index of Names and Subjects

Virginity. *See* celibacy

voluntary associations: compared to early Jesus assemblies, 195–212; as ethnic gatherings, 112; honoring the gods by, 196, 197–98, 203–4; feasting with friends in, 196, 202–11; moral behavior expected of members, 185–86, 200–201; rituals of, 5, 201–11; types of, 5, 174, 196–98

wealth and poverty: economic level of early Jesus followers, 173, 175–81; economic resources of the *humiliores,* 172–75; wealth of the *honestiores,* 171–72

widows: assisted by assemblies, 166, 180, 188, 213, 243; assisted by other widows, 166, 169, 181; Paul's advice to, 154, 159, 234, 237; vulnerability of, 180

Zeus: Alexander the great as son of, 15, 86; Barnabas mistaken for, 81, 95; Cynic philosophers sent by, 155; designated *Theos Hypsitos,* 98, 204; disguised as a human being, 92; Heracles as son of, 130; as the high god, 52; immortality granted by, 85; indigenous deities identified with, 83; sacrifices to, 95; voluntary associations and, 199, 204

Index of Scripture and Other Ancient Texts